P9-COO-623

CANADIAN
PRIVATE SECURITY MANUAL

Revised Edition

THE CARSWELL
LAW ENFORCEMENT SERIES

The Complete Guide to Police Writing
KAREN JAKOB

The Police Officers Manual
GARY P. RODRIGUES

The Police Manual of Arrest, Seizure and Interrogation
ROGER E. SALHANY

Understanding Criminal Offences
BARRIE J. SAXTON and RONALD STANSFIELD

Canadian Private Security Manual

Revised Edition

Kenneth N. Smith & Robert J. Prouse

CARSWELL
Toronto • Calgary • Vancouver
1989

Canadian Cataloguing in Publication Data

Smith, Kenneth N., 1941–
      Canadian private security manual

(The Carswell law enforcement series)
Rev. ed.
Includes Index.
ISBN 0-459-33571-5 (bound) ISBN 0-459-33581-2 (pbk.)

1. Police, Private—Canada. 2. Security systems—
Canada. 3. Police, Private—Legal status, laws,
etc.—Canada. I. Prouse, Robert J., 1947–
II. Title. III. Series.

HV8290.S55 1989   363.2'89'0971   C89-094315-X

All rights reserved. No part of this publication may be reproduced
or transmitted, in any form or by any means, electronic, mechanical,
photocopying, recording or otherwise, or stored in any retrieval
system of any nature, without the prior written permission of the
copyright holder and the publisher, application for which shall be
made to the publisher, The Carswell Co. Ltd., 2330 Midland Avenue,
Agincourt, Ontario, Canada, M1S 1P7.

©The Carswell Company Limited
1989

Preface

We began writing this book mainly because, after an exhaustive search, we could not find a Canadian publication on the subject of security. This disturbed us, as the private security field in Canada has evolved into a major Canadian employer.

We are two individuals, one employed as a Teaching Master of private security at a community college and the other as a Director of Security for a major pulp and paper manufacturer, who felt that more education, from a Canadian viewpoint, is required.

There are any number of American texts on the market; however, because of differing laws and viewpoints on the two sides of the border, they do not accurately reflect the situation in Canada. In fact, they are, in many cases, misleading from the perspective of individual powers and authorities as they exist in Canada. As an example, most American security guards are allowed to, and do, wear firearms, which is prohibited, with a few exceptions, in Canada.

We would be remiss if we did not give credit to certain persons who helped us considerably in our long and frustrating period of writing: our wives, Sella and Dianne, who put up with our tantrums and disappointments, but also were more than willing to help us as needed; Ken's thirteen-year-old daughter, Tracie, who assisted on all the drawings for the book; and Rick Mortenson, who so willingly acted as a resource person for certain portions of this book, which could not have been written without him.

This book was not written in the context of being the ultimate authority on Canadian security, but as an attempt to simplify the misnomers that have existed between Canadian and American perspectives. This is basically an attempt to simplify the areas that have been of concern to the private security industry.

We would appreciate receiving any comments you may have concerning the content.

Table of Contents

Preface v

Chapter 1   **What Is Security?** 1

    1. Contract Security 3

    2. In-House Security 3

    3. Contract/In-House Security 6

Chapter 2   **Contract Security and Licensing** 11

    1. The Licensing Function 14

      (a) Purposes of Licensing 14

    2. The Licensees 14

      (a) Who Must be Licensed 14

      (b) Documentary Requirements 15

      (c) Investigation of Applicants
            for Licences and Verification 16

Chapter 3   **Supervisory Management in Security** 29

    1. Selecting a Security Manager 29

    2. What is a Security Manager? 31

    3. How Does the Security Manager
       Accomplish His Goals? 35

    4. Security Management and
       the Budget 36

    5. Security Management in Contract
       Security 38

    6. Proper Deployment of Manpower 41

      (a) Figure A 42

      (b) Figure B 43

      (c) Figure C 44

      (d) Figure D 44

Chapter 4   **The Selection of a Security Guard** 55
Chapter 5   **Purchasing Process** 59
Chapter 6   **Authority For Enforcement** 75
Chapter 7   **Effects of Grievances, Arbitration
               and Collective Agreements on
               Security** 85
Chapter 8   **Property Protection and the
               Occupiers' Liability** 91
               1. The Trespass to Property Act 93
Chapter 9   **Security Survey** 97
Chapter 10   **Security and Safety of the Individual** 123
Chapter 11   **Report Writing** 129
Chapter 12   **Investigational Procedure** 137
               1. Classifying Complaints 142
Chapter 13   **Security Patrols** 149
Chapter 14   **Radio Communications** 155
Chapter 15   **Security Hardware** 161
               1. Communications 162
               2. Transport 163
               3. Fencing 164
               4. Alarm Systems 167
               5. Safes and Secure Cabinets 168
               6. Closed Circuit Television (CCTV) .... 17(
               7. Lighting 171
               8. Access Control 172
               9. Locking Devices 174
Chapter 16   **Document Security** 177
Chapter 17   **Retail Security** 185
               1. Types of Shoplifters 185
               2. Preventive Suggestions 187
               3. Tell-Tale Signs 190
Chapter 18   **Hotel Security** 195
               1. Visiting Dignitaries 201
Chapter 19   **Fire** 205
               1. Suggested Procedures to Combat a
                  Fire 210
Chapter 20   **Security For Disaster Emergency
               Situations** 215

1. Disaster Plan Outline 216
2. Classification Method of
   Casualties 225
3. Bomb Threats 226
4. Instructions to Recipients of Bomb
   Threats 229

Chapter 21   **Surveillance** 233
1. Surveillance Reports and
   Notemaking 242

Chapter 22   **Drug Awareness** 255
1. Alcohol 255
   (a) What is Known About
       Alcohol? 255
   (b) Short Term Effects 256
   (c) The Hazards of Alcohol 256
   (d) Who Uses Alcohol? Why? 257
2. Solvents 257
   (a) What is Known About
       Solvents? 257
   (b) What Are the Active
       Ingredients? 258
   (c) What Are the Methods of
       Use? 258
   (d) What Are the Effects of Solvent
       Abuse? 258
   (e) How Long Does the Effect of
       Solvent Abuse Last? 259
   (f) Who Abuses Solvents?
       Why? 259
3. The Narcotic Control Act 261
   (a) Definitions 261
   (b) Offences 262
4. Food and Drugs Act, Part III—
   Controlled Drugs—Schedule
   "G" 264
   (a) Definitions 264
   (b) Offences 264

    5. Food and Drugs Act, Part IV—
       Restricted Drugs—Schedule
       "H" 265
      (a) Definitions 265
      (b) Offences 266
    6. Food and Drugs Act—
       Schedule "F" Drugs 266
    7. Cannabis 272

Chapter 23 Transportation and Regulation of Dangerous Goods 277
    1. Classification 287
      (a) How to Classify Goods 287
        (i) Goods received from a
           manufacturer 287
        (ii) Goods generated by your
           company 288
      (b) Information Required for
        Classification 288
        (i) Proper shipping name 288
        (ii) PIN/UN number 289
        (iii) Classification and
           division 289
        (iv) Sub-classification 289
        (v) Packing group 289
      (c) Packing Requirements 289
      (d) Safety Markings 290
      (e) Documentation 291
    2. Dangerous Goods
      Documentation 292
    3. Reporting 293
    4. The Driver's Responsibilities 294
    5. Receiving Information 295
    6. Reporting Coordinators 300
      (a) 30-Day Reporting 302
    7. Registration 303
    8. Emergency Response Plans 304

Chapter 24 Human Rights 321

1. Discrimination 324
   (a) Direct Discrimination
       (section 8) 324
   (b) Indirect Discrimination
       (section 8) 324
   (c) Discrimination Because of
       Association (section 11) 324
   (d) Constructive Discrimination
       (section 10) 324
2. Harassment 325
   (a) Harassment in Accommodation
       (section 2(2)) and Employment
       (section 4(2)) 325
   (b) Sexual Harassment
       (section 6) 326
   (c) Responsibility for Preventing
       Harassment 326
3. Procedure for Processing
   Complaints 327
   (a) Fact-Finding Conference 327
   (b) Extended Investigation 328
   (c) Formal Conciliation 328
   (d) The Ontario Human Rights
       Commission 329
   (e) Reconsideration 329
   (f) Board of Inquiry 330
Chapter 25 **Conclusion** 333
Index 335

1

What Is Security?

Security can be generally defined as the quality or state of being secure, freedom from danger or aggression, caution, or the pledge and assurance of protection. This definition must be translated into a working definition of what constitutes private security as it applies to modern standards and requirements.

To begin with, certain distinctions must be made within the general context of security. The following types of security are classified in a category generally referred to as the public security sector: police, fire, customs, immigration, excise, park wardens, by-law enforcement, etc., provided by federal, provincial and municipal levels of government. The public security sector, which gives us security according to the above definition, is financed by public funds that are generated by taxation and other general forms of revenue, such as grants and fines in court.

A large portion of security, which is not funded by public monies, can be classified in the broad perspective of what is commonly referred to as private security.

Private security, for the purposes of this book, may be categorized into sub-classes. One sub-class is that which

applies to such groups as railway security police and auxiliary police. These particular agencies, and others like
them, have been granted certain special police powers by
the various governmental powers, but are, in effect, private agencies employed specifically for the purpose of protecting property belonging to their respective employers.

The area upon which this book will focus is the remaining broad spectrum of private security, being what
are commonly known as corporate (private) and in-house
(private) security. The differences between these two diverse but related fields will be discussed in more detail elsewhere in the book. Both of these fields share many things
in common because of their great similarities, but in many
aspects they are totally unrelated. Areas in common include provision of guard services, fire control, patrol services, store security, courier services, alarm respondents,
accounting auditors, alarm and fire installation and general
security consulting.

Some elements, such as guard and patrol service, are
the same in both the public and private security segments
and are activated to perform the same function, this being
the prevention of some type of loss, whether it be to property or life. Control of these losses may take the form of
theft prevention, fire prevention, industrial espionage, accident prevention and the well-being of the individual. Private security has the additional responsibility over public
security for the protection of property and safekeeping of
the employer.

Now that the narrow meaning of security has been
expanded, a meaningful definition of private security can
be obtained. Private security is the method of protecting
one's assets, be they individual or corporate, through total
loss prevention techniques, and having this protection paid
for by a non-governmental body.

The appropriate definition can now be applied to the specific areas of contract and in-house security.

1. CONTRACT SECURITY

Contract security, as it applies to the private security industry, prevents losses to the client who contracts out this loss-prevention desire to the contractor providing security. This is achieved by the individual (or individual company) paying to the security company a fee for services rendered. This is normally done on a contract basis for a specified period of time and services to be supplied listed therein. The security company then provides the agreed manpower and equipment to perform the desired duties.

2. IN-HOUSE SECURITY

In-house security is established to provide the same protection; however, the methods of achieving the end are reached by a different process. In this particular manner, the individual (or individual company) maintains full control over the security function by employing his own personnel and supplying his own equipment. The individual then bears the responsibility for establishing all functions related to loss prevention, including such diverse fields as training of the security staff, setting pay standards and establishing a means of internal accountability.

In both instances, the ultimate result is the establishment of a loss prevention service paid for by the private sector with non-government funds. One exception to this rule, albeit a small one, is where a government agency may extend a contract to a private agency (for example, security of a government building).

Bearing in mind the concept that private security is

security that enforces all aspects of loss prevention in the private sector, the obvious question that arises is, "Why employ private security"?

Companies have always been concerned with preventing all forms of loss, be they the result of theft, fire or natural disaster. Losses affect both profits and the general harmony of the worksite. Public security has neither the manpower nor the resources to extend full assistance to the private sector because of its duties to the general public.

Using the definition of private security, the key word contained therein is prevention. Public security must, by its nature, play a more reactive than preventive role than what is required by the private sector. This is not to say public security does not attempt to perform a preventive role. This it does well with such programs as Neighbourhood Watch, Crimestoppers, and Operation Identification, as well as routine patrol functions. However, with relation to private industry, it must, by necessity, play a reactive role.

When losses occur, such as theft, assault or an act of vandalism, public security remains the appropriate authority for notification and investigation. It will, at that time, take the initiative and follow through to the ultimate conclusion, normally a court action. The actions taken are those dictated by the justice system in force throughout Canada. In this context, all action taken is a reactive response rather than a preventive action.

On the other hand, with private security, the main objective is to protect your assets through *total loss prevention techniques*. This means the private security employee is devoting all of his time and effort to the protection of his employer's assets and aiding the employer in achieving his aim of greater profit and harmony.

Now that the reasons for having private security are known, the next aspect which must be considered, from the employer's point of view, and considering the state of economy, is the price—"Is it cost effective"? Unless the protection is for a valuable, mobile asset, security in itself may not be totally cost effective. A comparison can be made here between a warehouse containing 500-kilogram rolls of newsprint for commercial purposes and a display of expensive jewellery. Obviously, very few persons would be interested in stealing the newsprint; however, many thieves would show a keen desire to obtain the jewellery, because of it being easily-disposed-of merchandise that could be readily hidden with little effort.

Security will be required for the protection of both of these assets, the jewellery because of the high mobility and relative ease of theft if unprotected, and the heavy rolls of newsprint not because of theft but the existing potential of a major loss through fire. In these two instances, the type of private security utilized and the expense involved would no doubt differ substantially.

Both in-house and contract security must be a combination of many loss prevention techniques. Both must become a collaboration of fire and theft prevention services and in most cases must be capable of providing emergency first aid at the worksite location. This combination has a desired result in reducing the insurance premium of the employer, as it substantiates to the insurance carrier that the employer is concerned with, and taking remedial action to prevent, total or major loss. With a full loss-control service in place, private security will become cost effective or, at the very least, substantially reduce expenses to the employer through losses and the subsequent reduction in insurance premiums.

3. CONTRACT/IN-HOUSE SECURITY

As previously discussed, contract and in-house security are in many ways similar. The main difference between them is the fact that one is formed by the individual (or individual company) while the other is brought into the workplace by contract with actual personnel and equipment supplied on an as-needed basis. Each type has distinct advantages and disadvantages which differ from case to case; however, the end result generally applies to the over-all field.

In-house security, which is security wholly sponsored and supervised by the individual, has the distinct advantage of giving the sponsor full control over his particular duties. The individual can implement whatever job description he wishes, hire any particular staff with the qualifications he desires them to possess and have full control over any specialized equipment he may require. On the other hand, unless the individual is a large company with a particularly costly product to protect, he may quickly find the cost of establishing and maintaining such a system to be prohibitively expensive. The time required to set such a system in place also may not be practical if the end result—full protection at a suitable cost—cannot be justified.

Contract security is exactly what its name denotes. By this we mean a private company which is in the business of providing any number of security personnel and equipment to companies or individuals for a designated period. This method of obtaining security can have many advantages, the main one being cost. By having someone else provide the security force, the initial outlay for items such as training, uniforms, equipment and having to provide such things as administrative backup are avoided.

The individual need simply contact any agency providing contract security, explain his needs and have whatever is required provided when and as needed. Most contract security agencies, being in business for the sole purpose of providing that service, would be quick to provide needed personnel and necessary equipment on relatively short notice. As there are a large number of agencies in existence, competitive prices are easily obtained.

The main difference between the two types—in-house and contract security—is the degree of control exercised over the end-product. With in-house security the individual is maintaining complete control over his system. He has the power to change personnel, amend specific job descriptions and shift responsibilities as and when required.

By purchasing the security system from a supplier he is surrendering the right to amend the final product by what is contained in the contract. If, for example, the individual is not happy with the quality or appearance of the personnel supplied, there is very little he can do about it other than contacting the supplier and complaining. Should the individual, not receive satisfaction, his only recourse may be to obtain the services of a new agency, or if possible, to amend the existing contract. Unless he could amend the existing contract, to his satisfaction, he would be forced to accept a new service which would initially be unfamiliar with his needs.

The matter of supplying necessary equipment is very costly with both options and must be considered closely before opting for either in-house or contract security. The initial cost outlay for in-house security can be extremely high if it is not being utilized on a long-term basis. The actual per annum cost could be relatively minor, when both heavy usage and depreciation allowances are taken into consideration.

On the other hand, if contract security is utilized, the initial cost would not be a factor. Contract security must, of course, make a profit. Therefore, the cost of the equipment will have to be taken into consideration by the supplier. Inevitably, over a period of time, the equipment will be paid for a number of times over. However, as the equipment is owned by the contract security firm, it is responsible for all repairs and upkeep, reducing the cost to a reasonable level.

As can readily be seen, which type of security—in-house or contract—is best for any particular business, is a matter to be carefully considered and can vary immensely from situation to situation. Quite often, a company will opt for a security staff composed of both in-house and contract employees. In cases such as these, the in-house staff is normally delegated a responsibility for the more personal aspects of security, such as internal investigations and the design of new controls. The contract staff will normally be given the more mundane duties, such as routine patrols and manning alternate exit/entry checkpoints.

One area in which contract security can be of considerable assistance to in-house security, is having the ability to provide, on a consulting basis, security experts with a more diversified background than those employed directly by an individual. This expertise, provided on a short-term basis, can considerably enhance the overall performance of the in-house security staff because of their newly-gained knowledge.

The discussions in this chapter have centered on what private security is and why such systems exist. The view has been offered that private security is security that incorporates total loss prevention and maintains harmony with the service being paid for by the private sector rather than the general public. Prevention is the key word, rather than reaction. Private security alone may not be cost effective, but when combined with total loss prevention, it becomes a viable tool to promote profit. The overall growth of private security as a necessary part of private industry sustains the theory that it is both a practical and desired segment of a company function.

2

Contract Security and Licensing

As has been seen, a comparison has been made between in-house and contract security guards. The first chapter dealt basically with the facts affecting the employer and avenues that he can pursue to achieve the type of security department that best suits his needs.

With respect to in-house security, the security member is employed by one employer for the needs of that employer only. With this mandate the employer assumes all the responsibiity for training, development and structuring security authority as it would affect his company.

The in-house security member would have to meet the hiring standards of that company, and his type of dress would depend on the needs of the employer. The employer may decide that he will provide a type of uniform suitable to his company or allow the security employees to dress as they see fit.

In contrast, the contract security companies must follow strict standards to apply for and receive the appropriate licences that will allow the contract security company to operate a business.

For the purposes of this chapter we will examine the

Private Investigators and Security Guards Act of Ontario (R.S.O. 1980, c. 390). Other provinces have similar regulations that we will highlight as well.

As a general rule, the term "private investigator" means a person who investigates and supplies information for a fee and would include someone who makes background inquiries concerning an individual's character and actions, their type of employment or source of funds, and conducts inquiries for missing persons or property.

The interpretation of "security guard" normally means a person who is employed, for a wage or other type of remuneration, to guard or patrol and protect persons or designated property.

The Act does not apply to private investigators and security guards who are permanently employed by one employer in a business or undertaking other than the business of providing private investigators or security guards and whose work is confined to the affairs of that employer. (This application directly refers to the in-house security employee.)

When an individual wishes to start a private investigator and/or security guard business he must apply for a licence. Each branch office must have its own licence and each employee must be separately licensed as either a security guard or private investigator. He must display his licence in a conspicuous place in the office or branch office of the business for which it is issued.

After a licence has been issued, the holder of the licence cannot use any other name than that on the licence. The private investigator cannot have in his possession or display any badge, shield or card or any other identification or evidence of authority except the prescribed identification card issued under the particular Act of the province, but may have a business card if it contains reference to licensing under the particular Act. Every private investigator must, while investigating, carry on his person an identification card issued to him and shall produce it for inspection at the request of any person.

In the province of Ontario no person shall act as a private investigator unless he is twenty-one years of age or over and no person shall act as a security guard unless he is eighteen years of age or over.

After acceptance as a security guard the employee shall wear a uniform while acting as a security guard and shall carry on his person the prescribed identification card that was issued to him, and if required produce it for inspection at the request of any person.

No security guard shall hold himself out in such a manner as performing or providing services or duties connected with the police and the security guard while on duty shall not have in his possession or display any evidence of authority except his uniform and the prescribed identification card issued under the Act.

In the Private Investigators and Security Guards Act of Ontario there is a penalty section that states:

32.–(1) Every person who,
    (a) knowingly furnishes false information in any application under this Act or in any statement or return required to be furnished under this Act or the regulations;
    (b) fails to comply with any order, direction or other requirement made under this Act or the regulations; or
    (c) contravenes any provision of this Act or the regulations,
is guilty of an offence and on conviction is liable to a fine of not more than $2,000 or to imprisonment for a term of not more than one year, or to both.

(2) Where a corporation is convicted of an offence under subsection (1), the maximum penalty that may be imposed is $25,000 and not as provided therein.

1. THE LICENSING FUNCTION

(a) Purposes of Licensing

Licensing in the security field leads to certain needed controls being placed on those who choose this profession and desire to provide this needed service. The licensing function does, by its very nature, control access to dedicated individuals, controls the continued participation of these firms, and has the added benefit of ensuring that basic standards are upheld.

All provinces regulate the security industry; however, each province has its own rules, which offer a great variance. Before beginning an agency, the appropriate provincial authorities should be contacted. This may save a great deal of confusion at a later date.

2. THE LICENSEES

(a) Who Must be Licensed

Although each province has its own terminology, there are basically four areas under which a person can be licensed with more than one company. The four areas are private investigation (or detective) agencies, private security guard agencies, private investigators (detective) and private security guards. A company may acquire a security license that permits it to carry on a security business in more than one area. No province allows the licensed employees to be licensed with more than one company.

An agency may have anywhere from one employee upwards; however, the same rules apply to all. Saskatchewan and Quebec differ in the wording of their rules, as they both allow the term of "private detective" and "detective agency" to be used. These two terms, popularized by television, are not allowed anywhere else in Canada.

One notable exception, which does not have to be licensed, is that of the "security consultant". This is a company, or individual, that will come to given premises and offer its expertise in establishing guidelines, for a fee. As it is not providing an ongoing service, it is exempt in most provinces from having a "security" licence.

A further type of firm that is exempt, based on the duties performed, is that of cash carriers. These are firms which will transport cash and valuables from a given location, such as business premises, to a bank. They are considered to be temporary employees of the firm, working on a contract basis, and as such are considered to be part of the company's in-house security force.

(b) Documentary Requirements

Every province differs in the information required to obtain either an agency or individual licence, with Ontario being the most detailed. In most cases, all that is required is basic information, such as name, age, address, references, experience and previous convictions. Ontario requires that fingerprints (as do some other provinces) and a photograph be submitted as well, whereas Quebec has the power to request a copy of the birth certificate (or citizenship document) as well as proof of physical or mental capability of duty performance.

As the particular Act governing security agencies is under provincial jurisdiction, as opposed to a federal governing agency, various methods are taken to ascertain the reliability of a person or firm licensed. However, all do a thorough records check for any past criminal activity.

All provinces require that the individual and officers of the firm give truthful information on their applications, and any deviance can, and will, be severely punished.

(c) Investigation of Applicants for Licences and Verification

Every province follows a slightly different approach in its investigation of applications; however, all do a thorough background check of the individual (especially in the case of a new agency applying), which consists not only of a check of existing records but also detailed inquiries of all officers' backgrounds, through checking their characters, reputations and possible criminal involvement in the community. If the person is found to have a dubious, or questionable, background, enquiries may well be made for a number of years after a probationary licence has been granted.

For comparison purposes, application forms from the Provinces of Ontario and Manitoba are reproduced below.

FORM 1

Manitoba

THE PRIVATE INVESTIGATORS AND SECURITY GUARDS ACT

APPLICATION FOR PRIVATE INVESTIGATOR OR SECURITY GUARD
BUSINESS LICENCE

☐   Renewal

Application for a licence to engage in the business of providing private investigators or security guards is made by the following person(s) carrying on business under the trade name of: _____,

at _____

(address)

1.   Particulars of applicant including each partner of a partnership:

    (a)   Name: _____

        Address: _____

        Place of Birth: _____ Date of Birth: _____

    (b)   Name: _____

        Address: _____

        Place of Birth: _____ Date of Birth: _____

        (If more space is required, use separate sheet of paper)

2. The business in Manitoba is conducted from: (Show the address to which this application applies)

    (a) Head Office: _____

    (b) Branch Office: _____

3. Has the applicant been convicted of an offence under the Criminal Code (Canada) or the criminal law of any other state or country or are there any proceedings now pending that may lead to such a conviction? If 'yes', give the particulars.

    _____

    _____

    _____

4. Has the applicant been refused a licence as a Private Investigator or Security Guard in Manitoba or any other Province, state or country, or has any such licence been suspended or cancelled? If 'yes' give the particulars.

    _____

    _____

5. Has the applicant ever used, operated or carried on business under any name other than the name given in this application? If 'yes' give the particulars

    _____

    _____

6. The business reputation of the applicant(s) is well known to the following three persons, not related to the applicant(s).

    1. Name: _____

        Address: _____

        Occupation: _____

    2. Name: _____

        Address: _____

        Occupation: _____

    3. Name: _____

        Address: _____

        Occupation: _____

7. Address for service: _____

Dated at _____ this _____ day of _____ 19_____.

_____

_____

FORM 3

Manitoba

THE PRIVATE INVESTIGATORS AND SECURITY GUARDS ACT

APPLICATION FOR LICENCE TO ACT AS A PRIVATE INVESTIGATOR OR SECURITY GUARD

☐ RENEWAL — Application is made by:

Name: (in full) _____

Address: _____

Place of Birth: _____ Date of Birth: _____

for a licence to act as a private investigator or a security guard as an employee of _____

_____ a person (firm) licensed

(employer)

to carry on the business of providing private investigators or security guards in Manitoba.

1. The name and place of business at which the applicant is to be employed to act as a private investigator or security guard.

   _____

2. Has the applicant been convicted of an offence under the Criminal Code (Canada) or the criminal law of any other state or country or are there any proceedings now pending that may lead to such a conviction? If 'yes' give the particulars.

   _____

   _____

3. Has the applicant been refused a licence as a private investigator or security guard in Manitoba or any other Province, State or Country, or has any such licence been suspended or cancelled? If 'yes' give the particulars.

   _____

   _____

4. Has the applicant ever used, operated under or carried on business as a private investigator under any other name than the name given in this application? If 'yes' give the particulars.

   _____

   _____

5. The character of the applicant is well known to the following persons, none of whom are related to the applicant:

   1. Name: _____
      Address: _____
      Occupation: _____

   2. Name: _____
      Address: _____
      Occupation: _____

6. Address for service _____

Dated at _____ this _____ day of _____ 19___.

_____   _____
            Witness   Applicant

FORM 5

MANITOBA

THE PRIVATE INVESTIGATORS AND SECURITY GUARDS ACT

AFFIDAVIT

I, _____

of the _____ of _____ in the Province of _____

☐   1.   I have made application for a licence to engage in the business of providing private investigators or security guards.

☐   2.   That I am employed by _____, to act as a private investigator or security guard.

      3.   I have not been convicted of any offence under the Criminal Code (Canada), or the criminal law of any other state or country and there are not any proceedings pending that might lead to such a conviction — other than the following:

_____

_____

      4.   I have not been refused a licence to act as a Private Investigator Security Guard in Manitoba or any other province, state or country, nor has my licence been suspended or cancelled (other than on the following occasions):

_____

_____

      5.   I have never used a name other than the name given in this affidavit (other than on the following occasions):

_____

_____

Sworn before me at the   )

_____ of _____)

in the _____)

this _____ day of _____ 19__.)

)

)   . . . .

_____)

A Commissioner for Oaths in and for the)

Province of Manitoba.)

My appointment expires on the _____)

day of _____ A.D. 19____.)

Form 5

Private Investigators and Security Guards Act

APPLICATION FOR LICENCE TO ENGAGE IN THE BUSINESS OF PROVIDING PRIVATE INVESTIGATORS OR SECURITY GUARDS

(If application is for renewal of licence, complete paragraphs 1, 2, 15, 19, 20, 23, 24, 27, 28, 29 and 31)

Date of Application...................., 19....

The Applicant is:

    i. an individual who will carry on business alone ☐

    ii. a partnership ☐

    iii. applying for a branch office licence ☐

    iv. a corporation ☐

PART 1

(To be completed by an Applicant who is an individual or a partnership or is applying for a branch office licence)

1. Last or Family Name.....................

    First Name.........Middle Name.........
    (indicate name commonly used)

2. Residence address......................
    (number and street)

    ....
    (city, town, village)   (postal zone)

    Residence Telephone number...............

3. Nationality...............................

4. Occupation ....

5. Date of Birth...........................
    (day)   (month)   (year)

6. Place of Birth..........................
    (city, town, village)

    ....
    (province, state)   (country)

7. If born outside Canada, arrival date in Canada

    ....
    (day)   (month)   (year)

8. Physical description......................
    (height: feet inches)

    ....
    (weight)   (eyes)

    ....
    (complexion)   (hair)

9. Marital Status: Married ☐ Widower ☐
                Divorced ☐ Single ☐

10. Record of Education:

    i. Primary School........................
       (name and address)

    Year: from.............to............

    Last Grade completed...................

    ii. Secondary School......................
       (name and address)

    Year: from.............to............

    Last Grade completed...................

    iii. Other (give particulars):.................

    ....

11. Places of residence during past fifteen years:

    (Commence with present address)

Address	Year From To	Indicate if residence Rented or Owned
....	....	....
....	....	....
....	....	....

12. Employment Record during past fifteen years:

    (Commence with present employment)

Employer's Name and Address	Name of Dept. or Supervisor	Type of Work	Year From To	Reason for Termination
....	......	.....	.....	......
....	......	.....	.....	......
....	......	.....	.....	......

13. The business reputation of the applicant is well known to the following persons. References must not be related to the applicant and must not be former employers.

Name	Address	Business or Occupation	Length of time known
i.	....	....	....
ii.	....	....	....
iii.	....	....	....

14. Trade name under which applicant wishes to carry on business. List in order of preference.

   i. ....

   ii. ....

   iii. ....

15. Does the applicant hold a permit authorizing him to carry a firearm issued by any police authority in Ontario, or any other province, state or country?

   Yes ☐   No ☐

   If yes, give particulars.

16. Summary of experience and training in investigation. Furnish particulars:

   i. Police Force.

   ii. Armed Services.

   iii. Insurance Company or Insurance Adjuster.

   iv. Investigation Agency.

   v. Similar experience or training.

17. Summary of experience and training as a security guard. Furnish particulars:

   i. Police Force.

   ii. Armed Services.

   iii. Security Guard Agency.

   iv. Similar experience or training.

18. Chartered bank or trust company where applicant has been known during past ten years

   ....
   (name and address) (length of time account maintained)

19. i. Is the applicant an undischarged bankrupt?

   Yes ☐   No ☐

   If yes, give particulars:

   ....

   ....

   ii. Has the applicant ever been involved as an official in any company which is a declared bankrupt or is in the process of bankruptcy?

   Yes ☐   No ☐

   If yes, give particulars: ....

   ....

20. Has any judgment of any Court been issued against the applicant?

   Yes ☐   No ☐

   If yes, give particulars:

   ....

   ....

21. Does the applicant have any financial or other interest in any other business providing private investigators or security guards?

   Yes ☐   No ☐

   If yes, give particulars:

   ....

   ....

22. Address of business.........................
   (number and street)

   ....
   (city, town, village)   (postal zone)

   Telephone Number............

   i. Is this an office building or similar business premises?   Yes ☐   No ☐

   ii. Is this a private residence? Yes ☐ No ☐

   If yes, is office set apart from dwelling?

   Yes ☐   No ☐

   If yes, is office readily accessible to the general public by means of a separate entrance?   Yes ☐   No ☐

23. Address for service.........................

24. Has the applicant ever been charged, indicted or convicted of any offence under any law of any province, state or country?   Yes ☐   No ☐

If yes, give particulars:

....
(place)   (date)   (police department)

....
(offence)   (sentence)

25. Does the applicant intent to operate a business on a full time ☐ basis?
part-time ☐ basis?

If part-time, state other occupation..........

26. What type of investigation does applicant intend to carry out?

Domestic ☐   General ☐   Industrial ☐
Insurance ☐   Retail Store Checking ☐
Surveillance ☐

If other, specify:

....

....

27. i. Has the applicant ever applied for a business or personal licence as a private investigator or security guard in any province, state or country?   Yes ☐   No ☐

If yes, give particulars:

....

....

ii. Has the applicant ever been registered or employed as a private investigator or security guard in any province, state or country? Yes ☐   No ☐

If yes, give particulars:

....

....

28. i. Is the applicant a member of a Police Force?

Yes ☐   No ☐

ii. Is the applicant a member of an Auxiliary Police Force?   Yes ☐   No ☐

iii. Is the applicant appointed as a Special Constable?   Yes ☐   No ☐

29. Has the applicant ever used, operated under or carried on business under any other than the

name in which this application is submitted?
Yes ☐   No ☐

If yes, give particulars:

....

....

30. Does the applicant intend to apply for a licence to act as a private investigator Yes ☐   No ☐
security guard   Yes ☐   No ☐

31. i. Is the applicant an individual who will carry on business alone?   Yes ☐   No ☐

ii. If yes, will any other person have any financial or other interest in the operation of the business?   Yes ☐   No ☐

If yes, give particulars:

....

....

32. i. Is the applicant a partnership?
Yes ☐   No ☐

ii. List the names and addresses of all partners:

....

....

iii. Attach a copy of the partnership agreement.

iv. Will any person, other than a member of the partnership have any financial or other interest in the operation of the business?
Yes ☐   No ☐

If yes, give particulars:

....

....

33. If the applicant is applying for a branch office licence complete the following:

i. Name and address of applicant's head office

....

ii. Name of manager of branch office........

....

iii. Residence address of branch manager......

....
(number and street)

....
(city, town, village)   (postal zone)

iv. Address of branch office.................
(number and street)

....
(city, town, village)   (postal zone)

....
(telephone number)

34. Length of time branch office manager,

i. has been employed by licensee;

ii. has acted as manager of branch office for which application is now being made for licence.

35. If manager has been in charge of other branch offices, give particulars:

....

....

36. Is applicant applying for a branch office licence to engage in the business of providing:

private investigators ☐   security guards ☐

37. The branch manager will operate the branch office on a full-time ☐ basis
part-time ☐ basis

If part-time, state other occupation:

....

....

AFFIDAVIT

(By individual applicant, or by one of the partners or by an applicant for a branch office licence, as the case may be)

Province of Ontario:	I,....................,
County of............	of the.................
To wit:	in the County of........
	make oath and say:

1. I am the applicant (or partner of the applicant) herein for a licence to engage in the business of providing private investigators or security guards, or for a branch office licence.

2. The information given by me in the application is true.

Sworn before me at the

....

in the County of.......

this......day of......,

19....

....
A Commissioner, etc.

Part 2

(To be completed by an officer or director of a corporation)

38. Has the applicant ever used, operated under or carried on business under any other than the name in which this application is submitted?
Yes ☐   No ☐

If yes, give particulars:

....

....

39. Has the applicant ever been registered or licensed to engage in the business of a private investigator or a security guard in any province, state or country?   Yes ☐   No ☐

If yes, give particulars:

....

....

40. Does the applicant have any financial or other interest in any other business providing private investigators or security guards?
Yes ☐   No ☐

If yes, give particulars:

....

....

41. Chartered bank or trust company where applicant has been known during past ten years:

....
(name and address)

....
(length of time account maintained)

42. Is the applicant an undischarged bankrupt?
Yes ☐   No ☐

If yes, give particulars:

....

....

43. Has any judgment of any Court been issued against the applicant?   Yes ☐   No ☐

If yes, give particulars:

....

....

44. Address of business...........................
(number and street)

....
(city, town, village)   (postal zone)

....
(telephone number)

i. Is this an office building or similar business premises?   Yes ☐   No ☐

ii. Is this a private residence? Yes ☐   No ☐

If yes, is office set apart from dwelling?
Yes ☐   No ☐

If yes, is office readily accessible to the general public by means of a separate entrance?   Yes ☐   No ☐

45. Address for service...........................

....

46. Has the applicant ever been charged, indicted or convicted of any offence under any law of any province, state or country?   Yes ☐   No ☐

If yes, give particulars:

....
(place)   (date)   (police department)

....
(offence)   (sentence)

47. Does the applicant intend to operate a business on a full-time   ☐ basis?
part-time   ☐ basis?

If part-time, state other occupation:

....

48. What type of investigation does applicant intend to carry out?

Domestic   ☐   General ☐   Industrial ☐
Insurance   ☐   Retail Store Checking ☐
Surveillance ☐

If other, specify:

....

49. If the applicant is applying for a branch office licence complete the following:

i. Name of manager of branch office........

....

ii. Residence address of branch manager......

....
(number and street)

....
(city, town, village)   (postal zone)

iii. Address of branch office.................
(number and street)

....
(city, town, village)   (postal zone)

....
(telephone number)

50. i. Length of time branch office manager,

has been employed by licensee.........

has acted as manager of branch office for which application is now being made for

licence ....

ii. If manager has been in charge of other branch offices, give particulars:

....

....

iii. Is applicant applying for a branch office licence to engage in the business of providing:

private investigators ☐
security guards   ☐

iv. The branch manager will operate the branch office on a full-time   ☐ basis
part-time   ☐ basis

If part-time, state other occupation:

....

51. The applicant is a corporation,

i. whose head office is located outside Ontario

at ....

ii. whose Ontario head office is located at

....

52. The applicant is a corporation,

i. whose head office is located in Ontario at

....

ii. whose branch offices are located at ....

....

53. The names, residence addresses and telephone numbers of the Corporation directors and officials are set out below:

Name in Full	Residence Address	City or Town	Resi- dence Tel. No.	Officials
......	......	....	.....	President
......	......	....	.....	Vice-President
......	......	....	.....	Secretary
......	......	....	.....	Treasurer or
......	......	....	.....	Directors

State whether active or nonactive as a private investigator or a security guard.

54. Do any officers or directors of the corporation have any financial or other interest in any other business providing private investigators or security guards?   Yes ☐   No ☐

If yes, give particulars:

....

....

55. Has the applicant received its charter?
   Yes ☐   No ☐

If yes, give date of Letters Patent ....

AFFIDAVIT
(of Director or Officer of Corporation)

PROVINCE OF ONTARIO   I,.....................,

County of.............   of the.................

   To Wit: in the County of........

                        make oath and say:

1. I am......................................
   (state position in corporation)

   of the applicant herein and I signed the foregoing application.

2. The information given in the application is true.

SWORN before me at the

....

in the County of.......

this......day of......,

19....

....
   A Commissioner, etc.

R.R.O. 1970, Reg. 690, Form 6.

Form 6

Private Investigators and Security Guards Act

APPLICATION FOR EMPLOYEE LICENCE

Application for Employee Licence Under the Private Investigators and Security Guards Act form (Ontario).

EDUCATION RECORD

NAME OF SECONDARY SCHOOL LAST ATTENDED	DATES ATTENDED FROM	CIRCLE HIGHEST GRADE SUCCESSFULLY COMPLETED
ADDRESS	TO	9 10 11 12 13

SPECIFY ANY POST SECONDARY DIPLOMAS OR DEGREES YOU HOLD

SPECIFY OTHER SKILLS YOU POSSESS RELATIVE TO SECURITY

LIST THREE (3) PERSONS NOT RELATED TO YOU (EXCLUDE EMPLOYEES) WHO ARE COMPETENT TO JUDGE YOUR CHARACTER AND WHO HAVE KNOWLEDGE OF YOUR QUALIFICATIONS AND FITNESS.

	FULL NAME	ADDRESS	OCCUPATION	NO YEARS KNOWN
1				
2				
3				

FINANCIAL INSTITUTION WHERE APPLICANT KNOWN DURING PAST 10 YEARS	BRANCH	ACCOUNT NUMBER

DO YOU HAVE ANY FINANCIAL OR OTHER INTEREST IN ANY BUSINESS PROVIDING INVESTIGATIVE OR SECURITY SERVICES
☐ NO   ☐ YES - SPECIFY

HAVE YOU EVER PERSONALLY DECLARED BANKRUPTCY, OR ARE YOU IN THE PROCESS OF BANKRUPTCY
☐ NO   ☐ YES - SPECIFY

HAVE YOU EVER BEEN INVOLVED AS AN OFFICIAL IN ANY COMPANY WHICH HAS DECLARED BANKRUPTCY, OR IS IN THE PROCESS OF A BANKRUPTCY   ☐ NO   ☐ YES - SPECIFY

HAS ANY JUDGEMENT OF ANY COURT BEEN ISSUED AGAINST YOU
☐ NO   ☐ YES - SPECIFY

"CAUTION" Any person who knowingly furnishes false information in any application under the *Private Investigators and Security Guards Act* is guilty of an offence.
In addition the licence may be refused.

"DECLARATION AND AUTHORITY FOR RELEASE OF INFORMATION"

I hereby certify that the information set out by me in this application is true and correct to the best of my knowledge and belief and authorize the release to the Registrar of Private Investigators and Security Guards or any person authorized by him, of any or all information required under the Private Investigators and Security Guards Act with respect to my financial status, bank records, etc. and also pertinent information from my former employers.

_____   _____
SIGNATURE OF EMPLOYEE   DATE

This application is made on behalf of   by ....
                                                              (name of employer)

....
        (name of employee)   (employer's signature)

O. Reg. 52/78, s. 8, *part.*

3

Supervisory Management in Security

1. SELECTING A SECURITY MANAGER

In the past a Security Manager was routinely selected by traditional means; that is, the qualified manager for a Security Department usually was a retired military policeman or from the ranks of the public police. This was as a result of the "old-boy system", based on selecting a manager because of contacts from his previous occupation. As you are aware, some information that a Security Manager may require is obtained from police sources and in some cases is confidential. This information is obtained from "old working buddies" who previously knew the Security Manager and trust him with this information.

The irony of this system is that the successful applicant for the position of Security Manager in private industry usually knows little about industrial security, a fact that may be overlooked by the individual himself, and in most cases the transition can be made from the public sector to the private sector with a considerable amount of research and study being completed by the new incumbent.

Industry at that time did not have a drawing pool to choose applicants from as it does today.

In today's society many young people are continuing their education and choosing professions in the security field. Some of the more common fields of study are Criminology courses offered in universities and Law and Security courses offered through many community colleges.

These courses of study give the student some important insight into the world of private security, and at the very least provide a comparison to public police. Students who enrol in these courses usually find employment in their chosen fields, or ones closely related. These related courses have come a long way, but must advance further from their earlier stages to promote the expertise to allow the students to compete for management positions in industry today. The drawing pool that will result will consist of the highly motivated young people the industry will require in the future.

It is true that there is no teacher like experience, but relevant education plus experience offers the market more from which to choose.

It is suggested that the Security Director or Manager should have this type of background. The employer could then consider persons other than retired policemen. The usually younger Security Manager will have more time to offer the company and can grow with management through periods of transition.

Ideally, if you have an ex-policeman with a community college background and some related experience in private enforcement, you will have an excellent applicant. However, this is unlikely to happen and management will have to decide among the applicants who will better suit their needs.

It is not suggested that retired or ex-policemen should be ruled out, but merely suggested that in today's society there are extremely qualified people who are not police-men.

2. WHAT IS A SECURITY MANAGER?

This is an area that is complex to understand and define. The role of security management differs greatly when management centres around contract security in comparison to in-house security. However, when a Security Manager provides a complete security package that covers an industry, and only that industry, he may be considered as part of that industry's management team.

With this in mind the established role of the Security Manager must be defined carefully by the industry for which he is providing the coverage. The Security Manager may be looked upon as part of the top management team or possibly as part of the subordinate group of middle management.

Whatever the placement of the Security Manager, he should report directly to the executive level. This would enable him to be free from external pressures by middle management who may wish for compromises when a security matter affects their department.

The placement in the chain of command of the Security Manager would quickly define whether he is considered a professional or merely the caretaker of a group of watchmen.

Management in relation to contract versus in-house differs to some degree and we will discuss the factors affecting both.

Security management in relation to in-house can be very complex. Depending on the position in the chain of command, the issues become even more complex. With this in mind we will look at security management which ideally should report directly to the executive level.

Two cases may exist: the first case is that of the new appointment of a Security Director who inherits a department, and the second that of the newly-appointed Director who forms a new security department.

With both cases in mind the appointment of the Security Director must be considered carefully, as the new Director must exhibit confidence, good common sense and maintain at all times a professional stature.

The Security Director or Manager must take these qualities and establish a rapport with upper management. Once his position has been established he must proceed to put in place policies for the good of the company and all employees. This type of authority should jump the gap that may result from the Security Director coming into departments that may resist any attempt to interfere. If the Manager can rely on the support of upper management, it will give him further confidence to forge on even in the face of resistance. The Security Manager must sell his product to all levels of management and all departments within the company's jurisdiction.

The new Manager must have goals established, giving himself a reasonable time-frame in which to accomplish his objectives.

If the Security Manager inherits a security department, he must first review all of the security policies in place, then evaluate and implement changes as required. He may see areas that have not been covered and must implement policy to cover the area of concern until formalized policy changes can come into effect. When an established department is taken over, in some cases that department has not experienced radical change for a long period of time. This scenario produces further, even greater, problems. In most cases he will be the "new man on the block" and be greatly resented with any new change or review that is requested. He may well be faced with the all-too-familiar quote, "Well, we never had to do it before". If this attitude is present he may have genuine problems in developing a professional team.

If the attitude is that of resentment he has several options open to him. First, he may call a meeting and carefully discuss his analysis of the department with all of the security staff. In this analysis, all the current good points, as well as the bad, should be pointed out. He must be prepared to outline his goals and define the course he now wishes the security department to take. In this meeting he must be frank and request input from the working staff. In some cases he may be surprised to learn that suggested policies, or something similar, have been tried in the past and have not worked. This is not to say that these changes cannot be implemented, as he may have a new approach to the situation. It is hoped that this meeting will allow the staff to get to know who he is and what he wishes to achieve.

After the meeting, sufficient time should be allowed to elapse before re-evaluating the staff. It may now be found that several, if not all, have adapted the enthusiasm for change. If there still persists the nagging problem of security employees not wishing to change to do the job as the new director sees fit, then he must consider disciplinary action. On this path there is little leeway. Should the employee not respond to verbal and written warnings, then the director may have no alternative but to terminate his employment. The problem of discontent will never go away while one or two employees constantly question his authority and policies.

With this exercise completed he should now have a remaining crew who either voluntarily or with pressure have changed their outlook. It is hoped, if it was with pressure, that in time they will come to realize that his policies were for the betterment of themselves and the industry.

If he has formed a new department, with new employees, he will already have selected employees who, he feels, will be prepared to accept new concepts and are willing to adopt a professional work style. When policies and procedures are properly explained to them they will in most cases respond with a positive attitude.

The role of the Security Manager is to direct, plan, organize, control and coordinate the Security Department. He will bring it into the mainstream of the industry he has been charged to protect. He will carefully blend his policies with that of existing policies and goals already established by the company to promote harmony.

The Security Manager must be realistic in his approach to problems, as he must be cost effective, provide a service and, if necessary, take chances in areas in which he has never been before. He must always be cognizant that he may not always get what ideally he wants and must be prepared to trade-off certain ideals if management resists the spending of a considerable amount of money for certain projects. He may be forced to settle for second-best, if necessary, to provide some sort of protection. This is not to say that he must abandon the project because he was refused, but monitor the progress of what he put into effect and report back to management on its progress. Management may feel it will be in a position to afford the expense at a later time and will give the go ahead when money is available.

The Security Manager must always be in a state of flux. He must never settle for a policy the way he drafted it, but must constantly review policies and objectives to improve their quality. By carefully monitoring the industry, he will find that his policies may or may not be working. If they are not, changes must be made.

3. HOW DOES THE SECURITY MANAGER ACCOMPLISH HIS GOALS?

The Security Manager cannot do it alone. He must select supervisors with whom he can work. If he has a new department this will be relatively easy. If he has taken over an existing department it may be a little harder. There may be supervision already in place. If there are supervisors in place they must be willing to implement the new policies and goals. If they are not willing to do this then they must be replaced with either new employees or employees presently on staff who are willing to take the step. If there is supervision in place, he can now proceed. He must tightly control and direct his supervisors. He must be honest with them and, if necessary, quite frank when he feels that the job is not being done the way he feels it should be done. In most cases it will be found that it will be done better than ever imagined. He should direct the staff to take an existing policy and come up with a better one if they can. This can sometimes be quite revealing. Areas never considered by the Security Manager may be covered and presented for consideration.

Once he has established a rapport and common working relationship with his supervisors, he must coordinate all their energy in one direction. Nothing is worse than a lot of work being done for nothing. Supervisors should inform him of their progress and he, in turn, must advise them where their suggestions are going. Either agree or disagree with them but let them know. If they feel there is no feedback they will lose interest and progress will be defeated. He must ensure that they represent the remaining security staff and they keep the staff informed of possible changes or new policy that may take effect. He should have them obtain the views of the remaining employees, whether positive or negative. The important point to remember is not to allow the avenues of communications to crumble. He will have a greater chance of success if all parties feel they have a say in their direction, but he should never lose sight of the fact that he is accountable at all times and must have the final word on any matter affecting the department.

The Security Manager must set the course of the department. To accomplish this he must have pride in himself and pride in his profession. He must instill pride and professionalism in his security staff. Unfortunately, Security Departments must break the image of the old watchman ready to retire on the gate. This image resulted from industry demanding that the Security Departments in the past take on employees from outside the Security Department who could no longer work in their respective areas. Some were previously injured in some cases, but in a majority of cases the employees were near pensionable service and could no longer perform the rigors of their previous job. This image is being eroded, although much too slowly. Industry has realized that the Security Department needs to be independent of the rest of the company it has been charged to protect. The hiring of young, aggressive people with higher education, mostly from community college courses on Law and Security, has greatly improved this image.

4. SECURITY MANAGEMENT AND THE BUDGET

One of the jobs that security management is required

to perform is to establish guidelines in policy and spending.

Budgets are usually based on a year-to-year period. Some companies use January 1 to December 31 of any given year as a block, and others use April 1 to March 31 of the following year. Neither poses any different problems, as the period is still for twelve months. A company may wish for a five-year projected budget and this becomes a little more difficult.

Several factors must be considered when preparing a budget:

1. Expense budgets. This may include personal expense accounts and other expenses from personnel.
2. Miscellaneous expenses. This may include items such as uniforms or day-to-day operating expenses not planned for.
3. Office supplies.
4. Labour costs (full time). This would include departmental costs affecting full-time staff. The labour costs would be based on the number of shifts full-time security employees would be required to provide coverage. Absences through sick time, vacations, and statutory holidays must be taken into consideration. Benefits included in the salary must be taken into account if management requires it. Benefits may include coverage paid directly by the employer, such as dental, medical and prescription drug plans, etc.
5. Labour costs (part time). This would be based on the number of shifts that must be covered by full-time absences. In these calculations, benefits, as a rule, would not be a factor.
6. Equipment costs. This would apply to mobile equip-

ment, such as costs involving transportation. A vehicle may be required for the detex route or for emergency transportation. Costs would be gas and regular maintenance. Other equipment costs may include alarms, monitoring equipment, such as cameras and audio video recorders, etc.

7. Cleaning supplies. These may be required to clean and maintain equipment, including gatehouses.

8. Capital budgeting. This would include large expenditures of capital, such as a request to build a new gatehouse.

Once the budget is in place, the Manager must be prepared to live with it. It is usually too late to request additional manpower because it was forgotten to budget for this necessity. Always remember that senior management may request a cut back in your expenses should the need arise and a constant vigil should be maintained of the financial understanding on a monthly basis. The Manager should request printouts of the labour and administrative costs to evaluate the current position. In this manner it will be ·possible to refrain from overspending in unnecessary areas, or in months where it would have been possible to cut expenses.

5. SECURITY MANAGEMENT IN CONTRACT SECURITY

This area poses several different problems when compared to supervision for in-house security. There is no change in the chain of command with respect to the contract Security Manager being held responsible to a senior manager in the company that he has been paid to protect. The chain of command may be reporting to middle management or directly to the executive level. In all likelihood, if the service is contract, the manager of the contract security firm will answer to middle management or the in-house Security Director.

Contract security firms in most cases bid on a contract. These bids normally take the form of tenders and several contract security firms are requested to submit bids. These tenders usually refer to a clause stating that not necessarily the lowest bidder will be accepted, but in most cases it is. This poses problems with the working staff that the contract Security Manager must provide for the client. To get a contract the offer in most cases is the lowest possible. This must be translated from the contract Security Manager's point of view to paying employees a low wage, which must be done to cover operating expenses, and if the contract security firm is to survive it is absolutely necessary. With this problem you will restrict the type of applicants you would normally receive should the wage be considerably higher. There is nothing that can be done in this instance unless you remove yourself from the submissions for tender and strictly provide a higher quality service. This will add to your costs as you will be required to pay higher wages; however, if a quality service is provided, this will quickly become known and will tend to offset any contracts that may be lost through not tendering at a low rate.

In the contract security industry, providing motivation to your employees can be extremely difficult. With the wage that is usually paid, in some cases the employee working will not give that little extra that is most often desired. To achieve a highly motivated employee in this circumstance you will have to attempt promotion and always offer more money. If you do not do this the employee will not grow. Because of this factor there is a high turnover rate in the contract security field. Most employees in this particular part of the profession are looking for other work in their chosen field that pays more money and offers a more promising future. One application that may provide motivation is to allow the keen employee the opportunity of working more shifts or working at a more desirable location, thus allowing him to earn more take home pay or work in a better environment, while not raising his labour rate. This is, however, a band-aid solution that will only work for a short period of time. Industry today would see further changes in manpower should the economy be better, but as we all know jobs are hard to find in today's market place. This allows the contract Security Manager the temporary feeling of security as his employees have nowhere to go and are forced to remain in his employ.

These points are a problem in today's industry and until we break free of these practices we will never break the idea that contract security employees are people who are low paid, without motivation and merely waiting until they can find better jobs.

If we break free of this image, industry will be forced to deal with a better quality contract security industry which has better paid, educated and motivated people. With better pay and higher educational standards the product will still be cheaper than the public police. The industry will continue to grow because of its flexibility and enforcement centering around prevention. A higher quality contract security company may enable the company employer a better insurance premium, lower deductible with respect to theft and a lower premium with respect to insurance for fire.

The contract security industry can only motivate itself. It provides a unique service and it must overcome the fear that it will overprice itself. Once the contract security industry has accomplished these steps the old views and traditions will be broken down once and for all.

6. PROPER DEPLOYMENT OF MANPOWER

To properly deploy manpower the Manager must ascertain firstly what positions have to be manned to provide adequate coverage. Once this has been achieved, a dollar figure can be placed on the protection package.

After considering manpower requirements, a shift must be put into place. Some people dread this aspect; however, there are certain shifts available on the market today and these can be modified to suit any particular need. Several examples will follow. When establishing the shifts, it must be remembered there are several rules that will benefit both the Manager and the manpower who must work the shifts:

1. Establish the shift so that the employee rotates from day to evening to midnights, for example. There is nothing worse for morale than having to work all nights when fellow employees, who have the same seniority, work straight day shifts.
2. Project the shift for as long a period of time as possible. The examples that follow are for periods of one year.
3. Establish permanent crews in these shifts and allow them to switch between themselves, if operationally possible, days in their private lives that conflict with their shift schedules. However, their supervisors must always be suitably informed of these changes and their approval received before any changes take place.
4. Should there be twelve men required on each shift, except, for example, during the night when an additional

four men are required, it may be better to have the extra four positions covered by part-time personnel. This will enable you to rotate your shifts with little problem, leaving the extra four night positions to be covered by part-time employees.

(a) Figure A

This is an example of a three-shift rotation. Day shift is from 8:00 a.m. to 4:00 p.m., evening shift is from 4:00 p.m. to 12:00 midnight, and midnight shift is from 12:00 midnight to 8:00 a.m. There are three shifts working at all times while one is on rest. This particular shift was designed for a 24-hour operation, seven days per week, for one year in duration. The work stretch is seven days on shift, two days on rest, seven days on shift, two days rest and seven days on with three days on rest. This can be ascertained, for example, by looking at the 12–8 shift from Employee B. Follow the B for seven days and you will notice the B drops down to the area marked OFF. Employee B has come off a midnight shift, has two days off, then goes to the 4–12 shift, which is called afternoon shift. Proceed along this line for seven days again and Employee B drops to OFF again for two days off. Follow the B now to 8–4 shift which is days and he is working the day shift for seven days and following this he drops once again to OFF, where he will be rewarded with three days off, or what is referred to as a long weekend. This shift is based on a 42-hour work week.

Now break from the shift area in Fig. A, where the days of the month will be observed along the left side. Imagine you are an employee of A Shift and it is now January the 12th. You have been asked to attend a wedding on June the 12th and would like to do so. In this case drop along the column until you see the first JUN. Follow JUN to the 6, which is the 6th day of May, across the line until you see the 1 and 2. This is the 1st and 2nd of June and you will have to drop down to the following JUN, which starts at June the 3rd. Follow this line across to the right until you come to the 12. This is June the 12th. From the 12th, go up towards the top of the page past the 15 May, 17 April, 20 March, 20 February, and 23 January until you reach the shift area at the top of the page. Now look for the position that A Shift is in and you will observe that A Shift is off on the 12th and 13th of June so you will be able to attend. If you were not off you may be able to switch shifts with someone, but by following the schedule you would be able to determine who would possibly be available to switch with you.

(b) Figure B

This represents a 12-hour shift, or what is called a compressed work sheet. This is also based on a 42-hour work week; however, in some weeks this does work out to 60 hours, while in the following week it only comprises 24 hours. In the Province of Ontario permission must be granted to work employees the extra length of time, and similar legislation is applicable in other provinces.

It will be noticed in the shift area at the top there is 8AM to 8PM. and below that is 8PM to 8AM. This is due to the fact that there are only two shifts working on any given day instead of three shifts working and one on rest. This 12-hour shift removes the afternoon shift noted in Fig. A as 4–12. There are still four shifts, namely A, B, C, and D; however two shifts will now be on and two will be off. A Shift and C Shift may work opposite each other, while B and D will be on time off. This 12-hour shift works fundamentally the same as the Fig. A shift in ascertaining when someone is working or on rest. To explain this, look at the month of December on the bottom line. Observe the man on D Shift does not work December 1, 2, 3, 4, as he does not appear on the top under the shift area. Notice that D Shift appears on 5 and 6 December on day shift 8AM to 8PM and then on 7 and 8 December works 8PM to 8AM. This is followed again by four days off.

(c) Figure C

This is another example of a 12-hour shift, or compressed work week, based on 42 hours a week. The longest period worked by any Group is three consecutive shifts. Under the shift area at the top of the page there are four Groups as well. Two work and two are off. Groups A and C are usually working opposite each other, as well as B and D Groups doing the same. To ascertain if someone is working on September the 23rd in Group A, the principle is the same as the other examples. Look down the left hand side of the shift until you find the month of September, then go right until you come to 23. Follow this line up towards the top of the page until you see the shift area. Group A is Off on rest.

(d) Figure D

A lot can happen in the period of a year that will affect a shift and a staff member. Figure D will eliminate this problem plus provide a shift for part-time call-in people.

Notice on the top the space marked June. This is where the applicable month would be filled in. Next are the dates and, as can be seen, this period is for a week. This shift would have been drafted and posted for circulation usually on the previous Wednesday or Thursday, thus providing ample time for the people to find out when they are working. On the left going down the page you will observe Main Gate – Days, Main Gate – Nights, Security Van – Days twice and Security Van – Nights twice, Broadway Gate – Days, Broadway Gate – Nights, Kraft H.C. – Days, Kraft H.C. – Nights. These positions can be substituted with titles more applicable to the individual situation, for example, Main Gate may be referred to as Headquarters, etc. Notice under Security Van it has two spots. This indicates that this position is filled with two security staff.

Follow through with the shift for part-time employees who are working the week of June 2 to 8. Notice that no relief is needed the 2nd or 3rd as these spaces are not filled in. On the 4th of June, Number 7098 is in the position of Security Van – Days. This indicates that Employee number 7098 is working the security van on day shift. To find out why, look under the category of holidays and it will be seen that 2373 is on holidays the 4th of June. Therefore Employee 7098 is taking his place. On the 5th of June there are no part-time workers except on the Security van – night shift. This part-time employee is payroll 6979 and the explanation is that another full-time employee, payroll number 2379, is on a floating holiday.

A floating holiday is given in some instances to employees who worked on a statutory holiday and are given a day off for working on the holiday. The 6th of June has no part time employees working, but the 7th of June has payroll 7247 working two shifts, that of the 7th and 8th of June. He is working two day shifts in the Kraft H.C. position.

Notice that another full-time employee is off for the week, Employee 1649, who is on First Aid Training.

Under Distribution it can be seen that the shift is

going to the appropriate locations for posting.

This part-time shift is completed to keep record of shifts worked and changed, as well as to submit time worked for the part-time employees, so they will receive their correct payment.

It must be pointed out at this time that shifts are only an outline that can be changed at any time to bring about better efficiency to the Security Department. If it is necessary to move people around to eliminate overtime and other costs, then this must be done. You are not locked into a shift because you have posted a shift for a period of one year. This is a guideline only and for the benefit of the security staff that you employ. A shift for one year is basically a guideline only for the benefit of the employee, although it should be adhered to as closely as possible.

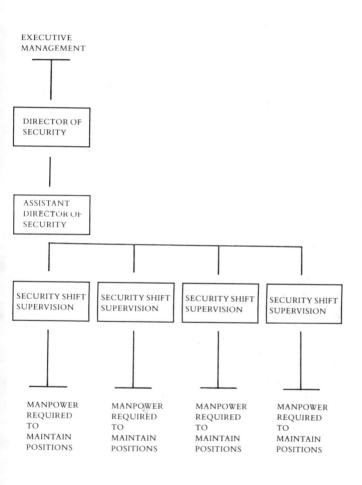

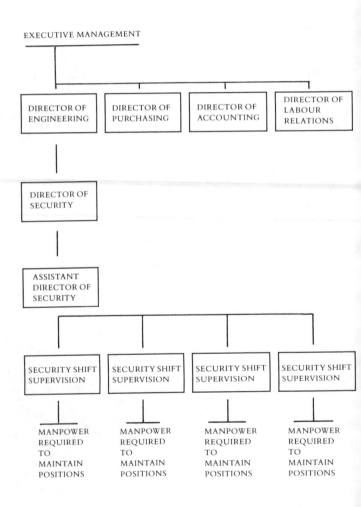

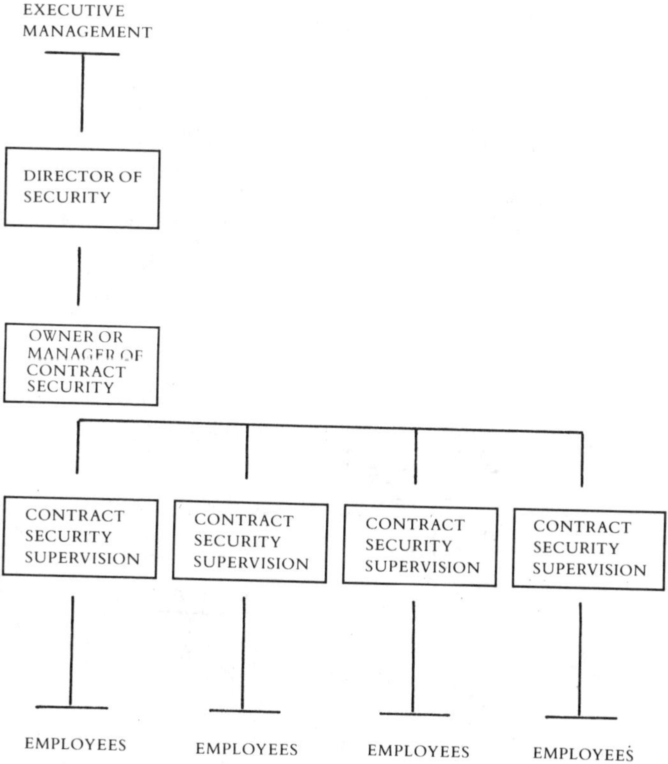

EXECUTIVE
MANAGEMENT

DIRECTOR OF
SECURITY

OWNER OR
MANAGER OF
CONTRACT
SECURITY

CONTRACT
SECURITY
SUPERVISION

CONTRACT
SECURITY
SUPERVISION

CONTRACT
SECURITY
SUPERVISION

CONTRACT
SECURITY
SUPERVISION

EMPLOYEES

EMPLOYEES

EMPLOYEES

EMPLOYEES

FIGURE A

SHIFT	8-4	4-12	12-8	OFF	JAN	FEB	MAR	APR	MAY	JUN	JUN	JUL	AUG	SEPT	OCT	NOV	DEC	DEC
S	C	D	A	B		13	10	10	7	5	2	30	28	25	22	20	17	15
S	C	D	A	B		12	9	9	6	4	1	29	27	24	21	19	16	14
F	C	D	A	B		11	8	8	5	3	31	28	26	23	20	18	15	13
T	B	D	A	C		10	7	7	4	2	30	27	25	22	19	17	14	12
W	B	D	A	C		9	6	6	3	1	29	26	24	21	18	16	13	11
T	B	C	A	D		8	5	5	2	30	28	25	23	20	17	15	12	10
M	B	C	A	D		7	4	4	1	29	27	24	22	19	16	14	11	9
S	B	C	D	A		6	3	3	31	28	26	23	21	18	15	13	10	8
S	B	C	D	A		5	2	2	30	27	25	22	20	17	14	12	9	7
F	B	C	D	A		4	1	1	29	26	24	21	19	16	13	11	8	6
T	A	C	D	B		3	31	28	28	25	23	20	18	15	12	10	7	5
W	A	C	D	B		2	30	27	27	24	22	19	17	14	11	9	6	4
T	A	B	D	C	1	29	26	26	23	21	18	16	13	10	8	5	3	31
M	A	B	D	C	28	25	25	25	22	20	17	15	12	9	7	4	2	30
S	A	B	C	D		27	24	24	21	19	16	14	11	8	6	3	1	29
S	A	B	C	D		26	23	23	20	18	15	13	10	7	5	2	30	28
F	A	B	C	D		25	22	22	19	17	14	12	9	6	4	1	29	27
T	D	B	C	A		24	21	21	18	16	13	11	8	5	3	31	28	26
W	D	B	C	A		23	20	20	17	15	12	10	7	4	2	30	27	25
T	D	A	C	B		22	19	19	16	14	11	9	6	3	1	29	26	24
M	D	A	C	B		21	18	18	15	13	10	8	5	2	30	28	25	23
S	D	A	B	C		20	17	17	14	12	9	7	4	1	29	27	24	22
S	D	A	B	C		19	16	16	13	11	8	6	3	31	28	26	23	21
F	D	A	B	C		18	15	15	12	10	7	5	2	30	27	25	22	20
T	C	A	B	D		17	14	14	11	9	6	4	1	29	26	24	21	19
W	C	A	B	D		16	13	13	10	8	5	3	31	28	25	23	20	18
T	C	D	B	A		15	12	12	9	7	4	2	30	27	24	22	19	17
M	C	D	B	A		14	11	11	8	6	3	1	29	26	23	21	18	16

FIGURE B

8 AM TO 8 PM / 8 PM TO 8 AM — Left schedule

Shift		M	T	W	T	F	S	S	M	T	W	T	F	S	S	M	T	W	T	F	S	S	M	T	W	T	F	S	S
8 AM TO 8 PM		C	B	B	C	D	D	A	A	C	C	C	B	D	D	A	A	C	C	A	D	D	B	A	A	C	C	B	C
8 PM TO 8 AM		A	C	C	D	B	B	D	D	A	A	A	C	B	B	D	D	A	A	C	B	B	C	D	D	A	A	C	C
JAN/FEB		24	1	2	3	4	5	6	7	8	9	10	11	12	-3	14	15	16	17	18	19	20	21	22	23	24	25	26
FEB/MAR/APR		25	26	27	28	1	2	3	4	5	6	7	8	9	-0	11	12	13	14	15	16	17	18	19	20	21
APR/MAY/JUNE		22	23	24	25	26	27	28	29	30	1	6	7	8	5	10	7	8	9	10	11	12	13	14	15	16
JUNE/JUL/AUG		17	18	19	20	21	22	24	25	20	26	1	2	3	50	5	6	9	10	11	12	13	8	9	10	11
AUG/SEPT/OCT		6	7	8	9	10	11	12	15	16	21	26	27	28	20	25	26	27	28	29	30	31	7	1	2	6
OCT/NOV		1	2	3	4	5	6	7	10	11	16	21	22	23	20	20	21	22	23	24	25	26	27	28	29	30
DECEMBER											11	12	13	15	14	17	18	19	24	25	31	1	2	7	28

8 AM TO 8 PM / 8 PM TO 8 AM — Right schedule

Shift		M	T	W	T	F	S	S	M	T	W	T	F	S	S	M	T	W	T	F	S	S	M	T	W	T	F	S	S
8 AM TO 8 PM		B	D	A	A	C	B	C	D	D	D	D	A	A	C	D	B	D	A	A	A	D	C	C	A	D	D	A	S
8 PM TO 8 AM		D	A	D	A	B	C	A	C	C	D	D	A	A	C	B	C	B	D	B	D	D	B	C	D	B	B	D	D
JAN/FEB		27	28	29	30	31	1	2	3	4	5	6	7	8	9	10	11	12	13	14	15	16	17	18	19	20	21	22	23
FEB/MAR/APR		24	25	26	28	29	30	31	1	2	3	4	8	9	6	7	8	9	10	14	15	13	14	15	16	17	18	19	20
APR/MAY/JUNE		19	20	22	23	24	25	30	29	31	26	27	30	1	2	4	5	8	9	10	11	7	2	6	7	8	13
JUNE/JUL/AUG		14	16	17	18	19	20	25	16	18	22	23	24	25	29	28	29	30	31	25	26	1	5	6	7	12
AUG/SEPT/OCT		9	10	11	12	13	14	15	16	17	18	19	16	17	22	23	24	30	31	20	21	26	27	2	7	8	13
OCT/NOV		3	4	6	6	7	8	9	10	11	12	13	14	15	16	17	18	23	24	25	20	21	22	27	28	3	4	5	30
DECEMBER		29	30	31	7																								

FIGURE C

SHIFT	M	T	W	T	F	S	S	M	T	W	T	F
"A"	0	0	D	D	0	0	0	N	N	0	0	D
"B"	N	N	0	0	D	D	D	0	0	N	N	0
"C"	0	0	N	N	0	0	0	D	D	0	0	N
"D"	D	D	0	0	N	N	N	0	0	D	D	0
JAN.	13	14	15	16	17	18	19	20	21	22	23	24
FEB.	10	11	12	13	14	15	16	17	18	19	20	21
MAR.	10	11	12	13	14	15	16	17	18	19	20	21
APR.	7	8	9	10	11	12	13	14	15	16	17	18
MAY	5	6	7	8	9	10	11	12	13	14	15	16
JUN.	2 / 30	3	4	5	6	7	8	9	10	11	12	13
JUL.	28	1 / 29	2 / 30	3 / 31	4	5	6	7	8	9	10	11
AUG.	25	26	27	28	1 / 29	2 / 30	3 / 31	4	5	6	7	8
SEP.	22	23	24	25	26	27	28	1 / 29	2 / 30	3	4	5
OCT.	20	21	22	23	24	25	26	27	28	1 / 29	2 / 30	3 / 31
NOV.	17	18	19	20	21	22	23	24	25	26	27	28
DEC.	15	16	17	18	19	20	21	22	23	24	25	26

S	S	M	T	W	T	F	S	S	M	T	W	T	F	S	S
D	D	O	O	N	N	O	O	O	D	D	O	O	N	N	N
O	O	D	D	O	O	N	N	N	O	O	D	D	O	O	O
N	N	O	O	D	D	O	O	O	N	N	O	O	D	D	D
O	O	N	N	O	O	D	D	D	O	O	N	N	O	O	O
				1	2	3	4	5	6	7	8	9	10	11	12
25	26	27	28	29	30	31									
							1	2	3	4	5	6	7	8	9
22	23	24	25	26	27	28									
							1	2	3	4	5	6	7	8	9
22	23	24	25	26	27	28	29	30	31						
										1	2	3	4	5	6
19	20	21	22	23	24	25	26	27	28	29	30				
												1	2	3	4
17	18	19	20	21	22	23	24	25	26	27	28	29	30	31	
															1
14	15	16	17	18	19	20	21	22	23	24	25	26	27	28	29
12	13	14	15	16	17	18	19	20	21	22	23	24	25	26	27
9	10	11	12	13	14	15	16	17	18	19	20	21	22	23	24
6	7	8	9	10	11	12	13	14	15	16	17	18	19	20	21
4	5	6	7	8	9	10	11	12	13	14	15	16	17	18	19
1	2	3	4	5	6	7	8	9	10	11	12	13	14	15	16
29	30														
		1	2	3	4	5	6	7	8	9	10	11	12	13	14
27	28	29	30	31											

FIGURE D

SECURITY SHIFT SCHEDULE	June	MON 2	TUE 3	WED 4	THUR 5	FRI 6	SAT 7	SUN 8
MAIN GATE – DAYS								
MAIN GATE – NIGHTS								
SECURITY VAN – DAYS				7098				
SECURITY VAN –								
SECURITY VAN – NIGHTS					6979			
SECURITY VAN –								
BROADWAY GATE – DAYS								
BROADWAY GATE – NIGHTS								
KRAFT H.C. – DAYS							7247	
KRAFT H.C. – NIGHTS								7247

HOLIDAYS 2373 – 4 JUNE	FLOATERS 2397 – 5 JUNE	LIEU DAYS 2745 – 7 & 8 JUNE

DISTRIBUTION
MAIN GATE & VAN
BROADWAY GATE
KRAFT HEALTH CENTRE
CHIEF SECURITY OFFICER
FILE

SECURITY STAFF TRAINING
1649 – First Aid Training

4

The Selection of a Security Guard

We have discussed in another chapter the qualities of a Security Manager with his duties and responsibilities, and now we must approach the area of selecting the proper work force.

The qualities of a successful applicant must be different for the various positions he would apply for.

The qualities of a good security guard are similar to his counterpart in the retail sector; however, both will have different job responsibilities. The retail security guard may be required to maintain surveillance for the entire shift, while the security guard's duties will, in most instances, be more diversified, revolving around such duties are loss prevention and fire protection. This would be similar to the qualities of a security employee who is applying for the retail sector; however, not all positions are similar.

The following general qualities apply in most cases:

1. Education in a related field is an asset and should be considered. Applicants from a community college, Law and Security course, should receive added points due to the fact that they have some experience in understanding private security and how it works. This is not to

say that another person of average education should not be considered, but someone with a little knowledge may require less on the job training, thus saving money that would have to be spent for needed training.

2. Good eyesight. Consideration should be given to a qualified applicant who has normal eyesight (with or without corrective lenses). This is obvious should the applicant be applying for the position on a surveillance team. If he cannot see he will be of little use. This same applicant may, however, fit into the organization in an office capacity where normal eyesight is not required and he can compete with qualities appropriate for the position.

3. Good hearing is an asset, especially if the applicant is working in an industrial site where there are dangers and risks involved when touring the area. Should the applicant have to enter an area that has an emergency siren activated due to a chemical spill he would not hear it. This would present a danger to him as well as to others. Corrective measures, such as hearing devices, would be acceptable should the hearing standard come close to a normal level.

4. Good physical condition. This is an absolute requirement for the security member who must walk long periods of time, up and down stairs and ladders, etc. The security applicant must be in excellent physical condition at all times, as his life or the life of an employee may be in jeopardy should he not be in a position to execute a rescue due to physical limitations. This is not to say that this same applicant would not be suitable in the position of gate attendant who would be responsible for signing in visitors and answering the phone if required.

5. Good character or background. This is essential should

an applicant be required to be bonded. If bonding is not required then the discretion of the employer is advised. Everyone has made mistakes in his past and circumstances should be weighed in all instances. The gravity of the individual's past activities and his recent behaviour would be major factors in arriving at the correct decision.

6. Age can be a factor in some instances. This would be coupled however with other requirements. A younger man may be of benefit when the number of years he will be able to contribute to the Company are considered. However, age should be of no barrier if the applicant is healthy and can, in the employer's opinion, perform the job as he is instructed. The employer, for example, should not hire an applicant with a bad back and other related ailments if, for example, that employee is required to check an office complex hourly, where there are numerous stairs. This employee may be perfectly capable of performing gatehouse duties if that is all the position demands.

7. A non-smoker would be preferred should the position be that of a guard in a warehouse containing, for example, oxygen cylinders. This may be a requirement of the insurance underwriter and may be out of the hands of the employer.

8. Character references must be checked. All too often character references are not contacted even though they are listed on the resume. It should be considered whether the applicant has references who are in the security field. These character references may know the requirements of the job the applicant is applying for and can offer insight into his abilities. The character reference in some cases may advise you that the applicant is not suited for the job he is applying for but more than

qualified for another position in your department.

9. Previous job experience is always an asset if it is in the same area as the position applied for. But do not rule out an applicant who is not educated to your standard if he has an excellent work record.

The security industry today has more to choose from than the security industry of yesterday. Higher paying jobs require applicants to be more qualified and competition is very keen in the industry today.

Bear in mind that the requirements above are only a list and are not to be considered the only requirements. The feel of the interview is a great part of the hiring process. An applicant who does not possess all of the requirements that your standard has established may still be qualified if given a chance to prove himself. This may be established during the interview.

All applicants must be given the same chance to compete for a position regardless of their sex, age, or physical handicap, if any. An applicant for one position may not be the best suited, but may be more than qualified in another position should it come open. You must advise the applicant of the position that is open and the requirments of that position. You owe it to their safety to advise them that dangers may be present if they suffer from a problem that may hinder their performance.

5

Purchasing Process

Purchasing, receiving and inventory controls are major parts of the security field. In most cases these departments do not come under the control of the Director of Security but are administered by the controller's department or internal audit. These people may be classed under various categories, but their main function is to exercise control by means of security and accountability.

To explain this complex process, we must start at the lowest part of the chain, that being the department head.

What takes place when a department head wishes to order an article? We will refer to this level as the requisitioner.

The requisitioner must have budgeted certain amounts of money at the beginning of the operating year. This money approximates the cost to the owner of the company that it will take to run that department. The owner then adds this cost to the costs of other departments that he employs to give him a total overview of the coming year. If he has done this then the process can begin. If this is not in place, then the department may have to approach this problem in a different manner or do without until the money is available.

In order to understand the process better we must follow what is called a paper (audit) trail. A paper trail is the path that documentation would take through various stages of a process or processes involved in performing a certain function. In this case the paper trail would consist of the documents indicating the person who wants an item, through to ordering, receiving the item, and paying for it.

The requisitioner (the one wanting to purchase a certain item) would fill in and complete what we will refer to as a purchase requisition. This is usually filled out in duplicate. One copy remains with the requisitioner and the other copy is forwarded to the company purchasing department. A sample purchase requisition is attached and we will dissect it generally. The requisitioner would complete the line date ordered. This gives the purchasing department the date you filled it out. The required delivery date indicates when delivery is needed. The requisition number is the number that will follow the paper trail. Requisitioned by would be the one wanting to buy the item. The place of delivery must be written as your department may be away from the main building and the item, when received should be delivered to the requisitioner. The account number would be the department ordering number of the requisitioner as, even though the company pays for the item, accounting must know which department expended the money and thus charge to its budgeted amount. The purpose must be reported so the managers above the requisitioner can determine if the expense is warranted. The requisitioner then completes the description of the item(s) requested and the number of the items required. The requisitioner, if he is department head, signs the form on the bottom left-hand corner. The completed form by the requisitioner is then forwarded to the level of management that is required to approve the requisition. Depending on the size of the expense, various companies have various levels of authority. For example, a purchase of flashlight batteries by the Director of Security may require the signature of a chief engineer who has been delegated authority up to $5,000. However, if the Director of Security requires a new vehicle for his department, which would cost approximately $24,000, the next level of authority may be the President of the company. When the approvals have been met the purchase requisition moves to the next step in the process, to the purchasing department of the same company.

The purchasing department then fills out the remainder of the original purchase requisition. The purchasing department obtains quotes for prices and indicates the successful vendor. To go back to the purchase requisition the purchasing department completes the vendor number, suggested vendor and the requisition date. The member of the purchasing department fills in his name in the ordered-by block and also fills in who took the order (this may not be the name of the owner, but an employee for the vendor's company who received the call and confirmed the order). The applicable tax terms would be added as well. Before sending the document forward they would assign one of the purchasing department order numbers, which is shown in the top right hand corner of the purchase requisition.

A purchasing department clerk typist then completes a four-part purchase order by entering the data on the computer. The original is forwarded to the vendor and is signed by the manager of the purchasing department of the company or the person designated as a purchasing agent acting on behalf of the manager. The second copy would go to the company accounts payable department, which will later be responsible for the payment of the item requested. The third copy would then be filed by the purchasing department in alphabetical order, while the fourth copy of the purchase order goes back to the requisitioner to attach to his copy of the purchase requisition. When the requisitioner wants to follow up on an order he can quote the purchase requisition number and the order number.

At the same time a Material Receiving Report (MRR), which is a mirror image of the purchase order, is forwarded to the company receiving department to await delivery of the goods.

Upon receipt of the goods, the receiving department matches the MRR amount and the packing slip (if included) along with a physical count of the items, to make sure that it received the correct amount ordered. The MRR is signed and a copy is kept for the receiving department's records. The original MRR and packing slip are forwarded to the accounts payable department, where the MRR is matched to the second copy of the purchase order.

The accounts payable department retains the second copy of the purchase order (PO2), MRR and packing slip and matches these with the invoice, which is mailed to the company for payment. A cheque is prepared based on the MRR, invoice, and packing slip, which are filed alphabetically. One copy of the cheque is filed by the accounts payable department and the cheque itself is sent to the vendor.

As you have been shown, there is a process to purchase items in industry. The processes may differ in various locations and types of industry, but the main point is that there is control. You cannot phone and order an item without approval and accountability. If you do not have this type of accountability, then you must re-evaluate your process.

Let us review the basic check point plan to ensure that there are no abuses:

1. management must approve the purchase requisition and it is recommended that higher levels of management approve higher purchase requests;
2. purchase managers must approve purchase requisitions;
3. you must match the shipment details to the Material Receiving Report (MRR);
4. the matching of all documents before payment of the invoice;
5. one of the most important factors, if not the most important, is the *division of duties*; you must ensure that different individuals are performing functions at each level of the process.

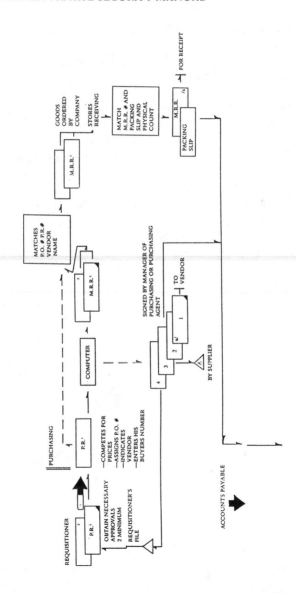

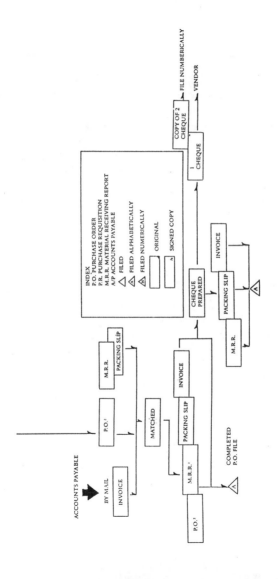

PURCHASE REQUISITION

ORDER NUMBER _____

VENDOR NUMBER _____

REQUISITION DATE _____

SUGGESTED VENDORS _____

SHIP TO _____

F.O.B. _____

SHIP VIA

DATE ORDERED			REQUIRED DELIVERY DATE			REQUISITION NUMBER (INTERNAL USE ONLY)	REQUISITIONED BY	DELIVER TO (APPLICABLE BILL OR WOODLANDS LOCATION)
DAY	MONTH	YEAR	DAY	MONTH	YEAR	607322		

	DIV.	CHARGE NO.			ORDERED BY	ORDER TAKEN BY (VENDOR)
ACCOUNT NUMBER		DEPT	FUND		ACCOUNT	

REQUIRED FOR WHAT PURPOSE?

QUANTITY	UNIT	STOCK CODE NO.	DESCRIPTION		PRICE	UNIT

PAYMENT TERMS	FEDERAL SALES TAX	ONTARIO RETAIL SALES TAX	FILE NUMBER
FUNDS			

REMARKS:

REQUISITION NO. (INTERNAL USE ONLY)

607322

DEPARTMENTAL APPROVAL	MANAGEMENT APPROVAL (WHEN APPLICABLE)	

REQUISITIONER

PURCHASE REQUISITION

ORDER NUMBER _____

VENDOR NUMBER _____

REQUISITION DATE _____

SUGGESTED VENDORS _____

SHIP TO _____

F.O.B. _____

SHIP VIA _____

DATE ORDERED			REQUIRED DELIVERY DATE			REQUISITION NUMBER (INTERNAL USE ONLY)	REQUISITIONED BY	DELIVER TO (APPLICABLE MILL OR WOODLANDS LOCATION)
DAY	MONTH	YEAR	DAY	MONTH	YEAR	607322		

ACCOUNT NUMBER	DIV	TO USE	CHARGE NO				ORDERED BI	ORDER TAKEN BY (H+000)
			DEPT	FUND		ACCOUNT		

REQUIRED FOR WHAT PURPOSE?

QUANTITY	UNITS	STOCK CODE NO.	DESCRIPTION		PRICE	UNIT

PAYMENT TERMS	FEDERAL SALES TAX	ONTARIO RETAIL SALES TAX	FILE NUMBER
FUNDS			

REMARKS:

REQUISITION NO. (INTERNAL USE ONLY)
607322

DEPARTMENTAL APPROVAL   MANAGEMENT APPROVAL (WHEN APPLICABLE)

PURCHASING DEPARTMENT

SUBMIT ORIGINAL INVOICE TO:

YOUR COMPANY NAME

THIS NUMBER MUST APPEAR ON ALL PACKAGES, PACKING SLIPS, BILLS OF LADING, AND INVOICES

ORDER NUMBER ▶

VENDOR NO

TO •
    •
    •
    •

SHIP TO •   YOUR COMPANY NAME AND ADDRESS
        •
F.O.B. •
SHIP VIA •

DATE ORDERED		REQUIRED DELIVERY DATE	REG. NO. (INTERNAL USE ONLY)		REQUISITIONED BY	DELIVER TO (APPLICABLE MILL OR WOODLANDS LOCATION)
ACCOUNT NUMBER ▶	DIV DEPT. FUNC ACCOUNT ID		607322 SUB-LEDGER ORDERED BY			ORDER TAKEN BY (VENDOR)

REQUIRED FOR WHAT PURPOSE?

QUANTITY	UNIT	STOCK CODE NO.	DESCRIPTION	PR QU	PRICE	/UNIT

PAYMENT TERMS	FEDERAL SALES TAX (EXPLANATION OF CODES ON REVERSE)	ONTARIO SALES TAX (VENDOR'S PERMIT NO. 65663018Q)	ORDER NUMBER
FUNDS			YOUR COMPANY NAME

NO BACK ORDERS ALLOWED

BY ACCEPTING THIS ORDER THE VENDOR/CONTRACTOR AGREES TO THE GENERAL TERMS

AND CONDITIONS ON THE REVERSE SIDE OF THE PURCHASE ORDER.

PURCHASING AGENT

ORIGINAL

YOUR COMPANY NAME

SUBMIT ORIGINAL INVOICE TO:

THIS NUMBER MUST APPEAR ON ALL PACKAGES, PACKING SLIPS, BILLS OF LADING, AND INVOICES

ORDER NUMBER ▶

VENDOR NO

TO ·

SHIP TO ·   YOUR COMPANY NAME AND ADDRESS

·

·

F.O.B. ·

SHIP VIA ·

·

DATE ORDERED			REQUIRED DELIVERY DATE			REQ. NO. (INTERNAL USE ONLY)		REQUISITIONED BY	DELIVER TO (APPLICABLE MILL OR WOODLANDS LOCATION)
ACCOUNT NUMBER ▶	DIV	DEPT.	FUNC.	ACCOUNT	ID	607322			ORDER TAKEN BY (VENDOR)
						SUB-LEDGER	ORDERED BY		

REQUIRED FOR WHAT PURPOSE?

QUANTITY	UNIT	STOCK CODE NO.	DESCRIPTION		PRICE	UNIT

| PAYMENT TERMS | FEDERAL SALES TAX (EXPLANATION OF CODES ON REVERSE) | ONTARIO SALES TAX (VENDOR'S PERMIT NO. 856630180) | ORDER NUMBER |
| 426 | | | |

YOUR COMPANY NAME

NO BACK ORDERS ALLOWED

BY ACCEPTING THIS ORDER THE VENDOR/CONTRACTOR AGREES TO THE GENERAL TERMS

AND CONDITIONS ON THE REVERSE SIDE OF THE PURCHASE ORDER.

PURCHASING AGENT

ACCOUNTS PAYABLE

YOUR COMPANY NAME

SUBMIT ORIGINAL INVOICE TO:

THIS NUMBER MUST APPEAR ON ALL PACKAGES, PACKING
SLIPS, BILLS OF LADING AND INVOICES

ORDER
NUMBER ▶

VENDOR NO

TO •

SHIP TO •   YOUR COMPANY NAME AND ADDRESS

F.O.B.   •
SHIP VIA   •

DATE ORDERED		REQUIRED DELIVERY DATE	REQ. NO. (INTERNAL USE ONLY) 607322		REQUISITIONED BY		DELIVER TO (APPLICABLE MILL OR WOODLANDS LOCATION)

ACCOUNT NUMBER ▶ | DIV. | DEPT. | FUNC. | ACCOUNT | ID | SUB-LEDGER | ORDERED BY

ORDER TAKEN BY (VENDOR)

REQUIRED FOR WHAT PURPOSE?

QUANTITY	UNIT	STOCK CODE NO.	DESCRIPTION		PRICE	UNIT

PAYMENT TERMS	FEDERAL SALES TAX (EXPLANATION OF CODES ON REVERSE)	ONTARIO SALES TAX (VENDOR'S PERMIT NO. 856030160)	ORDER NUMBER
JKBS			

NO BACK ORDERS ALLOWED

YOUR COMPANY NAME

BY ACCEPTING THIS ORDER THE VENDOR/CONTRACTOR AGREES TO THE GENERAL TERMS

AND CONDITIONS ON THE REVERSE SIDE OF THE PURCHASE ORDER.

REQUISITIONER

PURCHASING AGENT

GENERAL TERMS AND CONDITIONS–PURCHASE OF MATERIALS

1. Goods subject to inspection and rejection by purchaser notwithstanding prior payment. Rejected goods may be returned (transportation costs charged to Vendor's account) at the option of the purchaser for reimbursement, credit or replacement.

2. It is warranted that the design and manufacture of the goods delivered herein will be in accordance with any requirements for such materials imposed by the Occupational Health and Safety Act, 1978 and regulations thereunder and in accordance with any other applicable legislation. Goods delivered herein are further warranted to be of the kind ordered and to be of merchantable quality and condition and vendor agrees to replace FOB (applicable Mill or Woodlands location) any part or parts which prove to be defective, or not in accordance with the foregoing warranties within a period of one year from the date of putting the equipment into operation, reasonable wear and tear excepted.

3. Vendor will indemnify and save harmless the purchaser from all claims for damages of every nature and kind whatsoever which may result from the vendor's breach of express or implied warranties; or from any infringement of patents so as to ensure that the purchaser has continuous use of all the equipment at all times.

4. The supply of goods pursuant to this Purchase Order must be complete. No back orders allowed.

5. Vendor will issue one invoice in duplicate per Purchase Order (with original freight bills attached to invoice on pre-paid shipments) on same day as shipment.

6. Purchaser may reject goods and return in accordance with paragraph 1 when there has been an unauthorized substitution of goods.

7. Purchaser has the right to cancel this order or any part thereof if Vendor is unable to meet the specified delivery date. Vendor must advise promptly if unable to meet specified delivery date.

GENERAL TERMS AND CONDITIONS–PURCHASE OF SERVICES

1. The contractor shall observe and adhere to the Occupational Health and Safety Act, 1978 and Regulations for Construction Projects as well as all laws (and regulations made thereunder) of the Government of Canada, the Government of Ontario and all by-laws of the applicable city, township, municipality or district. The Contractor shall indemnify and save harmless the Company from all penalties, charges or other assessments of every nature and kind whatsoever made against the Company by virtue of the failure of the Contractor, his employees, officers and agents to comply with such laws (and regulations made thereunder) and by-laws. Any penalties, charges or other assessments made against the Contractor arising from the Contractor's performance of work pursuant to his contract with the Company shall be borne exclusively by the Contractor.

2. The Contractor shall be solely responsible for the faithful compliance and completion of all matters pursuant to this Agreement and the Contractor shall indemnify and save harmless the Company from all suits, actions, losses, expenses, costs or damages for every nature and kind whatsoever which the Company may suffer by reason of injury or death to any person or damage to any property resulting from the services performed herein.

3. (a) The Contractor agrees at his expense to keep in force at all times in which the Contractor is providing services pursuant to this Purchase Order an insurance policy in the minimum amount of ONE MILLION ($1,000,000.00) inclusive for property damage and public liability and also including the following coverages or extensions (unless waived in writing by the Insurance Department of Great Lakes Products Limited): (1) Products or completed operations coverage; (2) Fifteen (15) days prior written notice to the Company of any material change or policy cancellation; (3) Contractor's protective liability extension; (4) Contractual liability extensions; (5) Property damage on an occurrence basis; (6) Forest fire fighting expenses extension; (7) Attached machinery endorsement; (8) Non-owned automobile insurance.

(b) The Contractor shall also take out and keep in force during the term of this Agreement a standard owner's automobile policy covering all vehicles owned by and placed in the name of the Contractor to a level of liability of at least ONE MILLION DOLLARS ($1,000,000.00) inclusive for each vehicle. A Certificate of Insurance shall be filed with the Company before the commencement of work. This Certificate shall contain evidence that fifteen (15) days prior written notice of any material change or policy cancellation shall be provided to the Company.

(c) If the Contractor shall fail to pay any premiums or renewal premiums, the Company shall be at liberty to pay such premiums, charge such payments for premiums to the account of the Contractor and deduct the amounts from any monies due the Contractor under this Agreement.

4. The Contractor agrees to furnish all the materials and equipment necessary for the satisfactory fulfillment of the duties specified in the Purchase Order and that such materials and equipment will be subject to the General Terms and Conditions–Purchase of Materials herein.

5. The Contractor agrees that all services shall be performed by fully trained and competent personnel which personnel shall be fully covered by the Workmen's Compensation Act at the Contractor's expense.

FEDERAL TAX EXEMPTION CODES

1. Purchaser certifies that the goods ordered/imported hereby are to be used as outlined in Sections 1, 3, and 4 of Part XIII of Schedule III of the Excise Tax Act. Licence Number S0496638.

2. Purchaser certifies that the goods ordered/imported hereby are to be used as outlined in Section 2 of Part XIII of Schedule III of the Excise Tax Act. Licence Number S0496638.

3. Purchaser certifies that the goods ordered/imported hereby are to be used in, wrought into, or attached to taxable goods for sale. Licence Number S0496638.

6

Authority For Enforcement

The area of enforcement and its authorities is very complex and falls into grey areas of interpretation. We will examine various sections of different statutes that you will have to face to complete your task as a person employed in the private security sector. Before we start with these areas, we must identify and define certain terms to which all enforcement sections that we will be dealing with will refer.

All sections of the Criminal Code of Canada are divided into specific areas, only some of which carry penalties, the rest being of an interpretive nature. The penalty sections are of two types—summary conviction and indictable offences—with some sections containing clauses which allow for prosecution by either manner. An indictable offence, in Canadian terms, is a more serious offence against persons or property, with penalties ranging from a fine to life imprisonment. A summary conviction offence is a less serious offence compared to the indictable offence, with penalties ranging from a fine to a maximum of six months' imprisonment. All provincial offences are summary conviction.

A criminal offence is any offence against a federal, or

Canadian Government, law (statute). The penalty can be either summary conviction or indictment. Examples of laws would be statutes such as the Criminal Code of Canada, Narcotic Control Act and Food and Drugs Act. Criminal offences do *not* include violations of any provincial statute or municipal by-law. These carry their own particular summary conviction penalties and arrest authorities. Examples of these would be the Liquor Control Act, Highway Traffic Act, Petty Trespass Act and by-laws concerning pedlars.

Prior to establishing the grounds for arrest, the private security officer must be familiar with what an arrest is.

There are as many definitions or opinions as to when an arrest has begun as there are individuals learned in law. For the purpose of private security, the best rule of thumb to follow is the following: the arrest procedure has begun when the freedom of movement of a person is taken away against the person's will. This is accomplished by one person physically preventing another person from proceeding along his way, or alternatively, through the medium of words and/or tone of voice if the person feels compelled to obey those words.

The arrest procedure for all criminal offences (federal statutes) is, unless otherwise stated in the particular statute, based on the contents of the Criminal Code. There are a number of sections of the Criminal Code that outline the authorities and power for arrest. These fall into three categories—arrest by peace officers (including public police)—owners of property and their agents—and anyone (private citizen). Private security employees have two of these avenues open to them—that of the private citizen and as agent of the property owner.

The powers of a peace officer will not be dealt with specifically, as they do not apply to private security, except for a few exceptions (for example railway police). This position has been taken due to the fact that comparing private security powers to public police may cloud the issues that will be discussed. Should your career turn to the public policing area, you would at that time receive further training concerning your powers of arrest.

The Criminal Code of Canada (R.S.C. 1985, c. C-46) contains the following sections pertinent to the private security sector:

25.(1) Every one who is required or authorized by law to do anything in the administration or enforcement of the law
   (a) as a private person,
   (b) as a peace officer or public officer,
   (c) in aid of a peace officer or public officer, or,
   (d) by virtue of his office,
   is, if he acts on reasonable grounds, justified in doing what he is required or authorized to do and in using as much force as is necessary for that purpose.

25.(3) Subject to subsection (4), a person is not justified for the purposes of subsection (1) in using force that is intended or is likely to cause death or grievous bodily harm unless he believes on reasonable grounds that it is necessary for the purpose of preserving himself or any one under his protection from death or grievous bodily harm.

25.(4) A peace officer who is proceeding lawfully to arrest, with or without warrant, any person for an offence for which that person may be arrested without warrant, and every one lawfully assisting the peace officer, is justified, if the person to be arrested takes flight to avoid arrest, is using as much force as is necessary to prevent the escape by flight, unless the escape can be prevented by reasonable means in a less violent manner.

38.(1) Every one who is in peaceable possession of personal property, and every one lawfully assisting him, is justified
   (a) in preventing a trespasser from taking it, or
   (b) in taking it from a trespasser who has taken it, if he does not strike or cause bodily harm to the trespasser.
   (2) Where a person who is in peaceable possession of personal property lays hands on it, a trespasser who persists in attempting to keep it or take it from him or from any one lawfully assisting him shall be deemed to commit an assault without justification or provocation.

39. (1) Every one who is in peaceable possession of personal property under a claim of right, and every one acting under his authority, is protected from criminal responsibility for defending that possession, even against a person entitled by law to possession of it, if he uses no more force than is necessary.

    (2) Every one who is in peaceable possession of personal property, but does not claim it as of right or does not act under the authority of a person who claims it as of right, is not justified or protected from criminal responsibility for defending his possession against a person who is entitled by law to possession of it.

26. Every one who is authorized by law to use force is criminally responsible for any excess thereof according to the nature and quality of the act that constitutes the excess.

41. (1) Every one who is in peaceable possession of a dwelling-house or real property, and every one lawfully assisting him or acting under his authority, is justified in using force to prevent any person from trespassing on the dwelling-house or real property, or to remove a trespasser therefrom, if he uses no more force than is necessary.

    (2) A trespasser who resists an attempt by a person who is in peaceable possession of a dwelling-house or real property, or a person lawfully assisting him or acting under his authority to prevent his entry or to remove him, shall be deemed to commit an assault without justification or provocation.

42. (1) Every one is justified in peaceably entering a dwelling-house or real property by day to take possession of it if he, or a person under whose authority he acts, is lawfully entitled to possession of it.

494. (1) Any one may arrest without warrant
    (a) a person whom he finds commiting an indictable offence; or
    (b) a person who, on reasonable and probable grounds, he believes

(i) has committed a criminal offence, and

(ii) is escaping from and freshly pursued by persons who have lawful authority to arrest that person.

(2) Any one who is

(a) the owner or a person in lawful possession of property, or

(b) a person authorized by the owner or by a person in lawful possession of property,

may arrest without warrant a person whom he finds committing a criminal offence on or in relation to that property.

29.(2) It is the duty of every one who arrests a person, whether with or without a warrant, to give notice to that person, where it is feasible to do so, of

(a) the process or warrant under which he makes the arrest; or

(b) the reason for the arrest.

494.(3) Any one other than a peace officer who arrests a person without warrant shall forthwith deliver the person to a peace officer.

As can be seen from the foregoing sections of the Criminal Code of Canada, your authority for arrest is based on a combination of many sections; however, your main authority for detainment is section 494(2)(b).

When you arrest for a criminal offence that is both summary conviction and indictable (referred to in legal parlance as dual procedure), you are following the indictable procedure of the arrest. Only the Attorney General of the province or his designate may decide in which manner the offence wil proceed in criminal court. Even though the decision may be made to proceed by way of summary conviction, this will not affect your arrest if it was done following the necessary steps.

If we apply this practice of arrest and detention to the private security field, the following guidelines may assist you in deciding your avenue of approach.

Before making any arrest, you as a private citizen or representative of the company must see the criminal act actually take place. The theft of confidential, or classified, material, falls into a grey area and individual company policy should be predetermined before any action is taken. It is always better to be safe than sorry later. Taking the approach of arrest only after viewing the offence, will eliminate civil charges of false arrest, excessive force while effecting an arrest and subsequent expensive law suits against both you and your employer.

Should you receive prior information of an offence to be committed, it is recommended that you contact the particular public police force having jurisdiction prior to taking any action against the suspect(s) and have the police conduct the investigation jointly with the security personnel. Their powers of arrest are broader and have a greater magnitude than that given to the private security sector.

When a security employee observes a suspect in the act of commiting an offence, such as theft of an item, both the suspect and the item must be kept in sight until the moment of arrest. In doing this, two avenues are covered: one is whether the theft is legitimate or whether the person was simply moving the item from one location to another as requested by someone else or simply for the sake of convenience; and the other, and more important aspect, is whether he is acting in conjunction with someone else to effect the criminal act; for instance, by passing the item to a cohort who may be in a position to remove the article from the property more easily. In the second scenario, it may well be possible to stop an organized theft ring effectively, rather than arresting only one participant.

When making the arrest, you must identify yourself and advise the suspect he is under arrest and why he is being detained. It must be made very clear to him that his freedom has been curtailed. The most effective method is by physically touching him, where possible. When this action is taken, in conjunction with the reason for his detention, there is no chance of any misinterpretation on his part.

After making the lawful arrest, should the suspect attempt to flee, you have the legal authority to prevent his escape as long as excessive force is not used. If the stolen item is visible, you have the authority to remove it for safekeeping and possible evidence at a later hearing. Should the item be hidden, you do not have any authority to conduct a personal search; however, you can detain the person in visible sight until the appropriate police authorities arrive and they conduct the physical search.

The suspect must be made aware, at the earliest possible chance, of his right to contact a lawyer and must be given the chance to do so (that is, allowing him access to a telephone).

The Charter of Rights of Canada (Canada Act, 1982 (U.K.), c. 11) has stipulated that the following, or similar words to this effect, be told to any person charged with a criminal offence:

> "I am arresting you for (briefly describe the offence)
> It is my duty to inform you that you have the right to retain and instruct counsel without delay.
> Do you understand?

> You will be charged with   .Do you wish to say anything
> in answer to the charge?
> You are not obliged to say anything unless you wish to do so,
> but whatever you say may be given in evidence."

If a suspect is observed committing an offence, but the item is not removed from the property, an offence may still have been committed under the provisions of section 322(2) which states:

> A person commits theft when, with intent to steal anything, he moves it or causes it to move or to be moved, or begins to cause it to become movable.

Should this happen, it is suggested the appropriate authority, such as the Director of Security, be contacted before any action is taken. As the item has not been removed from the property, it is doubtful there is any urgency involved in effecting an immediate arrest. If possible, a cohort should be used to contact the Security Director while you keep the item and suspect under observation.

During the course of observation and eventual arrest, particular attention must be made to recording all pertinent information throughout. Such things as the location, time, date, description of the suspect, clothing worn, time of arrest, time any statements are taken, when the accused was advised he was under arrest and read his rights, when the police arrived, the officer's name, badge number and action taken by the police must be carefully recorded. Your notes may play an important role in any future court proceedings; therefore, detail must be taken to make them as full and accurate as possible.

In the area of search and seizure following arrest, you must remember that you do not have the legal right to search an individual. Only a peace officer has this power.

You do, of course, have the right to seize any item which is plainly in view. You do have the right to request the suspect voluntarily surrender any item to you; however, if he refuses, follow-up action can only be taken by a peace officer. Your duty at this time is to observe the accused closely to prevent him from removing the item from his person or in some manner destroying the item.

Should you come into possession of an item from the suspect, proper action must be taken to preserve it as evidence for future court action. The following steps should be followed to complete this action:

1. Place your name or initials, date and time of possession in an inconspicuous place on the item, or on a tag attached to the item;
2. If possible, place the item in a sealed container, such as a plastic bag with tie-top;
3. Store the item in a location to which only you have access, such as a locked container with yourself having the only key;
4. Should the item be turned over to someone else, obtain a receipt from that person and enter the details, such as time and recipient, in your notes;
5. Be prepared to fully and properly identify the item at any later date.

Always be certain your grounds for arrest are correct and the correct arrest procedure has been followed. A civil law suit can be both time-consuming and costly to you and your employer. Knowledge of the pertinent federal and provincial statutes and municipal by-laws is important. These should be reviewed on a periodic basis and particular attention paid to any new amendments that are periodically brought into being.

7

Effects of Grievances, Arbitration and Collective Agreements on Security

When establishing a Security Department, its goals, objectives, policy and procedures are affected by several factors.

One factor that establishes policy and procedures is the employer's industry and the working relationship with its employees. Is your company or industry union or non-union? If your company is non-union, the employees are protected by governmental legislation such as the Department of Labour. If the company is union, then in all likelihood rights and privileges of the employees are protected by a collective agreement. The union employee has the protection of both the collective agreement and the governmental bodies.

If your company has a collective agreement, your security department must be tailored around it to protect the interest of the employer as well as not to violate any agreement between the company and the union, thus causing labour unrest that could be costly to the company in time and money.

The Director of Security must combine forces with the employee relations department in the company and seek guidance as to the labour agreement and the company's wishes with respect to the proposed enforcement. For example, should there not be an agreement between the company and the union for security to stop and search an employee's lunch pail, then under no circumstances can you do it. This would violate the labour management collective agreement as well as the Criminal Code. However should provisions be made in the collective agreement that this procedure can be done then the Criminal Code of Canada would not apply. If there are certain provisions that you do not agree with or if you wish to add certain provisions in the collective agreement, this can be negotiated upon its expiry date at the end of the contract. You must remember that the union wishes a better standard for its employees and all the protection that it can provide, but union members also wish to promote harmony in the worksite and eliminate disturbing influences. The union realizes that management has the right to protect itself and usually meets the company on some sort of common ground to bring about a negotiated agreement.

Employee theft and vandalism hurts everyone and under the circumstances union members may wish to rid themselves of the troublesome employee as much as the company. Loss of productivity from theft and acts contrary to the good of the employer may result in more difficult bargaining when salary increases are negotiated. Safety is also a concern of management as well as the employee. Employees who place brother workers in jeopardy are usually dealt with severely both by management and the union.

Should your company have established a collective agreement or entered common ground by some means you may proceed with proposing your objectives, security policies and goals.

The following is an example that you will at some time or other have to deal with and will show how your policy would react to employee theft.

A theft takes place and you estblish your grounds, which is followed up with an arrest. In this instance the alleged thief is a company employee and at the time of his arrest you have advised him of his rights and freedoms under the Canadian Charter of Rights. Your involvement, including the facts in question, is properly recorded in your notebook. Your exhibit that was seized from the employee as evidence may now be used, providing the established procedures in the arrest, search and seizure chapter have been followed.

From this point, your Director of Security will have several avenues open to him.

One avenue may be the release of the employee back to his worksite without proceeding any further.

If you decide on proceeding with a form of prosecution you would have the following choices.

The first option under prosecution is that of proceeding criminally through the police and court systems.

The second option is that of proceeding with prosecution internally through the collective agreement, which we have already discussed earlier in the chapter.

The third option is that of proceeding with prosecution through the court systems and also internally through the collective agreement.

Whatever option you choose you must be prepared to proceed in a professional manner and all forms of the investigation will be reviewed with the Director of Security or his delegate. You may ask yourself, "Why must I be this cautious if I proceed internally?" If you proceed internally, the employee has the right to defend himself through the powers of the collective agreement and you will have to present your evidence at a hearing, in some cases similar to a court of law, where the independent head of the hearing will determine whether to support the company in whatever disciplinary action it took or to reinstate the employee and pay him for time and/or wages lost. Many employees have been reinstated because of faulty procedures followed in the termination or suspension of the employee. Employees have also been reinstated because an incomplete investigation took place and the investigator was not properly prepared to support the company or present his evidence properly.

A question you may ask yourself is, "Why proceed internally"? Depending on the circumstances, a more serious penalty may be achieved internally than through the court system. For instance, in the event of a minor infraction such as a theft of used nuts and bolts, it would not be in the interest of the company or court system to proceed with this matter criminally because of the minor nature of the offence. If the charge was laid and the employee was found guilty he may receive a form of discharge whether it be conditional or unconditional. Where the Security Department proceeded internally through the collective agreement and the evidence was presented professionally, all concerned parties, both union and company, may agree that the theft occurred and that theft is a problem which is to the detriment of both union and company employees, the employee may receive a suspension without pay. This option is a more practical avenue to proceed because the seriousness of the fine would reinforce the employer's position in regard to theft and this employee, as well as other employees, would understand that this type of behavior would not be tolerated.

On the other hand, this option would be changed should the theft be of a serious nature. The employer may instruct the Director of Security to proceed both criminally through the courts as well as internally through the collective agreement. In this instance the employer would probably be in a position to terminate the employee responsible for the theft and also feel that the offence was of sufficient seriousness to warrant criminal prosecution and the involvement of the courts.

As can be seen, decisions have to be made, and the more serious the infraction, the more complex the decisions. The options would be decided by the employer in all instances involving employees whose actions are contrary to the good of the employer, and these wishes would have to be carried out by the Security Department, whether in-house or contract.

8

Property Protection
and the Occupiers' Liability

The Occupiers' Liability Act of Ontario (R.S.O. 1980, c. 322) governs an occupier's liability to those who come onto his land. One of the main purposes of this Act, among other goals, was to strengthen the property rights and protection of land occupiers. The Act itself is quite lengthy, and only the main points will be commented on here. For detailed information you must acquire the complete Act from the Queen's Printer.

The occupiers of land or premises, usually owners or tenants, have a duty to take care of persons who are entering or are on their land that the occupier has control over. The duty to provide safe premises under the occupier's liability would apply in general to all buildings and structures, bodies of water and vessels, forms of transportation and residences.

When the occupier fails to meet a safe standard and the person is injured the occupier faces civil liability for any injuries that may result.

The basic duty of the occupier is to take such care as

in all the circumstances of the case is reasonable to see that persons entering the property are reasonably safe while on the premises. The occupier is to see that the person is not injured, and "reasonable" may be interpreted as a standard that would apply to what a reasonable person in that community would do in similar circumstances.

The legislation recognizes that there are exceptions which free the occupier from liability; however, the occupier is not free to create dangers that are likely to cause serious injury.

The person who enters into a situation where he willingly assumes the risk of being injured may be held responsible for his own actions. The owner of a hockey arena would not be liable if a person in the stands received an injury from a puck deflected in the stands. This person is there watching the game of his own free will and assumes the risk.

Criminal activity on an owner's property must be considered and the criminal who enters property to commit a criminal act, such as theft, also assumes the risk.

The Act also provides that anyone who, for example, uses an unopened road allowance assumes the risk. This would apply to a fisherman who wants to go fishing at a lake that he now can have access to by means of a cleared road that was not there before. This fisherman may have had access through a chain of lakes and because of this road, which may have been cleared by a lumber company, provides easier access. The Act states that anyone who takes their recreation without paying a fee will take care of their own safety and must accept the environment as they find it. Other examples would be private roads, properly marked, and recreational trails that also are reasonably marked. If the person has paid a fee then as a rule the occupier owes a duty to provide reasonable care.

All entrants who enter rural premises, such as land used for agricultural purposes, including land under cultivation, orchards, pastures, woodlots and farm ponds, vacant or undeveloped premises and forested or wilderness premises, who do not pay a fee for entry, assume the risks. Also included in the exceptions are trespassers, where entry is prohibited under the Trespass to Property Act and entrants who are neither prohibited, nor expressly permitted to enter or use the land. For example, a driver of a vehicle has a flat tire in the country. He knows he has passed a farmhouse and to request assistance it would be shorter to cut across an uncultivated patch of land that has not been posted or marked. He would be responsible for his own safety.

1. THE TRESPASS TO PROPERTY ACT

The Trespass to Property Act (R.S.O. 1980, c. 511) gives the occupiers greater control over the use of their property. It strengthens the occupier's position toward trespassers.

A person who is not acting under a right or authority conferred by law and who without the express permission of the occupier (the proof rests on the defendant) enters on premises when entry is prohibited under this Act, or engages in an activity on premises when the activity is prohibited under this Act and does not leave the premises immediately after he is directed to do so by the occupier or a person authorized by the occupier of the premises is guilty of an offence, and if convicted is liable to a fine of not more than $1,000.

The property that is being protected would be schools, lands and structures which would include water, ships and vessels, trailers and portable structures designed or used for residences, businesses or to provide shelter, forms of transportation such as trains, railway cars and aircraft (except when in operation).

In addition to a fine of up to $1,000, the trespasser may be found liable and the same court that convicted the trespasser may order the trespasser to pay for any damage that he did while on the occupier's property up to an additional $1,000. In addition to the penalty and possible compensation, if the occupier conducted a private prosecution and the trespasser is convicted, the trespasser will usually be liable for the reasonable costs incurred by the occupier in prosecuting.

The occupier or the person authorized by the occupier of the premises may arrest any person he has good reason to believe is trespassing. The Criminal Code and the Trespass to Property Act require that where the person making the arrest is not a peace officer (public police having jurisdiction) he must call for assistance and turn over the arrested person forthwith to the police. If the identity of the trespasser is known he need not be arrested because a charge can be laid against the person without an arrest having taken place.

There are areas where entry is prohibited without notice, where the public is taken to know better than to enter unless express permission is granted by the occupier. Examples of this would be a garden, field or other land under cultivation and including a lawn, orchard, vineyard, premises on which trees have been planted and have not reached an average height of more than two metres, woodlots on land primarily used for agricultural purposes, and enclosed in a manner that indicates the occupier's intention to keep persons off the premises or to keep animals on the premises. The field or garden would be considered under cultivation when it has been tilled, whether or not it has been seeded. It is also under cultivation when the field includes winter crops covered with snow.

An occupier can give notice regarding entry and activities regarding entry either orally or in writing, by means of signs and by means of a new colour-making system.

Where entry is permitted without notice no marking need be used; however, red markings under the new system mean that any entry is prohibited and yellow markings mean that entry is prohibited except for certain activities. It is the entrant's responsibility to find out from the occupier what activities are permitted. To be effective, the red or yellow markings must be of a size that a circle ten centimetres (4 inches) in diameter will fit within. Markings can be larger if required but they must meet this minimum size. The signs can be located anywhere and placed on posts, new or old or natural objects such as trees.

Recreational activity signs have evolved because of the popularity of outdoor activities. The code, together with the marking system, is sufficient to give the occupier of land freedom to prohibit or permit activities on his land on a selective basis. For signs and markings to give legal notice, they must be posted or placed so that they are clearly visible in daylight under normal conditions from each ordinary point of access to the premises, or part of the premises, to which they apply.

A sign naming an activity, or showing a graphic representation of an activity, gives notice that the activity is permitted.

A sign naming an activity, or showing a graphic representation of an activity with an oblique line through it, gives notice that the activity is prohibited.

Notice that an activity is permitted prohibits all other activities and entry for that purpose. Any other notice indicating prohibition is for certainty only.

This material was obtained in part from the Ministry of the Attorney General, Property Protection and Outdoor Opportunities pamphlet.

9

Security Survey

Before any security system can be introduced to business premises, certain data must be collected in order to properly ascertain what is required for that particular area to be protected. Without having the necessary supporting figures, any system brought into being may well not meet the needs and be either too little or too much. If a system is brought in that is more than required, it is simply a financial loss to the business; conversely, a system that is inadequate is similarly a waste of money, by not properly doing the job required.

Two prime questions must be resolved prior to the implementation of a security system, these being the factors of "criticality" and "probability". With these two factors, it will be possible to prepare for an efficient and effective system.

Criticality means the loss that will result from a mishap, including the relative importance of this to the company. For example, a contained fire in a vacant field being held for expansion would have little impact, whereas the theft of classified documents may well mean the loss of future business.

Probability is the chance of something happening,

such as an accident on a construction site without safety standards. In most cases, by completing the security survey, it will be possible to identify the more common areas of security problems; however, if the probability is of a relatively low level or of such a major expense to correct it, the decision may well be made to leave the probability in place. Should this decision be made, the likelihood of the happening and the action which must be taken should be clearly identified and made well known to the appropriate senior personnel.

By answering the following questions prior to implementing a security system, you should be in a position to properly assess your needs. It is suggested a review, using the check list, be done periodically. In this manner, any shortcomings will immediately come to your attention.

The Check List has been divided into various categories, all of which do not necessarily pertain to every business. However, by utilizing those that do relate to your particular enterprise, you will be able to prepare an accurate survey.

All answers in the security survey should be as descriptive as possible. A straight "yes" or "no" is of no value when attempting to plan a system. All relevant information should be included.

Once the security survey has been completed, it should be treated as a classified document, especially once recommendations and future planning are included or attached.

SECURITY CHECK LIST

GENERAL

1.　　Purpose of the survey.

　　　_____

　　　_____

2.　　Name and location of the facility.

　　　_____

　　　_____

3.　　Role of the facility.

　　　_____

　　　_____

4.　　Summary of existing security measures.

　　　_____

　　　_____

5.　　Date of previous security survey and whether it was complete or partial.

　　　_____

　　　_____

6.　　Recommendations of the previous survey and whether these suggestions were implemented.

　　　_____

　　　_____

7.　　Description of government contracts and whether such work is classified.

　　　_____

　　　_____

8.   Maps or aerial photos of the facility.

_____

_____

9.   Description of local roads and rail, air or other transport systems.

_____

_____

10.   Description of facility installations, such as power plants, repair shops, fuel pumps and manufacturing and storage areas.

_____

_____

RESTRICTED AREAS

1.   Identification of restricted areas.

_____

_____

2.   Function and degree of restriction for each area.

_____

_____

3.   Types of access control systems in use.

_____

_____

4.   Types of physical barriers used in connection with the restricted areas.

_____

_____

SECURITY OF BUILDINGS

1.   Construction of facility buildings and whether they are fire and lightning resistant.

   _____

   _____

2.   Frequency of checks by patrols during silent hours.

   _____

   _____

3.   Buildings which are locked or unlocked when not in use.

   _____

   _____

4.   Buildings which house critical equipment or information and whether these buildings are checked more frequently.

   _____

   _____

SECURITY OF INFORMATION

1.   Systems for the protection of classified information and equipment.

   _____

   _____

2.   Systems that ensure access to such information and equipment is restricted to authorized personnel.

_____

_____

3.   Systems for securing such items during temporary absences, such as lunch breaks and weekends.

_____

_____

4.   Storage receptacles available for documents and whether there is an adequate quantity.

_____

_____

5.   Safe and lock combinations restricted to authorized personnel only.

_____

_____

6.   Safe and lock combinations changed regularly or when an employee leaves.

_____

_____

7.   Regulations in effect to ensure that confidential information and equipment are not removed from facility property except with written consent from management.

_____

_____

PERIMETER BARRIERS

1. Description of the type of barrier in use.

   _____

   _____

2. Condition of barrier, including repairs needed.

   _____

   _____

3. Safeguards for all windows and doors, when outside walls form part of the barrier.

   _____

   _____

4. Locations of conduits or tunnels where penetration of the facility could occur. Describe and include protective measures.

   _____

   _____

5. Description of intrusion alarm devices used in conjunction with the perimeter barrier.

   _____

   _____

6. Presence of clear zones on each side of the perimeter barrier.

   _____

   _____

7. Presence of warning signs along perimeter.

   _____

   _____

8.   Frequency of perimeter patrols.

_____

_____

9.   Regulations in effect to ensure that vehicles are not parked near the perimeter.

_____

_____

10.   Measures in effect to protect a body of water that forms part of the perimeter.

_____

_____

11.   Presence of storage areas near the perimeter and whether the materials in storage could be used to scale the barrier.

_____

_____

ALARM SYSTEMS

1.   Location of all intrusion and fire alarm systems used at the facility and who responds to them.

_____

_____

2.   Alarm systems to protect areas where confidential information and equipment are stored. If the alarm systems are inadequate, make recommendations.

_____

_____

3.   Other alarms used in the facility besides fire and intrusion alarms.

_____

_____

4.   Record any false alarms or malfunctions in the existing alarm system.

_____

_____

5.   Times when panels in connection with propriet-ary systems are monitored.

_____

_____

6.   Auxiliary power available for alarm systems.

_____

LIGHTING

1.   Are there protective lights of adequate illumina-tion?

_____

_____

2.   Is auxiliary power available for protective lights?

_____

_____

3.   Are lights controlled automatically or manu-
       ally?

       _____

       _____

4.   Are all switches and timers secured?

       _____

       _____

5.   Is perimeter lighting adequate?

       _____

       _____

6.   Is lighting at entrances and exits adequate?

       _____

       _____

7.   Are all areas housing critical machinery and
       equipment well lit?

       _____

       _____

8.   Are sensitive areas well lit?

       _____

       _____

9.   Are records kept of the date when light bulbs
       and vapour tubes were installed?

       _____

       _____

10.   Is an adequate supply of light bulbs and vapour
       tubes kept in stock?

       _____

       _____

11.   Is portable emergency lighting available?

_____

_____

ENTRANCES AND EXITS

1.   Number of entrances and exits and whether
           they are for vehicles, pedestrians, rail or others.

_____

_____

2.   Hours when entrances and exits are in use.

_____

_____

3.   . Protective measures of all entrances and exits
           when not in use.

_____

_____

4.   Description of locking devices and who con-
           trols the keys.

_____

_____

5.   Security arrangements when entrances and
           exits are in use.

_____

_____

SECURITY FORCES

1.   Organization of the security force and the responsibilities of supervisory officers.

_____

_____

2.   Number of security officers authorized by management and number of positions filled. Is the authorized strength of the security force adequate for the facility? If inadequate, make recommendations.

_____

_____

3.   Security officer training programme and any weaknesses in the course.

_____

_____

4.   Pre-employment security and qualification checks.

_____

_____

5.   Safeguards for firearms, if such weapons are used in a facility, and the adequacy of the firearms training programme.

_____

_____

6.   Briefing of security officers of their duties prior to an assignment.

_____

_____

7.   Quality and tailoring of the uniform.

_____

_____

8.   Salary scales in effect and whether these wages
       are sufficiently attractive to interest qualified ap-
       plicants.

_____

_____

9.   Number of supervisors on shift. Is this number
       sufficient for the number of security officers on
       a shift?

_____

_____

10.   Condition and adequacy of security equipment
       and vehicles. If inadequate, make recommenda-
       tions.

_____

_____

11.   Storage and issuance records for security equip-
       ment and vehicles.

_____

_____

12.   Number and location of stationary security
       posts, length of the shift of the officer on duty.

_____

_____

13.   Working relationship between the facility sec-
       urity force and the local police and fire services.

_____

_____

14.   Number, routes and frequency of patrols.

_____

_____

15.   Adequacy of all security communication systems, both stationary and mobile.

_____

_____

16.   Amount of space provided for the security headquarters and its adequacy.

_____

_____

SHIPPING AND RECEIVING

1.   Are shipping and receiving areas isolated from the rest of the facility by suitable perimeter barriers? If there are no barriers, describe access control systems.

_____

_____

2.   Are packages of visitors and employees checked at entrances?

_____

_____

3.   Are railway cars sealed after loading?

_____

_____

4. Is there adequate security supervision of shipping and receiving docks? Are security officers properly briefed concerning the number and kinds of goods coming on to and leaving the facility?

_____

_____

5. Is there a designated waiting area for trucks and drivers prior to loading and unloading goods?

_____

_____

6. Are goods stored on shipping and receiving docks? Are the storage areas orderly to facilitate checking? Is the storage area open or covered? How is the area protected?

_____

_____

7. Is there a high loss factor in shipping and receiving areas? How may security be improved.

_____

_____

8. Can visitors or unauthorized persons loiter in these areas without supervision?

_____

_____

ENTRY CONTROL

1. Are badges or other identification media used for employees, visitors, delivery men and other persons who are authorized to enter? Are these tamper proof and serially numbered? Include a sample with the survey notes.

   _____

   _____

2. Are there adequate systems for control and issuance of identification?

   _____

   _____

3. Describe the procedures if identification is lost or stolen.

   _____

   _____

.4 Are there entry control procedures for all restricted areas? Include a sample of badges used.

   _____

   _____

5. Are escort systems in effect for certain classes of visitors within certain areas?

   _____

   _____

6. Are visitors screened before they are admitted to restricted areas? What are the criteria for admission?

   _____

   _____

7. Are employee-owned vehicles parked within the perimeter? How are vehicles controlled?

_____

_____

8. Are parking lots provided outside the perimeter?

_____

_____

9. Are these controlled for the entry and exit of all classes of vehicles?

_____

_____

10. Is information about all visitors to the facility recorded in ledgers?

_____

_____

LOCKS AND KEYS

1. Is there a secure location for the storage of all keys at security headquarters or at some other controlled location?

_____

_____

2. Are all keys tagged and accounted for?

_____

_____

3. Are records kept of all key holders?

_____

4.   Are the names of people possessing master keys
        recorded?

        _____

        _____

5.   Describe the master key systems in effect. Does
        security headquarters possess all records of
        combinations to safes and the dates when these
        combinations were changed?

        _____

        _____

6.   Are there pick-resistant locks of sufficient force
        used in areas for which they are intended? The
        location of sub-standard locks should be noted.

        _____

        _____

THEFT CONTROL

1.   Are facility supervisors and foremen urged to
        report suspected theft or fraud?

        _____

        _____

2.   Are control systems in effect for scrap, salvage
        and garbage removal activities? Do security
        officers supervise these collections?

        _____

        _____

3. Is there adequate supervision of janitors and maintenance personnel?

_____

_____

4. Are package control systems in effect?

_____

_____

5. Are storage areas adequately designed to prevent crime?

_____

_____

6. Are inventories frequent enough to detect theft?

_____

_____

7. Are tools adequately secured in cribs and properly accounted for? Are employees permitted the use of facility tools on loan? Can employees buy material at reduced prices?

_____

_____

8. Is there a serious theft or loss problem in the facility? Make any recommendations for lessening these losses.

_____

_____

9. Is there a facility policy regarding employee theft? Are all employees informed of this policy?

_____

_____

10.   Are lunch boxes frequently inspected?

_____

_____

11.   Is there an "incentive system" in effect whereby supervisors and foremen receive bonuses for taking steps to eliminate losses?

_____

_____

SECURITY INDOCTRINATION

1.   Are all new employees briefed on the following?

A. The need for security.
B. Management policy regarding theft.
C. Economic consequences of large losses.
D. Powers and duties of the security force.
E. General facility regulations, including entry and exit control.
F. Arrangements for the loan of tools and the purchase of stock items.

_____

_____

2.   Is the information presented at the initial briefing of new employees available in pamphlet form?

_____

_____

3.   Are personnel in sensitive positions advised of their responsibilities concerning classified information?

_____

_____

4.   Is there a continuing security education programme? Is this programme made attractive by intelligent use of films and other instructional material?

_____

_____

5.   Are posters relating to good security distributed within the facility?

_____

_____

6.   Are employees encouraged to report any breaches of security?

_____

_____

FIRE PROTECTION

In those facilities where the fire department is distinct from the security department, this portion of the survey should be implemented by the Fire Chief.

1.   Does the facility have a fire department separate from the security force? What is the organization, training and equipment of this fire department?

_____

_____

2.   Is there good liaison between the security force and the local fire department?

_____

_____

3.   Is there an auxiliary fire fighting organization in the facility? How are the members trained?

_____

_____

4.   Are there sufficient fire alarm boxes throughout the facility?

_____

_____

5.   Are fire extinguishers adequate as to type and quality? Are extinguishers checked frequently?

_____

_____

6.   Are there buildings without automatic sprinklers?

_____

_____

7.   Are fire doors adequate, properly installed and kept free of obstructions?

_____

_____

8.   Are fire barriers adequate?

_____

_____

9.   Is there a fire prevention education programme? Is instruction given by qualified persons?

_____

_____

10.   Is there storage of inflammable and spontaneously combustible items in fire resistant containers?

_____

_____

11.   Is the electrical system properly installed and maintained?

_____

_____

12.   Are _no smoking_ rules enforced?

_____

_____

13.   Are proper fire precautions taken when welding
          or other such operations are carried out?

          _____

          _____   _____

14.   Has the facility been checked by qualified per-
          sonnel to ensure compliance with provincial fire
          safety laws?

          _____

          _____

15.   Are practice evacuation drills conducted fre-
          quently?

          _____

          _____

EMPLOYEE SAFETY

1.   Are instructions given to employees regarding
          safety regulations and practices?

          _____

          _____

2.   Are safety regulations enforced?

          _____

          _____

3.   Does the facility comply with provincial safety
          laws for industry?

          _____

          _____

4.   Are safety posters distributed within the facility?

_____

_____

5.   Is there a first aid clinic staffed by trained personnel located within the facility?

_____

_____

6.   Are first aid kits adequately distributed within the facility, particularly in areas where dangerous operations are carried out?

_____

_____

7.   Are employees adequately protected from noxious dust and gasses?

_____

_____

EMERGENCY PLANS

1.   Are there separate plans for all man-made or natural disasters, including all forms of labour unrest or other disturbances?

_____

_____

2.   Are plans reviewed and amended periodically?

_____

_____

3.   Are copies of these plans available to top man-
        agement, local police and fire departments, and
        Emergency Measures Organization?

        _____

        _____

4.   Are there periodic test drills and briefing for the
        security force?

        _____

        _____

5.   Do emergency plans adequately provide for the
        security of confidential information? Are copies
        of all essential documents stored in a secure lo-
        cation away from the facility?

        _____

        _____

6.   Do plans include succession lists for the delega-
        tion of responsibilities and authorities in the
        event that key security and management per-
        sonnel become casualties?

        _____

        _____

7.   Is there adequate labour unrest training for the
        security force?

        _____

        _____

10

Security and Safety
of the Individual

Both the courts and companies in Canada have long realized they have a legal and moral responsibility to ensure the safety of all persons on their property, particularly those who are employed by the company either on a permanent basis or a temporary function, such as a person making a delivery. Certainly customers must be considered as having to be protected as well. The performance and supervision of a given safety function is often placed on the security staff, as they are the ones who are most often visiting all areas of the company property while performing other duties, thus being in a position to observe any breaches of safety that should be rectified.

The responsibility of safety control is not a duty which can be taken lightly, mainly because of the very real repercussions inherent with the improper performance of this function. Failure to observe and subsequently correct a breach of a safety procedure may well result in serious injury to an individual and/or possible damage to company property.

Safety control does not have to be a time-consuming function if time is spent initially in completing a survey of the business premises and designing a safety check sheet. This form should not be cumbersome but contain, in a brief manner, all areas that require frequent checks to ascertain safety measures are being followed.

This form should not be restricted to security personnel, but should receive wide circulation throughout the company, with particular emphasis placed on supervisory personnel who are employed in a capacity where infractions would be quickly observed. The form, accompanied by a covering memorandum from senior management, should be circulated periodically throughout the company. People tend to become somewhat lax after a period of time, but by continually re-circulating the safety check sheet, their minds will be refreshed and the matter given the consideration it should receive.

A properly compiled check sheet should, of course, contain any element deemed to be a particular hazard for the individual company, such as precautions to be taken for the safe operation of specific equipment or the storage of any hazardous materials. The following general areas are those which should be included in a check sheet designed for any firm, regardless of size:

1. Lighting
2. Heating and Air Conditioning
3. First Aid Equipment
4. Safety Equipment
5. Fire-Fighting Equipment
6. Fire Routes

The portion of the check sheet dealing with lighting should contain mention of such items as the location of fuse boxes, where spare lightbulbs are stored, any particularly hazardous outlets (such as those designed for a higher-than-normal voltage) and emergency numbers to locate the correct personnel should they be needed. Particular attention should be given to the location of light switches and emergency power shut-off levers as well as the source of temporary (emergency) lighting, such as battery-powered lamps. The sudden lack of illumination can lead to confusion and disorientation by both employees and visitors alike, leading quite often to serious injury, especially in areas where there is a presence of dangerous equipment or in areas under construction or repair.

Heating and air conditioning may not seem, at first glance, to be of any significant safety hazard; however, the loss of full-function control can have dire consequences. Natural gas, a prime source of heating, being basically colourless and odourless, can cause serious injury and/or death if a leakage in the system is not quickly discovered. Similarly, the chemicals used in modern air conditioning systems can cause severe injury, especially to the respiratory system. Therefore, the close and continuous monitoring of the appropriate gauges and detection systems is imperative. In many companies, the loss of a constant temperature can quickly destroy products, especially computerized equipment, resulting, in some cases, in irreparable damage. As with lighting, all employees in a potentially affected area should be aware of the location of all gauges and shut-off valves as well as emergency numbers.

All personnel must be made aware of the location of all first aid and safety equipment and their location clearly identified by prominently displayed signs. In order to prevent confusion, it is suggested international symbols be utilized for this purpose. They are instantly recognizable and identifiable by anyone, regardless of language. Safety and first-aid equipment should be checked on a regular basis to ensure all is in working condition and easily accessible. Through non-usage, materials can become redundant and spoiled. A dangerous practice, which, unfortunately, is an all-too-common occurrence, is the placing of materials in front of or on top of the equipment, making it difficult if not impossible to get to in times of emergency.

Safety equipment is anything designed for the purpose of safety in a given work situation and may include items such as hard-hats and safety glasses on construction sites and in factories to leather climbing belts for persons working above ground. People tend to develop sloppy habits in the usage of such equipment and a rigid company policy, with severe disciplinary action, must be in place and rigidly enforced. It is in the employees' own interest to have a safe work site. Injuries are costly to both the employer and employee.

Fire-fighting equipment, for the purpose of this chapter, incudes not only fire hoses and extinguishers but alarm or call boxes as well. All equipment should be clearly marked as to location and type. As there are many types of fire with different origin, all requiring their own particular chemicals to extinguish them effectively, all equipment must be clearly marked as to contents and usage. Some chemicals do effectively help a type of fire rather than hinder its advance. The inherent danger of using the wrong chemical on the wrong type of fire cannot be stressed strongly enough. All personnel, especially the security force, should be extensively drilled in the use, control and location of all firefighting equipment.

All extinguishers and hoses need to be monitored on a regular basis to ensure they are in working condition and the contents are not outdated or of insufficient pressure. Fire alarm boxes need to be well located and easily accessible by all personnel working in a particular area. It does not make sense to place the boxes in a location that cannot be quickly and readily reached in time of emergency. Personnel working in the area must be familiar with both the location and correct usage of the fire alarm boxes.

A fire route is defined simply as an emergency evacuation space through which personnel can quickly leave a given area in times of need. It is vitally important that all routes be kept clear of obstruction at all times and they be well marked. The storage of equipment on a fire route may well result in persons being unable to leave a designated area in time to avoid serious injury in the event of a mishap. It is in the interest of all employees to maintain an open route; however, because of work expediency and lack of storage space, this rule is often neglected. The presence of a strong company policy and its rigid enforcement is encouraged.

11

Report Writing

Very few people enjoy writing reports; however, it is probably one of the most important duties of anyone employed in private security. Reports give a permanent record of what has happened in a given situation and, if the occurrence was important, will be referred to many times. Therefore, they must be clear and concise and cover the event in a factual manner.

For the individual, quite often the only way senior management will be aware of that person's work is through the medium of their written work. As such, a career can depend, to a large degree, on how well that person has presented himself on paper.

A report, regardless of its purpose, must contain some of the basic aspects of *who, what, when, where, why* and *how*. All reports, because of their subject matter, will not answer all of the questions. For instance, a report dealing with a theft may not be able to answer the question of *who*, but, as far as possible, all should be covered in as much detail as possible.

If you consider a report being like a story, it will be much easier to compile. Every report must have a beginning (introduction) and must end with some type of conclusion (the climax), although the conclusion may not be final, pending further action.

In between these points, you must cover all happenings, in the order that they happened. A good report, like a story, will not jump from event to event, but rather will flow smoothly, listing everything as it happened.

Opinion must be kept separate from fact. Should a matter go before the courts, your lawyer will be very upset to find that something you stated in your report is merely your opinion, not an accurate accounting of what took place. Opinions have no place in the legal system and can rarely be used.

That is not to say your opinions should not be given, only that they must be clearly shown not to represent fact and are merely the opinions of the person compiling the report.

Many reports in private security consist of completing preprinted forms, such as those used to record the entry of persons to a property, key controls, patrol scheduling, etc. Most firms keep these relatively simple; however, they must still be completed accurately. If, for instance, an incorrect licence number of someone entering the property is entered on the form and there happens to be a theft, it would be virtually impossible to ascertain who, in fact, has entered the property.

With forms, the main item that must be covered is accuracy. The five required items will all be answered if the form is completed accurately.

The explanatory report, covering events not properly dealt with on a preprinted form, offers the security officer his greatest challenge. Regardless of the subject matter, whether it be the reporting of a crime or a routine administrative manner, the report must stand by itself and be as complete and accurate as possible.

The actual style of the report may well be dictated by individual company policy; however, certain key methods are required.

When completing anything but the original report the investigator in most cases is designated by the Director of Security. This delegated member completes the report as per the security policy and the report is addressed to the Director of Security.

Every report should contain some identifiable characteristic, such as a file number, which will make it easier for someone to locate it at a future date or read more details leading up to this particular report. The ideal place for this number, barring any distinct company policy to the contrary, is at the top of the page, normally on the right side.

The beginning of the report should contain a brief introduction as to what is to follow. This can be done in two different ways—one is by using the "Re" (short for reference) or subject line. This is shown before the body of the report and contains such elements, in brief form, as *what* the following report will deal with, *who* it is talking about, *when* something has or is about to happen, *where* the subject-matter took place and *how* something happened.

For example, if a company employee named John Doe had stolen $50.00 worth of tools on January 4, 1986, while working on a project in building A and had been apprehended by the Security Department that day, the "Re" line would appear as:

Re: John Doe, Theft of Tools ($50)
      Building A, 86–01–04

This will instantly tell the reader what the report is about. Further details will be contained in the main body of the report.

If the particular company policy does not allow for the use of captions, then the first or introductory paragraph would contain the same information, in proper sentence structure, as that contained in the caption.

The main body of the report should state, in a clear, factual manner, what has happened. The report should begin with the first indication received as to what is about to happen. For instance, in the case of John Doe, did you receive information from someone that he was going to steal tools, was he observed taking them or was he apprehended as the result of an investigation? If the latter, who reported the tools missing and when were they first noticed to be missing?

Following this, what action was taken? Was Doe apprehended immediately or was an investigation conducted which eventually led to his apprehension? If an investigation was done, what steps were followed? Were interviews conducted? If so, with whom? If statements were obtained from persons interviewed, are copies attached? If not, where are they held? Was Doe advised of his rights? Who witnessed this? Were the public police notified or was this handled internally? Was his supervisor notified? Has Doe been in trouble like this before? What action has been taken concerning Doe? Have the tools in question been recovered? If so, where are they now? If they haven't been recovered but are believed to be at a certain location, is a search warrant being obtained? What authority do you have to obtain a search warrant?

In a case such as our example, no doubt the author would have opinions to offer, such as what punishment should be given, whether the matter should be referred to the public police or dealt with internally, what rumours he may have heard concerning Doe's character, etc.

The proper place for comments such as these is at the

end of the report, just before the summary. They must be clearly shown to be opinions, as opposed to actual happenings. If they are rumours, state this. Comments, rumours and opinions form an integral part of any report but must be clearly shown to be exactly that—comments, rumours and opinions. The receiver of the report must be able to readily and accurately separate the facts from the rest of the report. If company policy allows it, the sub-caption "Comments" preceding the portion containing opinions, etc., is an excellent idea.

The last paragraph(s) of the report should either summarize what has happened, if the matter has now been fully dealt with, or give a plan of action as a follow-up to the matter. If direction is being sought, it would also be asked for at this time.

When this report is completed and the Director of Security has reviewed the file he will then decide the distribution of that file. If not already done, the Director of Security will at this time assign it a classification. This classification may be anything from routine to secret. The Director of Security will then distribute the file to the individual(s) who will provide follow-up assistance or guidance, such as the Manager of Employee Relations, who may have to make the decision to proceed through the collective agreement seeking disciplinary action of the employee or to proceed through the court system. Should this be the case, the file will begin as follows:

Classification

To:	The Manager of Employee Relations
From:	The Director of Security
Re:	Theft of Tools. Suspect Jim Brown —Employee—Payroll number 1234

In most cases, after the Director of Security has received a report from his investigator or from those providing follow-up assistance, he must decide as to the course of action required. In this case the Director of Security may refer this report to an investigator and request further investigation and/or surveillance. When the Director of Security feels that the investigation is complete as far as possible to that date, he will complete a follow-up report himself. The report may be an overview of the investigation and offer his conclusions as a professional as to the causes, effects, and prevention of the incident.

The report that was submitted by the investigator is usually referred to in his master report and attached as an appendix. An example of this is a reference in his report to "the investigation by security investigator Brown who can state the following: . . . This report by Security Investigator Brown is shown as Appendix "A"." The Director of Security may have another report from security investigator Smith and will also refer to it in his report. The Director of Security may refer to this report by saying that the information was obtained by security investigator Smith and is attached as Appendix "B".

Appendices are not restricted to other reports, but may also take the form of supporting documents, exhibit reports, etc. Each individual attachment must, however, bear its own appendix number, in order to keep it distinct from all others and allow for easier reading by the receiver.

Reports should be written in a clear, concise manner. Where it is possible to state something in one sentence, two paragraphs should not be used. A report is not the Great Canadian Novel, but simply a statement of what has happened and what will happen in the future. A long, complicated report full of excess verbiage is difficult to understand and will not, in all likelihood, get the reaction you wish it to receive.

The report is an extension of the individual compiling it. As such, it is important that it be factual and a true accounting of what happened. In addition, correct grammar, punctuation and spelling are necessary. A poorly written report, containing grammatical and spelling errors, even if factually accurate, will reflect poorly on the individual, as well as making it difficult for the receiver to assess accurately what is being discussed.

If you have a poor command of the written English word, it is strongly suggested you obtain a good dictionary and refer to it frequently. As well, there are a number of good books on the market that explain, in simple terms, how to compose a good sentence and paragraph. With practice, you will quickly learn to write without these aids. Until then, use dictionaries and other material extensively. Remember, the report is a reflection of yourself.

12

Investigational Procedure

The most common complaint of a serious nature received by a Security Department is that of theft, although many other criminal matters may have to be dealt with on occasion. By simply changing the word "theft," the following general guidelines will apply to any criminal investigation.

Regardless of who initially receives the complaint, the Director of Security or his designate must be notified immediately. Any action taken would be under his direct control. The Director may well wish to investigate such matters personally, or, ideally, have an experienced investigator on each shift who would undertake the responsibility. Should this not be practical, or the matter of small import, he may well direct anyone on that shift to undertake the preliminary aspects. By following this latter procedure, the most junior member of the Security Department can obtain experience in investigational procedure.

The Director of Security should prepare a firm, written policy on how to conduct internal investigations. With this in place, there will be firm guidance provided to all members of the Security Department. Part of this policy should contain instructions that all facets of an investigtion that are unfamiliar to the investigator must be referred to him before action is taken. This will ensure that obvious errors, which could adversely reflect on future action, are avoided. Concurrently, there may be personnel within the company who do not wish to be contacted by other than the Director of Security. If these matters are elaborated upon, the chances of an unsatisfactory investigation taking place are minimized.

The policy should contain adequate instructions on how to carry out the investigation. The investigator would now be selected if there is adequate time. Some investigations, such as a theft happening at the moment, would, of course, have to be responded to immediately by available personnel. Whenever possible, the same investigator(s) should conduct the investigation through to its completion. This will provide a continuity and familiarity with all information received and action taken, thereby avoiding unnecessary duplication.

Normally, the initial stage to be followed would be an interview with the complainant. During this interview all details of the happening would be received in as much detail as the complainant is able to provide. Items such as the following should be expanded on: description of the stolen property, serial number, model number, colour, value, size and quantity. This information is important both for your investigation and for advising the local police department, who, with all this information, can place an adequate description on a centralized computer for future reference. Should the complainant not be in possession of all these details, it may be possible to obtain them from another department, such as the purchasing section being able to provide an accurate price or the maintenance department being able to give a detailed description of a motor.

Ascertain from the complainant when the item in question was last physically seen. This is quite important in determining a time frame during which the item could have been taken. If the complainant himself has not seen the item for some time, check as to whether someone else may have viewed it, even accidentally. Obtain a list from the complainant of all individuals who have had access to the area where the item was stored or in use for the period in question.

Most persons will readily discuss the theft and the trained investigator will listen carefully to them. They may well offer an insight into how the theft may have occurred or even offer the name of a suspect. His story may well be based on nothing but rumour or a personal vendetta and this must be borne in mind but not completely discarded until proven so by further investigation.

Establish whether the item is one that is easily obtained and has a ready market value or whether it is a specialized item for which only a select clientele is available. If the latter can be ascertained, it will greatly limit the area of your investigation.

From the list of individuals obtained, it may come to attention that persons employed outside the company, such as private contractors, may have had access to the area involved. If this is the case, the entry/exit gate to the worksite should be contacted with a view to establishing whether the item was removed by the contractor. Many thefts can be solved at this point as a legitimate error on the part of the contractors' employees removing items they felt belonged to them. Should the gate logbook not indicate the item leaving, careful attention should be paid to the time of departure of the contractor. If it is in the time period under question, the contractor should be interviewed. He will be in a position to clarify whether he does indeed have the item. If he does not, he will be able to supply a list of persons working for him who were in the area.

Should the item not be located at this point, it will be necessary to interview all employees and contractor's employees. These interviews should be conducted individually and in private surroundings. During the initial interviews, one employee may well come to attention as being somewhat suspect, however, it is doubtful any hard evidence will surface. Follow-up investigation would then be conducted on the suspect individual, including subsequent interviews with him and randomly selected individuals, in order not to raise his suspicion. Often, especially if the employee has not committed an offence before, he may voluntarily admit to the infraction.

Should nothing of value surface during your interviews, it will now be necessary to widen the scope of your investigations. Employees working in areas adjacent to the theft location should now be interviewed as well. They may have observed someone in the area or with the item in question who was not noted by the previously interviewed employees.

Should all these interviews be unsuccessful in solving the case, it may be necessary to broaden your investigation further by checking with other areas of the company. For instance, someone in an unrelated area may have simply borrowed the equipment without notifying the proper authorities and is still using it.

At this stage, one of two happenings has occurred—either your investigation has been brought to a successful conclusion or it is still not resolved. If the conclusion has been achieved, your file will now be complete. If the item has not been located, it may be necessary to keep your file active. Although you will no longer work on this case on a daily basis, a diary date system should be placed on it, whereby every so often the file will be brought to your attention by the registry. When you receive the file in this manner, a review should be completed and a short report concerning your present status of investigation submitted.

The fact the file has not been successfully resolved should not lead to discouragement. Many times a theft is so well planned it is virtually impossible to ascertain who the culprit is. However, given time, so-called "perfect crimes" are solved. Quite often, after a period of time has passed, the criminal will become more brazen and be apprehended for another crime. Investigation of that crime may well lead to a string of unsolved crimes being suddenly solved. Often, a friend of the culprit, or the culprit himself, will inadvertently say something concerning the event which will open new avenues of investigation. By having the file brought forward with a diary date the happening will not be forgotten and may well lead to a successful conclusion.

On occasion, investigations may have to be conducted on senior personnel of the company. Because of the obvious delicacy involved, only a senior member of the Security Department should conduct the investigation, and always in close co-operation and under the immediate supervision of the Director of Security. Normally investigations of this nature involve serious criminal infractions such as fraud and consequently must be handled with delicacy and experience. If the fact an investigtion is being conducted is revealed, the whole investigation may well be jeopardized. As such, as few people as possible should be advised and no official file opened until overt action can be taken. The file itself should bear a high security classification and be kept in a secure place where only the investigator and Director of Security will have access.

No investigation is easy and the obvious sometimes may well be concealing a deeper problem. The age-old questions of *who, what, when, where, why* and *how* apply to any investigation. Once these questions have been fully and properly answered, your investigation will be complete.

One of the initial steps the Director of Security must establish is the classification of the various types of criminal complaints. The classification would break down the complaints into areas of investigation: for example, theft or assault. Each classification would carry with it specific guidelines for the investigational procedure to be followed. For instance, an assault would have to be responded to immediately, whereas a theft that may have happened several days before being reported would be handled in a more standardized fashion.

The routine, but very necessary procedure of properly classifying the investigation into a records system would be done by a centralized person as soon as conveniently possible after the complaint is received. Without a proper records system, it would be virtually impossible to keep track of the investigation or discover any that may be similar.

1. CLASSIFYING COMPLAINTS

A system must be developed which will allow all complaints to be classified into various categories. This will present a more professional appearance and enable the Director of Security to obtain a more realistic approach to the types of problems presently facing the security staff. For example, if complaints were classified into thefts and vandalism separately, a quick glance at these two categories would immediately enable him to determine which is the more prevalent problem, as well as enabling him quickly to retrieve any particular file desired at a later date.

When a complaint has been received, it should be immediately entered into a general log book, containing the name and location of the complainant, who received the complaint, the name of the security officer dispatched and a short summary of what the complaint is about. Once the investigator has made his initial inquiries, he may be in a position to categorize the complaint into a select area, such as a legitimate theft or the mere misplacement of an item. When this has been established, the file, consisting of his report, can be placed into the correct category, such as, in our example, an actual theft requiring more investigation or completely concluded at that time because the item had been located without a theft having taken place.

When the initial report is submitted, one member, detailed with the responsibility, will categorize the file and assign it a file number in that category. This number will be obtained from a central ledger and cannot be reassigned to any other file. Should it become obvious at a later date that the classification should be changed, the initially-assigned number would be cancelled, but never reissued. It is vital that only one person have the authority to issue the specific numbers, or duplication may result, making the system misleading.

Coupled with the entry of the file number, an index card, to be placed in a main file system, would be completed, indicating the file number, name(s) of any individuals involved and the title of the file.

The file itself would be assigned a diary date; in other words, a day on which a further report is required and must be submitted, bringing any action taken so far on paper and included officially in the file. The file would not be considered complete until the investigation is successfully concluded or instructions to conclude the investigation are issued by the Director of Security. Normally, such an instruction would not be issued until all possible avenues of investigation have been thoroughly exhausted. Even then, the best approach would be to place a six-month diary date on the file and have it reviewed once again for any possible areas of investigation which may have come to light through other happenings in that period. Never forget, a thief will normally repeat his act and as such the successful conclusion of another investigation may solve the existing but unconcluded investigation.

Periodically, but not less than once a month, a chart should be prepared listing all complaints received in an easily understood style, such as that shown below. With a chart like this, you can establish at a glance the progress of all ongoing and concluded investigations. This form will also allow the Director of Security to have an immediate overview of all activities undertaken during the period in question.

CLASSIFICATION	ACTUAL	UNFOUNDED	CLEARED BY CHARGE	CLEARED OTHER- WISE
Theft 85–01A–136	1		3	
Theft 86–01B–7	1			1
Trespassing 86–03A–3		2		
Vandalism 86–02A–45	1			

The first box on the chart contains the classification of the type of investigation/complaint and the file number assigned to that particular complaint.

The next column lists the number of offences covered by that particular file number; normally this would contain the figure one only; however, it is conceivable that two thefts may have occurred simultaneously or may have been discovered at the same time, although they happened over a period of time.

The third column, captioned "Unfounded," covers the type of complaint that was found to be non-existent. For instance, in the chart above, Trespassing has the figure 2 for Unfounded. In this instance, a report was received by the security department that two persons were trespassing on company property. On investigation, it was learned the two individuals were actually contractors performing an on-site review prior to beginning new construction. As an investigation was conducted, a file should be open, even though no further action need be taken.

The fourth box, captioned "Cleared by Charge", in our example, shows three persons were charged with theft in this instance. The investigation portion of the file has now been completed and the only further action required will be an entry showing what penalty the three eventually received. The charge could be either of a criminal nature, with public police involvement, or an internal disciplinary action, such as an arbitration hearing.

In the final column, "Cleared Otherwise," it has been established the theft has taken place and a suspect is known, however, because of lack of evidence no charge can be proceeded with. A file in this caption is an example of the type that may well be disposed of later by utilizing a diary date system to refresh investigators' minds.

Another type of file disposition in this category is the type where, because of a particular management/union agreement, the charge cannot be proceeded with. In both of these examples, it may well be preferable to open a new file utilizing the suspect's name and placing it in an observation category, where the person would be watched closely for a period or be the subject of intensified investigation.

In the sample chart above, "Vandalism" is shown as "Actual," with no further comment. In this instance, an act of vandalism has taken place, but no suspects have been located. This same act, with the same file number, would appear on a subsequent chart should suspects be located. An example of this happening is shown under the first Theft on the chart, file number 85–01A–136. In that case, the theft was reported in 1985 and would have appeared on the form at that time as an actual offence; however, no suspects were located. During the period for which this chart was prepared, although it was in another year, three suspects have been charged. Consequently, the file is being reported on once again with the further column now being properly completed.

In our example on the chart, there were file numbers for each separate entry. The file classification used in this sample is a relatively simple one which can be adapted readily to suit any given situation.

Each type of complaint has been given a particular number; for example, 01A means a theft under $1,000, while 01B indicates the theft was over that amount. Every conceivable complaint can be classified accordingly. For instance, if vandalism were given the master code of 02, this could be further sub-divided by the addition of an alpha letter such as A for a vandalism against company equipment and B for damage to company buildings and C for damage to private contractors' equipment while on company property.

The number preceeding the code, shown in our example as either 85 or 86, simply indicates the year in which the investigation commenced. The last digit indicates the number of that classification being used for that particular file. By looking at the numbers, a person can readily see how many complaints in that category have been received to date.

The accompanying chart shows the file numbering system in a simplified form.

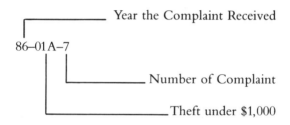

86–01A–7
Year the Complaint Received
Number of Complaint
Theft under $1,000

13

Security Patrols

The security patrol forms an integral and necessary part of the duties of the Security Department. Patrols must be done for a variety of reasons, ranging from the detection of crimes or other infractions to providing routine checks of certain areas for administrative purposes. When patrols are done in conjunction with fixed security stations, such as gatehouses and barriers, a more complete security package is delivered to the company, thus providing them with a more detailed security coverage.

Security patrols can be broken into five distinct types, these being:

1. Fixed foot patrol.
2. Random foot patrol.
3. Fixed vehicle patrol.
4. Random vehicle patrol.
5. Detex patrol.

Each of these types has its own distinct features and is established for a distinct purpose.

The fixed foot patrol is done by a security member covering a given area by walking. The purpose is to discover any infractions and establish an appearance. The dishonest employee will quickly become aware of the security presence at a given time and be alert to them. A definite side benefit of foot patrols is the contact between the security department and other employees. This can, if done correctly, greatly assist the security member by allowing him to have contacts throughout the area who will, on a casual basis, provide him with information concerning activities. During the fixed patrol certain predetermined functions will be completed, such as checking for doors that should be locked and potential fire hazards.

The random foot patrol is completed on an irregular basis through a preset timing as determined by the Director of Security. Its purpose is to detect happenings when the dishonest employee is least expecting it. The timing of these patrols is often set in conjunction with other department supervisors, who may have reason to expect an illegal happening; however, they are not in a position to observe the actual event. These may range from items missing to illegal use of company property, such as using machines for personal use. The very fact these patrols are not predetermined will often deter the dishonest employee, whereas the honest employee will not be bothered.

The fixed vehicle patrol is very similar to the fixed foot patrol, other than a wider area can be covered in less time. This is particularly important where the company complex is very large and contains isolated areas that must be observed, such as a water line that may freeze or a storage shed used only occasionally. Not only can the patrol cover a larger area in less time, but the member on patrol can quickly respond to any emergency. Although this patrol may seem superior, it does have its drawbacks. For instance, the lack of personal contact with other employees.

will not allow the member to develop the personal rapport so important to the security member's duties.

The random vehicle patrol is done for identical reasons as the random foot patrol. Where this becomes invaluable is the ability to service areas during periods when it has become obvious, through past happenings, events are happening in isolated areas, such as persons trespassing on company property.

The detex patrol is normally conducted in conjunction with the fixed foot and vehicle patrol. The planning of the patrol cannot be properly assigned until a security survey has been conducted to ascertain what areas require particular attention. The patrol is normally planned by the Director of Security in conjunction with the Fire Chief, if there is one, and the insurance company providing fire and loss prevention coverage.

The purpose of the detex patrol is to provide a permanent record of when any particular area was visited. In this manner, should, for example, a fire happen, it would be possible for the company to state unequivocally when the area had last been visited, allowing the insurance company to pay damages accordingly.

The detex machine is in the form of a clock with a keyhole, and is carried by the security member on patrol. Locked inside the clock is a paper disc, also with a clock face. At each location to be visited there is a permanently mounted key, which, when inserted into the detex clock, will punch the paper at the time visited. The key bears a code which tells where that particular key was located. The clock is virtually tamper-proof and its reliability is accepted by all insurance companies. Many insurance carriers, in fact, insist such a system be installed on site. The frequency of visits to any particular location will be set and must be strictly adhered to. A large fire loss resulting in a claim which the insurance company will not honour because of the failure to make the visit will result in a heavy loss of profit to the individual company.

Regardless of the patrol there are certain observations that must be made each time the patrolling member moves through various areas. Several factors must be taken into consideration and properly recorded in the patrolling member's notebook:

1. Casually observe the employees in the various areas and record any differences of personnel on return patrols.
2. Record the condition of the area; that is, clean, dirty, uncovered gas cans, solvents, etc. When you observe these factors you should contact the Department Head for that area and report your findings to him. Should he not take the necessary action and a fire results you have fulfilled your obligation to the Department and the Department Head responsible for that area of concern will have to explain his actions.
3. General temperature of the area and comparisons on your next patrol. Should an area be of normal temperature the first time but it seems colder than normal on your next patrol, make attempts to ascertain if there is a problem with the heating system. If you cannot find the problem notify the Area Head for follow-up action.
4. Doors that should be locked must be checked. If not locked you must lock same. Check on return rounds and if found open, lock the door and notify your Security Department shift supervisor for direction.
5. In no-smoking areas, check the floors for cigarette and cigar butts. This may reveal that unauthorized smoking by the employees is taking place between your rounds or when no supervision is present.

6. It is always a good idea to check fire extinguishers when on patrol as some may have expired and are not usable or an extinguisher has been used and not refilled. Check the condition of the fire hoses as well.
7. A general rule of thumb is to remember the condition of the area the last time it was checked. If there is a difference there has to be a cause. Some causes are justified; however, some are not, and early detection and prevention will protect the employer's assets.

To this point we have discussed the various methods of patrol as well as what to look for while on patrol.

The next obvious question to ask is, "How do I apply the theories to practice?"

With respect to the manufacturing industry as a whole, the important patrol is the detex patrol. This patrol will cover the prevention of losses through theft and fire and is a necessary requirement by the insurance underwriter. This patrol is a standard patrol and is usually set to a certain pattern as previously discussed. This routine will in all likelihood not prevent theft because of the routine nature. The pattern can be followed by the criminal over a period of time and a theft may result.

The Director of Security must look at his protection, and besides providing the mandatory prevention package must incorporate the unexpected. For instance, the Director of Security will establish his detex patrol for a certain hour. This patrol may take, for example, approximately thirty minutes. Instead of the vehicle or man patrol returning to the office it should be dispatched to a random vehicle or foot patrol or a combination of both. No set pattern should evolve and should never be repeated exactly the same. This patrol can be high profile, where the security members make sure that all employees see them wherever they go to establish a deterrent or lean the patrol towards the surveillance end or both in different areas.

The Director of Security, once he has maintained his fire and security protection through the detex method, can utilize any methods he chooses to provide extra protection to the employer. Use your imagination and the combinations are unlimited.

14

Radio Communications

Communication between both various members of the private security staff and their main control centre are extremely important and their necessity cannot be over-emphasized. The member on patrol is, quite often, in an isolated state, being in an area where there is no other form of verbal contact or physical assistance.

Should he encounter a situation where help or information is needed quickly, he must be able to communicate instantaneously. The only method of doing so is the properly functioning portable radio.

Portable radios, by their very name, are neither large nor cumbersome and can comfortably be carried in pouches designed for that purpose. They do not hinder the performance of the security officer in any manner.

Most modern radios on the market today are capable of having a broadcast function on more than one channel; however, normally only one channel is used internally, the other being reserved, with the permission of the local public police, for contacting them or the local fire department directly in case of an emergency only.

Many companies, because of their size, may have numerous employees, other than the security department, equipped with portable radios. In this case, normally the security department's main radio base has the capability of monitoring these channels; however, there is no possible way in which these personnel can monitor the channel reserved strictly for the security department.

All security department members should be trained in the proper operation and maintenance of the radios. This should include simple repairs, such as replacing worn-out batteries and broken antennas.

Because of the manner in which radio waves travel, often encountering interference from electrical lines, steel, etc., private security members must be instructed to simply move to another location as quickly as possible before attempting to rebroadcast. The distance required, in some instances, may be as small as two or three metres. Because of this, members must also be instructed to reply promptly to an inquiry, otherwise the broadcaster may assume his message is not being received and inadvertently move to an area where he will not be able to receive/transmit. Should the recipient be busy with other duties, a simple statement such as "Stand by" will alert the broadcaster that his transmission is being received.

Prior to implementing the usage of radios, each member issued with one and each permanent location where a radio is located (such as the main gatehouse and various security locations) should be given a designated number or letter, which will simplify broadcasting.

Proper radio prodecures should be clearly understood by all members of the security department and closely adhered to. The improper use of the radio may well impair an emergency broadcast from being made when required. As such, a few basic rules should apply:

1. Radios should be used for official business only, not for personal conversations.

2. Matters of a confidential or delicate nature should not be discussed over the radio. Any radio frequency can be monitored. If such a matter should come to the individual's attention, he should delay the transmission until he is able to pass the message verbally or by telephone.

3. Keep conversations as brief as possible. Lengthy conversations may well delay the transmission by someone else of an important message.

4. Remain cautious of anyone who may be within hearing range. Such a person will be in a position to monitor both sides of the conversation.

5. Memorize both the "10-Code" and phonetic alphabet (see diagrams) and use them accordingly. They are designed to assist the receiver and prevent an inaccurate conclusion being reached.

6. A radio issued to the security department should never be left unattended. If the radio should come into unauthorized hands, they would then be in a position to monitor the location and activities of the whole security department.

10-CODE SIGNALS (INTERNATIONAL)

10–1	Receiving poorly
10–2	Receiving well
10–3	Stop transmitting
10–4	Acknowledgement
10–5	Relay message
10–6	Busy, stand by unless urgent
10–7	Out of service

10–8	In service
10–9	Repeat
10–10	Request permission to change channels
10–12	Unauthorized person can overhear conversation
10–13	Weather and road conditions
10–16	Pick up prisoner at - - -
10–18	Complete assignment quickly
10–19	Return to Headquarters
10–20	What is your location?
10–21	Call - - - by telephone
10–26	Detained subject, expedite request
10–28	Vehicle registration information
10–29	Check records for wanted
10–30	Improper use of radio
10–33	Emergency
10–35	Major crime alert
10–36	Correct time
10–38	Investigation alert
10–45	Death or fatality
10–50	Accident (fatal, personal injury, property damage)
10–51	Tow truck needed
10–52	Ambulance needed
10–60	Subject is negative
10–61	Subject has record, not wanted
10–62	Subject possibly wanted
10–63	Subject positive record
10–64	Proceed with caution

10–65	Assist re: a 10–64 individual
10–66	Subject in observation category
10–67	Subject in parolee category
10–68	Subject in charged category
10–78	Need assistance
10–90	Bank alarm
10–92	Person in custody
10–93	Set up blockade or roadblock
10–95	Person believed dangerous
10–100	Bomb threat

PHONETIC ALPHABET

A–Alpha	N–November
B–Bravo	O–Oscar
C–Charley	P–Papa
D–Delta	Q–Quebec
E–Echo	R–Romeo
F–Foxtrot	S–Sierra
G–Golf	T–Tango
H–Hotel	U–Uniform
I–India	V–Victor
J–Juliet	W–Whiskey
K–Kilo	X–X-ray
L–Lima	Y–Yankee
M–Mike	Z–Zulu

15

Security Hardware

The term "security hardware" covers all types of equipment available to assist the security staff in performing its task. It is meant to include such things as alarm systems, safes, closed circuit TV, computer systems, fencing, etc.

In the not-too-distant past, it was sufficient for a security department to be equipped with a radio and possibly the use of a vehicle when nobody else needed it. Thieves have changed, and so has the equipment available to them; consequently, the modern Security Department must be adequately equipped if it is to perform competently and professionally.

One aspect which must be borne in mind, however, is the cost factor. Security detection equipment can be quite expensive, and it is easy to spend far too much or too little than is necessary equipping the Security Department. If the security survey has been completed correctly and realistically, you will be in a position to purchase what is actually required, bearing in mind that neither under- nor over-purchasing will satisfy your needs.

There are many reputable firms that are more than willing to assist you in your planning and completing the necessary installation of needed equipment. It is strongly suggested these companies be called upon in order to obtain the expertise and necessary training required. Modern equipment is quite sophisticated and without proper training is virtually useless in the hands of the inexperienced.

Some of the equipment available on today's market is discussed in this chapter. It is impossible to comment on all items available and as such a grouping system has been used of the more common items.

1. COMMUNICATIONS

Communications form a vital part of any security department, and close consideration must be given to obtaining the best equipment needed for the job required. All security personnel, while on duty, must be in constant contact with their particular headquarters.

Accordingly, they should all be equipped with two-way radios for instant communication. *There is little sense sending a person on patrol to observe any happenings if he is not able to report the findings quickly.* The element of safety to the individual also plays a major part here. If the security employee faces a serious situation, he must be in a position to call for assistance immediately.

Standard two-way radios have rechargeable batteries and a relatively long lifespan and once the purchase has been made, there is little maintenance required. A ratio of one radio for each security employee should be a minimum requirement. This will allow radios to be recharged while an employee is off duty.

In addition, each vehicle should be equipped with its own radio. When a security employee is any distance from the main base, his portable radio may not have the range for communication, whereas a radio mounted in a vehicle, with the proper antenna, will offset this shortcoming.

Care must be taken to ensure that the particular radios purchased are all on the same frequency, preferably one that is restricted to that particular company only. On application, a separate frequency can be obtained through the Federal Department of Transport and Communications. With a private frequency, there is no chance of waiting for someone to finish broadcasting before using the network.

Many buildings, because of their structure or internal equipment, will not allow reasonable transmission of all radio messages. Any communications equipment being cosidered for purchase should be carefully scrutinized and checked before purchase.

Consideration should also be given to equipping the Security Director and any senior security personnel who may be required for duty on short notice, with a paging system. This will allow them to move about freely on their leisure time, but still be in instant contact with the Security Department should there be an urgent requirement. These can be purchased outright and utilized by the security main base, or can be rented and controlled by a commercial firm at a relatively cheap rate.

2. TRANSPORT

If the security personnel are required to patrol any large area, they must be equipped with their own suitable transport. It is not sufficient, in most cases, for them merely to have access to a central car pool when a vehicle is required.

The vehicle should be kept at a location convenient enough to allow immediate access in the event of an emergency. All members of the security department must know how to operate this vehicle, including all equipment contained therein.

The vehicle should be well-marked with signs indicating it is a security vehicle. This will allow immediate access to all areas, as well as providing a visible sign of the presence of security personnel.

In addition to a radio, the vehicle should be equipped with emergency lighting on the roof. This may be flashing red or blue, depending on what is legally allowed in the particular area. Some provinces have regulations governing the color of any roof-lighting and this aspect should be checked closely before purchase. A spotlight should also be included, as well as a first-aid kit, fire extinguisher, tow rope, emergency cutting tools and emergency flares. Depending on the type of industry, other equipment, such as burn-paks, flame-retardant suits, stretchers, etc., may be required as necessary equipment. Although the vehicle is not an ambulance, and is not meant to be, it is normally the first vehicle to arrive at the scene of an accident, and as such should have all possible necessary equipment applicable.

A full and properly equipped vehicle will not only greatly assist the Security Department, but will allow the department to provide better and more efficient security to the company.

3. FENCING

Any company with property, as opposed to a building flush with other buildings, should have a security fence. The sole purpose of a fence is to prevent access by persons who have no right of entry.

Obviously, using the above reasoning, a short fence,

such as that used around a residence, is not sufficient. Any fence should be at least two but preferably three meters high and constructed of a material that is difficult to scale. A brick wall, for instance, is not sufficient because of the relative ease with which someone could use the jutting bricks to form a natural ladder. Chain link fencing is the most common type utilized, mainly because of its relatively low cost in relation to other materials, the ease of construction, long life expectancy and low maintenance cost. If a chain link fence is chosen, the space between the wire must be relatively small, no more than two to three centimeters. Anything larger than that will allow a person to place their foot in the space and scale the fence with relative ease.

A neutral area of approximately one meter should be constructed on each side of the fence. This area should be blocked by a lower fence and kept free of any debris and undergrowth. The purpose of this area is to prevent anyone from placing objects against the fence that would allow them ease of entrance, such as parking a truck against the fence and using the roof as a ladder, or employees inadvertently piling items to the top of the fence for storage. Any items placed like this would form a natural ladder for any dishonest employee wishing to throw something over the fence to a confederate or for later retrieval.

If a top is being placed on the fence, it should be of barbed wire facing outwards on a forty-five degree angle and consist of at least three strands.

Wooden fencing is utilized in some instances and should you be considering this, bear in mind the wood must be of a thickness to withstand someone easily breaking it and coming directly through. One deterrent to wood is its solidity. While this will give far more privacy than chain link—a highly desired quality for many companies—

the fact no one can see in also means no one can see out. This may necessitate operating a patrol outside the fence, thus increasing the manpower costs.

Whether a fence will encompass the whole property or only certain areas depends on the particular needs of the individual company. A common practice is having, for instance, the parking lot outside the fenced area, thereby forcing all vehicles, with the possible exception of delivery trucks, to remain off the sensitive area of the property. Conversely, it may be required by some companies to have a large area fenced and another fence within this, encircling particularly sensitive areas.

Wherever there is a fence, there naturally must be an opening, or access. A guardhouse should be erected at this point and should be manned at all times when access is permitted. The guardhouse should be just inside the fence if it is not going to be manned continually. In that manner, no access from the outside can be gained when the fence is locked. The guardhouse should offer a clear, unimpeded view in all directions, allowing the security officer to observe anyone approaching. It must contain, at a minimum, proper heating, lighting and ventilation and a form of communication, such as a telephone. If properly equipped, the guardhouse can serve as the main centre for all security personnel and the nerve centre during a disaster or other type of emergency.

The gate itself should be of a similar height to the fence and should be capable of being locked securely when not in use. In addition, a movable bar should be in place at all times when the guardhouse is functioning. Although such a bar is not sufficient to keep a determined person out, it will force all persons to either stop or risk damage to their cars by crashing through. The bar should be easily removable by the security staff to allow ready access and exit. A hinged bar with a well-balanced end will accomplish this easily.

Fencing should be inspected regularly by the security staff while on routine patrols, and any defects or damage should be promptly reported to the maintenance department for necessary repairs.

4. ALARM SYSTEMS

Alarm systems have advanced significantly in technology during the past few years and have now reached a point of sophistication which would have been unbelievable not ten years ago. Computerization has helped and many systems are now operated almost exclusively with the aid of a computer.

While alarm systems will not take the place of security members, they can do much to ease their duties, as well as providing security in areas which, because of isolation, are rarely visited.

While the term "alarm system" is generally conceived to be a burglar system, the importance of fire detection and the necessary monitoring equipment for this function should not be overlooked.

Systems can be designed to issue a loud warning, such as a siren, if they are penetrated, or linked to a central monitoring location where a member of the security department can take instant action.

The sensitivity of current equipment is adjustable, thereby eliminating the possibility of false alarms. A fire detection system installed in a foundry would, because of the heat, be continually emitting an alarm notice. However, with the proper setting, it would not react until a set temperature was reached. It could also be set to react only during certain periods, such as when the foundry is not operating. An anti-penetration system mounted on a fence can be set not to react to birds hitting the fence or small animals brushing against it.

Alarms can be designed to cover any individual or group area, such as the registry room in a building or the whole building itself. The actual design and installation should be done with the consultation and advice of reputable firms involved with security hardware, bearing in mind the cost involved of any system.

5. SAFES AND SECURE CABINETS

Safes are designed with two purposes in mind—to deny access to unauthorized personnel and to protect documents and valuables from fire, or a combination of both. Safes are built accordingly, and because of high costs, care must be taken in selecting the right one for the right job. A burglar-resistant safe is far more expensive than one designed solely to resist fire.

A safe designed primarily for the storage of papers and documents, such as that required for an accounting department, need not have a high resistance to physical attack. Paper burns when it reaches a temperature of 180 degrees Celsius; consequently an appropriate fire-resistant safe must not heat internally to this temperature.

In Canada tests are performed by the Underwriters' Laboratories of Canada, an independent agency, which, after performing specific tests, will determine the time period for which any safe will resist the internal temperature of 180 degrees Celsius. The tests are based on the time it takes before combustible material inside the safe will burn. At the end of the testing period, all material must be capable of being handled without disintegrating and being read under normal conditions. Their findings are universally accepted as being reliable, and, more importantly, are accepted by the various insurance companies when determining the amount to pay following a fire loss.

Once a fire-resistant safe has been fully tested, a label is affixed listing the time period before the material will burn. The period may be any time from thirty minutes to six hours. The longer the period is before paper will burn, the more expensive the safe; however, the protection offered is also that much more effective.

Should all records in, for instance, the accounts receivable department be destroyed in a fire, the chances of that company suffering severe financial loss, and even possible bankruptcy, are quite great. This important aspect must be taken into consideration when purchasing any fire-resistant cabinet.

Although fire-resistant safes do offer some protection from external attack, they do not have a high resistance to attacks by professionals. Should you require protection for valuables such as money or jewellery, the appropriate safe must be purchased.

Once again, Underwriters' Laboratories of Canada submits these to very strict testing. Two ratings are given, these being TR (Torch Resistant), which indicates how long it takes to burn a hole in the safe with an acetylene torch, and TL (Tool Resistant), meaning how long it would take to open the safe using conventional tools, such as pry bars and jack hammers. The symbol is followed by a numeral, such as 60, which means it would take sixty minutes to gain access.

The higher the number, the better quality of safe, but also the higher the cost. Therefore, careful attention must be paid to the resistance the cabinet is required to offer. If, for instance, only petty cash is stored on the premises, and this is kept in a safe on the second floor, fully protected by an alarm system, the resistance would not have to be as high as one containing valuable jewels on a main floor with direct access from the outside.

The location of a safe in the building is also of importance. Normally, safes should be firmly mounted into a wall with cement casing, making them that much more difficult to penetrate. If they contain any type of valuable, they should be surrounded by an efficient alarm system and placed in a lighted area. Thieves do not like lights, for obvious reasons, and will take care to extinguish the light before beginning their attack. An observant security official, noting a light missing, would quickly apprehend the would-be culprits.

Safes come in many varied sizes, ranging from the bank vault to the small safe for home use. The correct size and configuration you require can be ascertained through consultation with the many agencies available who specialize in these products. Regular maintenance must be performed by qualified personnel. Safes are like any other mechanical system and can break down.

6. CLOSED CIRCUIT TELEVISION (CCTV)

Closed circuit television is a private television network linked to a central location where the image produced by each camera can be viewed. It can be of invaluable assistance to the Security Department as it allows particularly sensitive areas to be constantly monitored without placing a member of the security staff in that area on a permanent basis. One centrally-located security employee is then capable of monitoring any number of areas at one time.

Modern technology allows CCTV to function under

almost any given circumstance. With infrared lighting, the cameras can operate in virtually total darkness. The cameras can also be preset to transmit an image only during given periods or even automatically, should there be any movement in the area under observation.

Cameras have also been developed that will operate while totally submerged in water. This can be particularly helpful to the company located on the waterfront. Not only will the cameras monitor any possible intrusion from this source (an unlikely event), but they can be used to check on the condition of the wharf or any vessel that pulls alongside for shipping purposes.

The cost of CCTV has decreased significantly over the years and is now a relatively inexpensive operation, when compared to the cost of maintaining security personnel in the area under surveillance. In addition, when coupled with a video recording ability, a permanent record can be made of the location, such as the interior of a bank.

7. LIGHTING

An integral part of any security system is adequate lighting. As mentioned earlier, thieves do not like brightly-lit areas and will pass over such an area for one that does not present the same problems.

Spotlights should be placed at intermittent levels along the length of any fencing, making it more difficult for anyone to gain access. Particular attention should be given to areas that are not frequently visible to the security department. This would include areas such as storage sheds and the far reaches of the property. Any areas used for storage of materials outside should also be well lighted. This will not only assist in security, but will also serve to minimize possible injury by employees who may trip and fall in a poorly-lit area.

The interior of all buildings should also be suitably protected. All lights do not need to be on during quiet hours, but a system of every third or fourth light left on will provide adequate visibility to anyone entering the area. Safes and particulartly sensitive areas, such as the computer section, should be fully lit at all times.

An adequate system of lighting is not difficult to design and rarely would any existing system have to be substantially altered to provide full and complete coverage.

8. ACCESS CONTROL

Security personnel, utilizing a gatehouse, can, if there is adequate financing and lighting in place, effectively control admission to the company's property; however, often there are areas within the company where access must be restricted to a small number of employees. These may be areas containing confidential material or where continued pedestrian traffic can upset the air control or delicate equipment, such as a computer centre.

There are basically two types of systems available on the market, both of which can be easily modified to fit virtually any need. The two systems utilized are generally known as a digital system and a card entry system or a combination of both.

The digital system is a locking device opened only by pushing control buttons in a pre-designated order. The system works similarly to that of a combination lock, other than it allows for quicker access. The door itself has a magnetic lock which is released when the right series of numbers are pushed, but will not open otherwise. The door can be set to open without any combination on the interior, allowing for quick exit should there be a fire or similar disaster.

The digital combination can be easily changed by anyone having access to the correct equipment. The Security Department should therefore change the digital sequence on a periodic basis, or more often if required, such as when an employee has been dismissed or no longer is allowed in the particular area for any reason.

The card entry system consists of a coded card given to employees requiring access. The card is inserted into a slot which automatically opens the door. Only employees having the correct card may gain access. The slot, which acts as a decoder, can be changed easily, with new cards containing the new code given to the affected employees. This system is superior to the digital system, as there is no number to remember or inadvertently be passed to a non-authorized employee.

The card entry system can also be adapted for computer-control. In this instance, each card contains its own unique code, allowing for an instant check of who may have entered the area at a given time. By a simple manipulation on the computer, any card can be instantly cancelled, thus denying any employee further access. This ends the necessity of having to retrieve coded cards from employees who may have left the firm and are difficult to locate.

The digital and card entry systems can be easily combined, if desired. In this method, a coded card would be inserted in a slot, following which the pre-designated code would have to be entered before access can be obtained. Removing the card would not allow anyone with only the coded number to gain entry.

With either system, the door can be set to lock itself

after a certain period of time, should the person having activated the system change their mind and not enter.

Which system, or combination, is best is a matter of judgment, taking into consideration what access control is required for any given area.

9. LOCKING DEVICES

Locks have always been considered a necessity for security, and rare is the company that does not utilize them in some capacity. Unfortunately, companies will, after spending large amounts to finish a new location and bring in expensive or confidential material, purchase locks that a five-year-old child could open with a rusty nail.

There are many locks available on the market, most of which are designed to perform a particular function. Before any purchase of locks is made, carefully ascertain what is required of the lock and make your purchase accordingly. If your present locks are insufficient, it may be possible to modify them without major expense by changing the cylinders (the actual working control of any lock) and leaving the handles, etc., in place. Any competent locksmith will be able to give you sound advice and complete the necessary changes quickly and efficiently.

Locks, with the exception of those opened by a combination, are operated by keys. Consequently, regardless of how good the lock is, security is only as good as those who have possession of the key. Most keys can be easily duplicated in any hardware store and, because of this, anyone wishing to have a spare, or the ex-employee who may wish to gain access, will have little problem gaining entry.

However, there are on the market a number of locks with keys that cannot be easily duplicated. In these instances, the necessary key blanks are tightly controlled by the manufacturer and a duplicate key cannot be made without proper authorization. Because of this, no employee can easily obtain a duplicate.

Although a tightly-controlled key blank system theoretically solves all problems, in fact it does not. There are still the problems of the ex-employee who does not, for whatever reason, return his key and the employee who loses his key. Both of these present potential security problems, but they are not insurmountable.

By equipping the Security Department with extra cylinders, a lock facing the potential of access mentioned above can be quickly replaced with a new cylinder, having its own keying system, which cannot be accessed with the old key.

Imperative with any keying system is the necessity of having a well-documented control system. This system, under the direction of the Director of Security, is composed of a list of every person who has been given a key. Each key would contain its own serial number, which would also be recorded. Beside each name would be a listing of which particular doors that key will open. In this manner, any unauthorized access to any area by a key, or the loss of a key, can be quickly covered. Should an employee leave the company without returning his key, it would be a simple matter to replace the particular cylinders on the locks his key would fit.

Many firms equip their Security Department with a key-making machine, which allows them to keep secure blanks on hand and simply duplicate existing keys should additional personnel require access to a given area. This allows for instant duplication, rather than waiting for the manufacturer to return a request for an additional key. If this system is utilized, the blanks should be under tight control and not easily accessible by other than designated personnel.

Because of the possible necessity of emergency access, the security department must retain a copy of a key to every lock on the premises. Although this may initially sound like a formidable task, it can be greatly simplified by using the same type of cylinder on all doors. From this, a master key, which will open all doors, can be produced. This key must, by necessity, be kept under extremely tight control and never loaned to anyone.

As some company personnel, such as supervisors, may require access to more areas than an individual employee, it is also possible to produce sub-masters, which will open any number of pre-designated doors. When such a key is issued, it must be stressed to the receiver of maintaining similar close control of the key and not lending it to someone. If an employee forgets his key at home, then the door should be opened for him, rather than lending him the master or sub-master. Given time, any key can be duplicated.

The above information is by no means complete and is given as a guide only. The security field is changing drastically and as such it is recommended competent security supply companies be contacted when new hardware is required. They will be able to offer professional advice and inform your company of what is currently available.

16

Document Security

All companies, regardless of whether they are manufacturers, retailers, wholesalers or suppliers of services, have written material which is considered, by them, to be of a confidential nature. The release of these documents to an unscrupulous competitor or, in some cases, the general public, would have an adverse effect on that company's ability to compete equally on an open market.

Documents are generally classified in five distinct areas, although this may well vary with the individual company. The particular classifications normally given are: Top Secret, Secret, Confidential, Restricted and Unclassified.

Top Secret is the highest of the classes and normally contains documents to which very few individuals would have access and thus will require the utmost protection. These documents should bear a distinct marking, such as a Top Secret stamp or coloured border, making it easily identifiable and preventing it from being accidentally stored in the wrong area.

Secret is normally the top classification given to documents by any company. Once again, they should be visibly marked and given the proper protection. Circulation will be limited to only those requiring access and having the proper clearance. They must be properly stored when not in use.

Unclassified documents form the bulk of paperwork in any company. These may take the form of handouts to the public, press releases, prospectus, etc. No protection is given to them as anyone, in or outside the company, has ready access to them.

Documents may take the form of sales reports, patents, price lists, competitive bids on new projects, projections for future expansion or deletion of services, etc. A rival company, coming into possession of a competitor's price list, for example, would be in a position to undercut the competitor on all future sales, putting the one company in severe jeopardy in future dealings. This can have the mushrooming effect of creating unemployment by the cessation of future orders and forcing the firm into a non-competitive role.

Companies working on sensitive government projects have the additional responsibility of fulfilling any particular security features placed on the work by the government and effectively safeguarding all aspects of that phase of their business, which may be quite different to that in place elsewhere in the firm.

The key to effect protection of all forms of documents, whether they be reports, blueprints, computer disks, etc., is an effective and tightly controlled central registry. If the registry has full control over the flow and whereabouts of all documents at all times, there is little chance of any material going astray or leaving the firm.

All personnel, regardless of what security clearance they may have, must be aware of the policy regarding documents and what is expected of them when dealing with them. Particular emphasis should be given to those employees having access to classified material.

All documents given a security classification should be listed on a control file kept by the registry. This control file would indicate the name of the file, the particular classification (that is, Secret, Confidential) and how many copies exist. This control file should be kept in the registry and access limited to very few individuals.

No individual employee should be allowed to receive any classified material without having the correct security clearance for that particular document. This must be a hard-and-fast rule and no exceptions allowed. If a particular employee requires a document urgently (which should be a rare occasion) a contingency plan should be in effect to allow him access under the supervision of somone having a legitimate right to review the document.

A classified document should not be given to any employee except directly by the central registry. In other words, a document should not be passed from one employee to another without the registry being properly advised as to its current whereabouts. This can be accomplished by simply having the employees in initial possession of the document notify the registry as to their actions and establishing the individual they wish to give the document to has the correct security clearance.

When a document is requested from the registry, a notation should be made containing the following: name of the recipient, date issued, name of the person issuing the document, what copy of the document was issued. When the file is returned a further notation will be made indicating when the document was returned, who returned it and who received it.

A further check by the registry staff can be done simply by maintaining a diary date system of all documents not presently in the registry. By reviewing the diary dates regularly, it will be possible for registry to ascertain who has what files and how long they have held them. If the period appears to be excessive, registry could then make the appropriate enquiries to see if the file is still required by the individual. More classified documents have been found in the bottom of work baskets than have ever been stolen.

Every individual who has access to classified material should have some means of safely storing the material in his absence. This can be accomplished by a small safe with only the individual (and an employee of central registry) having access to the combination. If this is not possible, then all documents should be returned to registry for safekeeping during periods of absence of the individual, especially during non-working hours. Under no circumstances should an employee be allowed to take classified material away from the building premises without both permission from a supervisor and a notation being made in central registry containing the employee's name, the date and period the material will be absent.

Copying machines exist in almost every business office and are extremely easy to operate, as well as being fast and efficient. From a security point of view, however, they are a deadly enemy. A classified document can readily be copied as many times as the individual wishes, thereby ruining any restriction placed on the document. To avoid this, all copying should be under the strict control of the central registry staff with no one else being allowed to use the machine. This can be, unfortunately, quite impractical in the modern business office. A partial solution, although not by any means as wholly effective, is placing the copying machine in a location where it can be readily viewed by someone in authority. As well, anyone using the machine would be required to enter in a ledger what they have copied and how many copies were made. An instruction should be issued allowing only the central registry to make copies of classified material. Both the above procedures are somewhat cumbersome and will not be greeted with great enthusiasm by employees; however, their lack of endorsement is greatly offset by the protection of the classified material.

The staff of a central registry has far-reaching duties concerning the security of classified material and must be above reproach. Particular care must be taken to ensure these employees do not possess any character weaknesses which would place them, willingly or unwillingly, in a position vulnerable to compromise. A common mistake made by employers is designating registry duties to a minor role, thereby leaving registry staff in a position of low respect. The employees must be given full control of all files and have the power to refuse any other employee, including senior management, access to any documennt for which they are not properly cleared. They must have free access to search any cabinets for missing documents without interference. Above all, they must be, in all matters, above reproach, circumspect in all dealings and possess a high level of maturity.

The registry location itself is of prime importance if full security is to be maintained. The ideal area would be on some floor other than ground level and not be abutting on an exterior wall. The reasoning behind this is quite simple: if an outside intruder wishes to gain access to the registry, he must first break into the main building, travel to another floor, then break into the registry itself. The time and complexity involved by themselves offer a basic element of security.

Access to the registry itself must be restricted to as few personnel as possible—ideally only registry staff. Any individual desiring access to a file should request the particular document either by telephone, following which a member of the registry staff would deliver it by hand, or the individual could come to the entrance of the registry but be denied entry into the actual room itself. This can be accomplished by either having a control desk outside the room with an intercom to the room or the installation of a half-door, allowing the person to talk to registry personnel without entering the room.

Registry personnel would gain access to the registry by use of an access card system. Only qualified personnel would be issued with the appropriate card, which would be taken from them when their duties change. By inserting the card in a slot, the door would automatically open. If an incorrect card is inserted, a warning device would automatically alert security personnel, who could then take the appropriate action to ascertain who was attempting to gain access.

During quiet periods when the registry is unoccupied, it should be protected by both an alarm system and a strongly locked door, preferably with a combination lock. The combination should be known by only the Head of Registry, with a copy held by the Director of Security. The copy held by Security should be in a sealed envelope and placed in his personal safe, to be opened only in the event of an emergency. Should the Registry Director be absent for any reason, such as holidays, another person in registry would be given the combination. On the return of the Director, the combination should be changed and a copy of the new number given to the Director of Security.

As mentioned earlier, documents should not leave the premises without registry being advised. Should they have to be transferred to an exterior location, such as a branch office, the transfer should be effected by qualified personnel, such as the security staff. Ideally, the documents would be carried in a locked container, such as a briefcase, by a member of registry, under escort by security personnel.

If the documents are required for use by an individual at an off-site location and it is not feasible to provide an escort, then registry must monitor the situation very closely, by ascertaining exactly when the documents left the premises and when they were returned. If the documents must be absent overnight, registry must be supplied with written documentation stating where they will be stored when away from the individual's immediate possession. The Head of Registry must be given the power to unilaterally reject any proposal that does not meet his preconceived criteria.

When classified documents are no longer required, especially when copies exist, they should be destroyed as soon as possible. This serves two purposes—preventing the possible leakage of material and preventing the storage and inherent security in central registry of unneeded material. Documents must be destroyed in an acceptable manner following strict guidelines approved by both the Head of Registry and the Director of Security.

The most commonly accepted methods of destruction are either burning or shredding or a combination of both. The most secure method is the combination.

Shredding machines are electrically operated and by inserting the paper into a slot, the paper comes out in a finely sliced format, usually about one centimetre wide and the length of the paper, although some machines will reduce the paper to one centimetre in both length and width. With paper being this size, it is virtually impossible to reassemble the material to its original condition. It is possible, however, for a dedicated operative with lots of time to assemble the material to a fairly readable form.

By burning the material it is reduced to a fine ash which is not possible to reassemble. Material should be burned only in an approved-style container. These are self-contained units with appropriate locks placed on the doors to prevent anyone from opening the door and retrieving any material inside, even if it is only ash. The top of the container has a fine screen to prevent any unburned material from escaping through the chimney. When burning is completed, the ashes are removed, given a final stirring to mix them completely, checked for any unburned documentation and disposed of in a routine manner.

The actual shredding or burning should be done by two properly authorized employees, with both of them certifying what documents were destroyed, the time and date of destruction and the method used. This information should then be placed on the control document held by central registry. It must be stressed that the individuals performing the destruction must have, at the minimum, the same security clearance as that required by anyone previously utilizing the documents. Ideally, this function would be performed by the Head of Registry and the Director of Security or their personally approved designate. The designate should be approved in writing in order to protect all persons involved.

17

Retail Security

Outlets dealing with the general public, such as department stores, have their own unique problems concerning security. Whereas an industrial complex can initiate tight controls over given areas and thus restrict access, stores must allow the general public to enter and leave freely.

Merchandise for sale must be displayed prominently and in many instances must be located where persons can actually handle it. Unfortunately, this allows the dishonest shopper to gain access to the merchandise more readily. By following a few basic rules, however, conditions can be such that the dishonest person will have more difficulty, whereas the normal shopper, who forms the vast majority, will not be inconvenienced.

1. TYPES OF SHOPLIFTERS

Shoplifters, who form the major problem for retail outlets, can be generally classified into unique groups, all of whom present their own problems and slightly different methods of handling.

The kleptomaniac is suffering from a legitimate illness

and steals compulsively, normally without any preplanning or attention to the particular merchandise they are taking. This person normally has money with him and is not stealing from need. Kleptomania is a very rare disease and does not afflict more than a tiny percentage of the overall population, although many shoplifters, when caught, will try to use this is an excuse.

The amateur shoplifter accounts for the majority of actual thefts, although not necessarily in dollar value. Most amateurs are female, which is not that surprising when one realizes the vast majority of shoppers are female. The amateurs can normally be spotted by their nervous actions and sudden movements. They normally work alone and steal items for which they have a genuine need.

The juvenile shoplifter generally steals as part of group pressure and will take items they can use, such as cassettes and records, makeup, jewellery and portable stereos. They normally work in a group and will closely check the area before actually stealing.

The professional shoplifter is without doubt the most difficult to apprehend. They normally work in pairs, with one person distracting the clerk while the other steals the item. They have checked the store in advance and are aware of all exists and the routine of the store. Normally they are equipped with such items as oversize handbags and parcels, often with false bottoms, and may even have hooks inside their coats to facilitate hiding objects. They do not exhibit any overt signs of nervousness.

The drug addict or alcoholic steals from a basic need to obtain money. They will steal any item for which they feel there is a chance for quick conversion to cash. Normally they are not too discreet and can be spotted by their haggard appearance and furtive movements.

2. PREVENTIVE SUGGESTIONS

Retail outlets, by following a few simple rules, will help considerably in deterring the shoplifter. Each store must be treated somewhat differently, mainly because of the style and value of merchandise being offered for sale. For instance, a jewellery store can store all merchandise in locked cabinets without upsetting the buying public, but a self-serve grocery store must have goods where the consumer can reach them.

One common error committed by many retailers is that of leaving small, expensive items next to exits. For instance, placing the jewellery or cosmetic sections, with their display of merchandise, by an uncontrolled exit. The temptation for any type of shoplifter is simply overwhelming and the losses can be staggering. A small bottle of perfume, easily held in the palm of the hand while leaving the store, can have a retail value of well over one hundred dollars. By rearranging the physical layout of the store, losses from external theft may be greatly reduced.

The number of items a person may take into a change room at one time should be closely monitored. The change room itself should have no hidden areas. Customers have been known to remove sales tags and hide them in areas such as the back of a mirror, then boldly wear the item out of the store, knowing it would be very difficult to accuse them of theft.

Customers should be served as quickly as possible after they enter the store. If this is not convenient because of attention being given to another customer at the time, the new arrival should at least be acknowledged. Not only will this deter the would-be shoplifter for fear of recognition, but the legitimate customers will appreciate the gesture. Professional shoplifters concentrate on the store where little or no attention is paid to the customer.

A store should never be left unattended, even for the briefest period. Many small stores feel they can easily take a coffee break or work in the stock room because they have a bell or similar device to alert them when someone enters the front door. The professional shoplifter has no difficulty entering without disturbing the device, whereas the amateur will simply grab an item and run out the door before the clerk can return to the store.

Every customer should be issued with a receipt for all purchases and a strict policy adhered to where no refunds will be given without the receipt. In this manner the shoplifter will not be able to return stolen items for cash. A central returning area is preferable to each individual department accepting its own returns. Not only does this allow the clerks to spend more time with the customers, but a person dealing with nothing but returns will develop an ability to spot the dishonest person.

Items which are sold in pairs, such as shoes, can be protected by simply displaying only one of the pair. If a customer wishes to try on a pair, then a clerk has them under control, making it virtually impossible for someone to steal them.

Small but valuable items should be kept under lock and key, with only one clerk having access to the keys. If these items are in glass display cases, they can be seen easily by the public and be removed for closer examination on request. Under no circumstances should a clerk leave the customer alone with a display of valuable items. It does not take long to take, for instance, a ring and place it in a pocket. The harried clerk may well not realize until later that an item is missing. Some stores have a habit of placing some type of sticker in each vacant spot left by a sale. By doing this, a clerk can readily see whether a vacant space does exist. Such a policy is not expensive to implement and as such is highly recommended.

Employees should be wary of the customer who is wandering aimlessly throughout the store and obviously not interested in purchasing anything. This may well be nothing more than a person bored with waiting for their spouse or friend to finish shopping or could likely be a potential shoplifter waiting for the right opportunity to steal something or checking the store's various security systems for a later visit by professional shoplifters.

Merchandise should not be placed in such a manner that it blocks the view of the clerks. Very high counters that a clerk cannot see over may display more merchandise, but they also allow the thief to hide from view and steal at their leisure. Similarly, counters running in different directions create 'dead' spots that allow the shoplifter to work with ease.

Merchandise should be arranged in such a manner that people have to physically pick it up, otherwise it is very easy to push it into a container surreptitiously. Similarly, larger items such as fur coats should be chained and locked, preventing their removal. Customers can still view them readily and if interested in purchasing will receive the personal attention of a clerk.

Packing bags should not be given to persons unless a purchase is completed. An empty bag can be used to hide stolen merchandise, while giving it a legitimate appearance. The same rule holds true for issuing bags too large for the purchase made.

Sales slips not taken by a customer should be immediately destroyed. A thief can steal an identical item to the one mentioned on the sales slip, place it in a bag and leave the store with little chance of being detected. It would be virtually impossible for the shoplifter to be convicted in court when he has possession of a sales slip.

Clerks should be instructed to keep cash drawers closed whenever they are not immediately being used. It is common practice in many retail outlets to open the cash drawer of the register immediately after completing the sale, then bagging the customer's purchase before placing the money received in the till and giving the customer any change due. By leaving the cash open to display like this, the dishonest person, by offering a small distraction, can quickly grab money from the drawer. The missing money probably won't be missed until cash is balanced later, at which time it is impossible to trace. A better policy might be to bag the merchandise first, thus removing any possible distraction, then complete whatever is needed with the cash drawer.

Clerks should be instructed to remove any loose packing inside objects purchased, such as paper stuffing in purses. Smaller items can be easily hidden within the stuffing and carried out.

Persons carrying large objects, such as a canoe or lawnmover out of a store should be asked to show proof of purchase. Items such as these have been stolen with clerks even holding the door open as a courtesy.

It must be remembered shoplifters are both bold and brazen. They act quickly and must be watched closely. There is no common rule to identify them—they come in all shapes, sizes and ages. Normally though, they all exhibit similar traits and accordingly persons exhibiting certain signs should be watched more closely.

3. TELL-TALE SIGNS

The following are some of the more common traits

by which most shoplifters can be identified by the clerk trained to watch for them:

1. persons leaving a given area quickly; they may well have a legitimate reason for doing so, and as such are not automatically guilty, but the chances are they are doing something wrong;

2. persons entering the store carrying large items with them, such as shopping bags or coats over their arm; these articles can be used to hide stolen items;

3. persons wearing unseasonable clothing, such as bulky jackets in warm weather, or persons wearing baggy items such as oversize pants; once again, these can be used to conceal merchandise;

4. persons who appear to be nervous and exhibit unusual traits such as a distinctive walk or scratching themselves; the nervousness can well be the sign of the amateur, while the walk may mean an item hidden between the legs or in a shoe and the scratching a way of hiding small items inside a shirt or blouse;

5. persons who enter areas obviously set aside for the exclusive use of clerks and persons who reach inside display cases; they may have a legitimate reason for doing so, but this is highly unlikely;

6. the person who is wandering aimlessly and without apparent interest through the store; this may be the bored husband waiting for his wife, or it may be the professional shoplifter;

7. the person who is questioning the clerk about an item in which he does not appear to be truly interested; this person could well be acting as part of a team to distract the clerk while a partner steals items;

8. the person who keeps a hand constantly in a pocket while in the store and leaving; items that would other-

wise bulge in a pocket can be covered easily by a hand;
9. the person who frequently uses the washroom; items stolen can be hidden with ease in the privacy of a wash-room;
10. the person who tries on items in a change room, comes out quickly handing items to the clerk and leaves the store in a hurry; the items returned to the clerk may be either less than taken into the change room or items worn by the customer into the store and exchanged.

In order to arrest a shoplifter effectively, certain steps should be followed to ensure an effective prosecution. The would-be shoplifter must be given every opportunity to pay for the merchandise. No action should be taken before the individual has passed the last possible location where payment may be presented; in other words, the last cash register. To be on the safe side, it is better to wait until the individual has actually left the premises before placing the person under arrest.

The person must be kept under close observation from the time they take the item until the time of arrest. Many would-be shoplifters change their minds and secrete the item in another area, or leave the item in a location for a confederate to later retrieve it. An arrest when the person does not have the item on them can lead to a civil action with a large lawsuit against both the security officer and the store.

The arrest must be done correctly, with the person ad-vised of their rights and the public police notified im-mediately. If possible, no search should be conducted until the arrival of the police. They are the only persons who have full authority to conduct a thorough search of the in-dividual. While awaiting for the police to arrive, the person must be kept under close observation to ensure they do not dispose of the stolen item. Requests such as having to go to the washroom should be treated dubiously and the person should be accompanied.

As many details as possible should be gleaned from the individual, such as their identity, whether they admit to stealing the items, and, if they are juveniles, where their parents can be contacted. If the suspect arrested is a female, a female should be present throughout the whole period. This will deter any later accusations of sexual harassment.

18

Hotel Security

Like the retail trade, hotel security has its own unique problems which are quite distinct from the industrial sector. Hotels, in many ways, are like a city unto themselves, and as such have all the security problems any city might have.

Hotel security has many distinct areas, all of which require a different approach. There are, for instance, the threat of employee theft, customer (or guest) theft, credit card frauds, bar disturbances and rooms being rented for illegal gambling or prostitution.

Hotels can be financially ruined by adverse publicity affecting happenings within, as guests will tend to stay away if the hotel has a 'bad name', therefore most problems must be handled with discretion and tact. Rarely are the police notified, unless the happening is of a major concern. The Director of Security in a hotel setting must be a diplomat as well as being thoroughly versed in all aspects of security.

Because of their type of operation, hotels are considered to give an implied invitation to everyone to enter and utilize the lodging facilities; consequently, it is difficult to refuse anyone access to the premises who is legitimately seeking lodging. However, this same right of access does not necessarily apply to persons wishing to visit the guests of the hotel or merely patronize the restaurant or bar.

If a registered guest should return to the hotel in, for instance, a drunken state, as long as he is not causing a disturbance, the hotel must allow him access to his room, although they do not have to allow him the usage of any other facilities. If the guest is accompanied by a friend also in an inebriated condition, this person could be denied access to the premises.

Hotels, by their very nature, have a large supply of expendable items that are relatively easy to steal, but do account for profit losses to the company. These items range from towels and bars of soap placed in every room to food in the kitchen and liquor in the bars. People have been known to check into hotels (under an assumed name, of course) and steal every piece of furniture in the room.

Because of the diverse types of security problems within a hotel, both types of security, contract and in-house, can be effectively utilized. Contract security, for instance, can be employed to guard the employee entrances and shipping/receiving areas and even make routine patrols throughout the hallways, leaving the in-house staff free to concentrate on the more delicate areas of guest theft and problems in the public areas (for example, bars and restaurants).

The varied duties within a hotel require a large staff to perform all functions. As with any activity of this magnitude, there is always the possibility of theft against the hotel from the staff. Accordingly, certain systems should be brought into force to offset this.

All employees should be instructed to enter the hotel through one entrance only, as well as parking their vehicles in a designated area. Not only will this allow for freer access by the guests, but it will allow security to monitor who is presently working in the hotel.

All parcels brought to the hotel should be checked and held by security. This will prevent employees from bringing empty bags or boxes filled with paper into the hotel and leaving with supplies owned by the hotel. These may take the form of towels and toilet paper being carried by chambermaids to foodstuffs smuggled out by kitchen employees.

A favoured trick of dishonest bartenders is to bring their own liquor into the hotel and sell it from the bar, pocketing the profits received and in effect stealing from the hotel. Once the bottle is empty, they simply take it out of the hotel with them and no one is the wiser.

The receiving area is always of concern to a hotel because of the large number of supplies required on a daily basis. Merchandise required by the hotel should be accepted in one central receiving area only and during specified hours. All suppliers should be advised accordingly and the receiving area should be closely supervised by a member of the security staff. If, for any reason, supplies cannot be delivered during the designated times, instructions should be given that they will only be accepted by a member of the Security Department.

A dishonest employee, working in collusion with an outside supplier or transportation company, can easily short-change the hotel with the loss possibly never being discovered.

The housekeeping department of any hotel must be given particular attention. The employees of this department have access to unlimited supplies of easily-disposed-of items, such as linens, towels and cleaning supplies. A dishonest employee, over a relatively short period of time, could remove voluminous quantities of these supplies.

Of even bigger concern, however, is the fact these employees are, by the nature of their duties, in a hotel guest's room without supervision. The chance for theft of valuables can be great, either by the employees themselves or by someone working with them and entering on their advice or with their pass keys.

Fortunately, the vast majority of housekeeping employees are honest. Nevertheless, care should be taken to obtain as much detail as possible concerning their background and a close check should be completed. New employees in this area should be closely supervised until their reliability can be ascertained. Not only will this offset any security problem, but it will allow the hotel to clarify the type of work they are capable of performing.

Employees and their immediate families should not be allowed to utilize the hotel facilities without the specific permission of senior management. The risk of possible abuse of hotel amenities is far too high; for instance, a fellow employee under-charging the person for food and beverages or allowing them to use a hotel room without payment.

The problem of guests obtaining lodging and failing to pay their bill is, with credit cards, not as prevalent as it once was. Most hotels follow the simple but effective policy of requiring guests to either pay in advance or leave an impression of their credit cards with the reservations desk on checking in. This is either completed or destroyed when the guest leaves. By having the credit card impression, the hotel can check with the issuing company as to the validity and amount of credit available. This is normally done by the night staff.

When the individual has reached the limit of his credit, he can be approached to settle his bill or arrange for extended credit. Although this may appear to be a security function, the duty is normally done by the credit manager. Security is notified mainly when the individual has left without paying or, for some reason, refuses to pay his bill. The Innkeepers Act of Ontario (other provinces have similar statutes under similar names) allows a hotel to seize and sell any goods belonging to a guest who does not pay his bill. Any excess profits, of course, must be returned to the individual.

Unfortunately, hotel rooms are often rented for illegal purposes. Because of the potential embarrassment to the hotel, these matters must be handled discreetly by the security department, in conjunction with the local public police force. Because of the type of offences, most police departments will offer full co-operation in handling the matter with as little public knowledge as possible.

Offences for which the rooms are normally rented are what are commonly referred to as the morality or "victimless" type, mainly prostitution and gambling. The reason they are termed "victimless" is simply that the victim willingly participates in the crime, as opposed to, for instance, a robbery where the victim does not condone the happening. By their very natures, these crimes are relatively difficult to discover, but their continuance will quickly establish a bad reputation for the hotel.

Prostitutes, both male and female, possibly working in collaboration with a member of the hotel staff, will rent rooms on a short-term basis, sometimes even a matter of a few hours, to ply their trade. When this becomes known to the general public, regular clients will often avoid the hotel, for fear of tainting their own and their companies' reputation. To prevent this, careful vigilance must be undertaken to watch for this activity. Many prostitutes, if not discovered, will ply their trade in the hotel's bars, often, if not checked, quite openly. Periodic checks by hotel security and, if needed, contract security operating under-cover, should be made of these areas.

Women who are overly-frequent guests of the hotel or who are observed spending long periods of time in the hotel lobby should be discreetly checked as to their true purposes. Many loyal and reliable guests may also follow these habits, therefore discretion is of paramount concern. Where it is established prostitutes are indeed using the hotel for their illicit activities, they should be warned in no un-certain terms that the hotel will prosecute for any offences on or in relation to their property.

Public police, who are also faced with the problem of prostitution, will most often co-operate fully with hotel security to identify and eliminate the problem of prostitu-tion.

The guest of the hotel, who returns after a "night on the town" with a known prostitute in tow, should be po-litely but firmly advised that his guest is not welcome in the hotel and will not be allowed to enter the rooms. If possible, this should be done discreetly, in order to avoid embarrassment to the guest and avoid the creation of a scene in the hotel lobby.

Professional gamblers will often rent a hotel room in order to carry out an illegal gambling operation. The reasoning behind this is quite simple; if they move their game often from location to location, the police will have a difficult time catching them.

Once the room has been rented, normally under a fictitious name, the gambler will contact his other players and advise them of the location. Often the gambler will frequent the hotel bar, looking for potential' players amongst the various patrons. The latter method is used quite frequently where the gambling operation is crooked, that is, using marked cards or other methods to give the gambler a distinct edge in the play.

Rarely is a complaint received by the hotel of an illegal gambling operation until a victim has lost all his money and realizes he was probably cheated. By their very nature, gamblers are a nomadic lot who will quickly disappear before anyone can react to the complaint. Although the Criminal Code of Canada is quite explicit on what constitutes illegal gambling, it is difficult for hotel security, acting on their own behalf, to obtain all necessary evidence to obtain a conviction. Close co-operation and liaison with public police will often cause a professional gambler to be located before he is able to utilize the hotel's facilities.

1.   VISITING DIGNITARIES

A problem of major concern to hotel security is the protection of visiting dignitaries. These people face serious threats, ranging from over-eager fans trying to touch rock stars to persons trying to kill political leaders.

While many of these persons may have their own personal bodyguards among their entourage, the primary responsibility for their safety while on hotel property is that of the hotel itself. Accordingly, the security department must be prepared to deal with this eventuality. If a procedure is put in place prior to the arrival of the dignitary, there should be little danger.

Depending on the size of the security department, it may be necessary to arrange for additional trained personnel from a contract security firm. These persons can be used in a crowd control capacity to prevent unauthorized personnel from gaining access to the hotel area where the dignitary is lodged.

Assuming the dignitary requires maximum protection, the following procedures should be adopted, subject to change for any particular situation.

Where possible, the individual should be placed on an upper floor and access to the floor prohibited to all but authorized personnel. This can be accomplished by shutting off the elevator to that floor, allowing it to work only with a key, and locking all doors to that floor.

A form of identification, either a picture card or symbol, should be issued to all personnel, both hotel staff and others requiring access to the floor. One security member should be stationed by the elevator to check all persons attempting to enter.

No other rooms should be rented on that floor. In extreme cases, rooms should not be given to guests on the floor above and below the dignitary.

The dignitary's vehicle should be kept in a secure location, under lock and key and guarded by a security member. This is a duty quite suitable for contact security.

All telephone calls should be screened before being forwarded to the individual. As well, any parcels addressed to the dignitary must be checked thoroughly before being forwarded to his floor.

Only well-trusted hotel personnel should be allowed access to the floor. The room, of course, must be cleaned and no doubt room service will be called upon. Therefore, individuals from these areas should be chosen in advance and only those so chosen should be allowed access. This would also apply to any kitchen staff involved in meal preparation for the dignitary. The kitchen must be spotless and should be checked in advanced by the appropriate health authorities in order to prevent any possible sickness.

Particular attention must be paid to the public areas of the hotel, such as the lobby, restaurants and bars. Unknown personnel frequenting these areas during the dignit-ary's stay should be questioned as to their purpose.

One of the most dangerous periods is when the dignit-ary is entering or leaving the hotel and, as such, particular attention must be given during these periods.

Whenever possible, entry/egress should be done through a seldom-used door, such as a side or rear entrance or parking lot. When this is not possible (political figures and movie stars in particular like to circulate amongst the crowds), extra precautions must be taken in all areas. A manned elevator should be ready and secured for use by the individual concerned. When possible, a second elevator should also be ready for use by support staff or if the first one should fail.

The dignitary should not spend any more time than is absolutely necessary in the public areas. With security providing necessary protection, the public areas should be quickly gone through. Details such as hotel registration can be looked after by a subordinate or by the dignitary himself after settling in his suite.

While these procedures may appear quite severe, they are suggested only as a means of providing full and proper protection to avoid any potentially embarrassing incident. They can be readily adapted to fit any given situation, re-gardless of the threat, real or perceived.

All hotel security personnel must be familiar with any evacuation plan that has been prepared. Whether the par-ticular need for the initiation of such a plan be for a fire, bomb threat or other disaster, all security personnel will become involved. Because of this involvement, they must be thoroughly briefed in advance on all procedures. They must be familiar with all exit routes to be utilized and the location of emergency equipment .

19

Fire

Fire in the worksite and at home is a devastating form of loss, one that the victim never fully recovers from. Losses can be both financial and personal. In the case of an industry, buildings, inventory and product may be lost and cannot be replaced for some time. This could result in the loss of potential and regular customers. The loss as shown can be more than physical. Recovering from a disaster, through fire, can involve insurance underwriters, public and private investigators, possibly the Department of Labour, and Fire Marshal's office. If a fire strikes, communications and records may be irretrievably lost. When fire strikes a large company the result could be rebuilding costs in the millions of dollars and even bankruptcy.

When fire strikes the homeowner, the effects can be far more reaching. Everyone in society knows the value of carrying insurance on homes and personal effects so that any financial loss can be overcome. The real damage comes from losing personal property, keepsakes, antiques, pictures, etc., that cannot be replaced and the memories that are attached to each item.

To deal with this problem the approach has to be the same as the mandate of the private security sector: *"preven-

tion rather than *reaction*". In industry, emphasis is placed on good housekeeping and identifying potential hazards. Regardless of the time and money spent on prevention, several factors can come into account where fires do in fact start accidentally. In most cases the fault is human error, and because of this certain steps have to be considered in establishing a fire-fighting strategy that will combat fire should it rise.

To prepare a good defence you must understand what fire is. Fire is a chemical reaction that occurs when material combines with oxygen so rapidly that a spark or flame is created. Fire is a combination of fuel, uniting with oxygen, producing heat. To combat a fire you must remove one of the three elements.

Usually it is quite dangerous to remove the fuel, such as wooden timbers once they begin to burn; however, flammable liquid may be removed in some cases by pumping the fuel to another tank, thus reducing the fuel that can burn. Once the remaining fuel has been spent the fire will go out. Should the fire be burning at the end of a pipe you may be fortunate to be in a position to shut off a valve to remove the supply of fuel.

To remove heat the most common method is water. Common fuel such as wood, when completely saturated with water, will not burn to any degree.

The third element that you will attempt to remove is that of oxygen. This can be done by smothering a fire with sand or material that will not allow oxygen to enter the fire. Gas, such as carbon dioxide (CO_2) and other similar gasses can be used because they are heavier than air. Various types of foam can also be used, depending on the circumstances.

Not all fires can be fought in the same manner. This is due to the fact that there are different types of fires and to combat each one successfully may take different methods. The wrong method can create even greater problems.

The first class of fire involves ordinary common materials such as wood, cloth, paper, etc., and can be combatted by the application of water. The water saturates the material, thus cooling down the fuel being consumed. The water would also be used to saturate the surrounding area to prevent the spread of the fire. This type of fire has been designated with the symbol Class A, which is green in colour. One purpose of defining the classes is to identify what type of fire fighting extinguishers are recommended. We will discuss this in further detail when we discuss fire extinguishers used to combat fires. For this type of fire you would use fire extinguishers with Class A on the label.

The next fire that may have to be combatted is designated a Class B fire, involving flammable liquids, greases and gasses such as car gas, paint, etc. Everyone knows that if car gas is on fire the danger of explosion is present due to the fumes. To successfully combat this type of fire you should use a type of dry chemical extinguisher, usually CO_2 or Halon. The type of fire extinguisher for this type of fire is designated Class B and is a vivid red in colour.

The third class of fire involves elements burning in Class A and B; however, they are related to electricity. An example of this would be gas-soaked rags lying around an electric fuse box and the fire is in progress. The Class C fire extinguisher prevents electricity from coming from the source to the firefighter. This may occur if the firefighter was using a water hose to combat an electrical fire as the water would conduct the electricity back, thus creating the danger of electrocution. The Class C fire extinguisher bears the label C and is blue.

There is a fourth class of fire, which is Class D. This

classification involves combustible burning metals, such as magnesium, titanium, zirconium, sodium and potassium; however, they are rarely encountered.

In most locations it is advisable to have a fire extinguisher which bears the identification of all three letters. This means that the extinguisher can be used to combat all fires. This is advisable for the home owner because it is most practical as he has all the elements in the home to create any type of fire. Running around to find the proper fire extinguishers would only allow the fire to spread even further.

There are several types of portable fire fighting extinguishers, such as the following:

1. Pressurized Water: these fire extinguishers are rated for Class A fires only.
2. Multi-Purpose Dry Chemical: (Pressure type and cartridge type) This variety can be used on all three classes of fires as it discharges a dry chemical powder called monoammonium phosphate. The cartridge type contains the chemical, but not under pressure. The extinguisher has a small cylinder containing nitrogen and when punctured, pressurizes the cylinder containing the dry chemical.
3. Standard Dry Chemical: (pressure type) Class B and C chemical fire extinguishers can be used on a Class A fire; however, they are not as effective as water. They work by removing the oxygen and do not allow electricity to conduct.
4. Carbon Dioxide: this is also effect on Class B and C fires. Carbon Dioxide forces oxygen from the fire by means of the gas leaving the wide nozzle at the extremely cold temperature of approximately -79C.
5. Halon: this type of extinguisher attacks the fire by cut-

ting off the oxygen supply. The extinguisher has a similar effect as CO_2 extinguishers but is lighter and does not require the same pressure in the cylinder. Halon is particularly effective in areas such as a clothing store or computer department, because it removes the oxygen without leaving any residue, thereby not damaging equipment or merchandise. One dangerous factor, however, is that all personnel must immediately leave the area because of the lack of oxygen. This extinguisher is effective on Class B and C fires; however, it can be used on Class A fires when the unit contains seven pounds or more of Halon.

Fighting a fire can be a dangerous exercise. The one aspect that the person fighting the fire has to confront is how to operate the fire extinguisher. Extinguishers are basically of the same design and contain a handle, trigger, nozzle and often a pressure gauge. Some extinguishers have directions on the body and all extinguishers have the class of fire that they are meant to combat on a label. After you find a fire burning and you see the fire extinguisher, make sure the extinguisher and the fire are compatible. Do not use the wrong extinguisher and create added danger to yourself.

If at all possible alert the fire department or fire volunteers for assistance. Some fires may be more complex than you realize and help on the way is better than none at all. When entering the area to combat the fire until help arrives, do not leave yourself without an exit and be careful that the fire does not circle around, cutting off possible avenues of retreat. Protect the lives of yourself and that of anyone else in the area. If the fire gets out of control then you must retreat immediately to safety and make sure that anyone else in the area leaves with you.

1. SUGGESTED PROCEDURES TO COMBAT A FIRE

For combatting a Class A fire, the first step is to ensure you have the proper extinguisher for that class of fire and that the fire extinguisher is in working order.

Approach the fire and get as close as you can, spraying the water around the area of the fire to prevent any spreading. When this is completed, spray the water back and forth across the source of the fire. Completely saturate the fire with water, and after the flames have gone out, spread the source of the fire if you can, adding water to make sure it is completely out.

In fighting a Class A and B fire you would use, in most cases, a dry chemical extinguisher. Approach the fire cautiously and when approximately three to four meters away from the source of the fire engage the extinguisher. Spray the powder back and forth across the top of the fire but remember do not be too high. Approximately fifteen to thirty centimeters would be appropriate. After you have cut the fire down, spray immediately into the fire near the front. Spray all around the fire to encompass the source completely. As the fire begins to come under control you may move in closer, but remember that the fumes may be toxic and extreme caution must be exercised. Completely check the fire source and make sure that the fire is properly out.

The next class is a Class C fire. Remember that this is associated with electrical equipment and every effort must be made to ensure that the power is shut off if possible prior to you entering the fire zone. Both CO_2 and Halon can be used; however, you must get as close to the fire as possible without endangering yourself. Because of the extremely short supply of fire fighting material in the extinguishers, you must act quickly. Aim the gas, sweeping through the fire from front to back.

The businessman and homeowner must not fall into a false sense of security and totally rely on a fire extinguisher as the cure-all to a fire situation in his home. Do not overestimate a fire and assistance should be called upon if there is time. Careful consideration should be given to locate the extinguishers in all parts of the home, but do not mount an extinguisher too close to a potential source of fire, such as a stove or furnace. Have the extinguisher a safe distance away, but within easy access. Attempt to mount the extinguisher high enough from the floor so that is it easily visible and in a conspicious place. Should someone be in a position to go for another extinguisher it is better placed in the open, in plain view, rather than in a closet or drawer. Consideration should be given to mounting the extinguisher near entrances as well, as you would normally have to walk into some room to combat a fire. Mount the extinguisher with the label forward to identify the type of extinguisher should you not have an all-purpose fire extinguisher.

Do not become so involved in fighting a fire that you lose sight of reality. Always assess the fire, have everyone leave the area for safety and if they are unable to move on their own, take them out. Call for assistance and when you have exhausted everything at your disposal, get out. When the professional fire department arrives on the scene, get out of their way, but remain close in case they require information.

The sure way to stop fire is to prevent it in the first place, through understanding, good housekeeping, and constantly maintaining that standard.

If you are in the position of designing a system for your worksite, bear in mind the type of equipment that will be in use and the appropriate extinguishing material needed.

Industry has established several preventive and responsible techniques to deal with the problem of losses through fire. In many cases industry has sprinkler systems, flooding techniques, fire hoses and hydrants to combat the potential threat of fire. Standards have been set on locations of fire extinguishers, fire hoses, etc., as well as the quantity of appropriate fire-fighting equipment required to combat fire as well as rcording inspections and maintenance.

Several books have been published with recommended standards. One of the most recognized is the *National Fire Codes, Recommended Practices and Manuals*, published annually by the National Fire Protection Association, 470 Atlantic Avenue, Boston, MA 02210. This material contains their established standards and should you be required to establish a fire-fighting strategy of this magnitude this material is highly recommended. Your local fire department should be contacted as well, as there may be certain specific standards required in your community.

TYPE	CLASS OF FIRE		
	A ORDINARY COMBUSTIBLES	B FLAMMABLE LIQUIDS	C ELECTRICAL EQUIPMENT
MULTI-PURPOSE DRY CHEMICAL Pressure Type / Cartridge Type Monoammonium Phosphate	EXCELLENT	EXCELLENT	EXCELLENT
STANDARD DRY CHEMICAL Sodium Bicarbonate / Pressure Type	Small surface fires only.	EXCELLENT	EXCELLENT
PYRENE "K" DRY CHEMICAL Potassium Bicarbonate / Cartridge Type	Small surface fires only.	EXCELLENT	EXCELLENT
HALON 1211 Bromochlorodifluoromethane	EXCELLENT	EXCELLENT	EXCELLENT
MONNEX Potassium Bicarbonate Urea	Small surface fires only.	EXCELLENT	EXCELLENT
CARBON DIOXIDE	Small surface fires only.	GOOD	EXCELLENT

20

Security For Disaster Emergency Situations

Disasters can take many forms and degrees, and because of their complexities, the overwhelming odds of successfully providing a working disaster plan are limited. No one knows when or if a disaster will ever actually take place during his career with a company.

However, in recent years, we have seen terrible disasters happen and the ways in which various companies have reacted to them. Industry itself, as well as governments, has insisted that companies prepare disaster plans that can be instituted as needed (as an example, refer to Chapter 22, entitled Transportation of Dangerous Goods). The particular strategy brought into play will centre on the security department as the catalyst, initiating communications, evacuation and initial implementation for the particular disaster.

The security department may not be involved in the drafting of the various plans to be followed, but the Director of Security should be delegated the authority for the commencement of the plan as needed, as well as having direct access to the appropriate senior management personnel for direction and consultation as to the correct measures to be implemented. By having this communication, the chance of overreaction by any one individual is greatly reduced.

You must remember that a disaster plan involves all levels of supervision and employees. All must be involved in the disaster plan for one to be effective and the procedures established must encompass prevention, reaction and implementation. The following disaster plan is simple and is only an outline in forming your own plan. The number and situations can be modified to suit your basic needs and the size of your company. One view that you must consider prior to establishing a plan is, "What do I want to achieve"? Do you want a plan that will really work or one that will be cosmetic and meet limited requirements. It may look good, but will it work? When you establish a realistic and workable plan, be prepared for a long and trying period with full co-operation needed from all levels of the company. If you adopt a realistic approach and attain the full co-operation of all employees, you will be in a position to prepare suitable disaster plans to cover any emergent situation.

1. DISASTER PLAN OUTLINE

A disaster can be defined as a sudden, unexpected destructive event which causes a large number of casualties relative to the resources available and the threat of extensive damage to property is present.

The major item which must be determined, with input from all Personnel, is establishing what constitutes a disaster for your particular Company, bearing in mind that, should your worksite be a chemical factory the causes would be vastly different than if it were, for example, a clothing factory.

The following areas must be considered in establishing any disaster plans. Each one may, depending on the individual circumstance, require their own particular plan, although there will be common denominators.

—Fire
—Chemical spillages
—Explosion
—Extreme weather conditions
—Severe worksite accident
—Accidental release of hazardous materials
—Air crash
—Train derailment
—Flood
—Bombs (The topic of bomb and bomb threats will be covered later in this chapter in more detail)

The categories listed below may offer assistance in your particular planning. These numbers are flexible and may well have to be adapted to suit your particular plan.

Minor disaster

25–100 casualties
10–50 persons requiring hospitalization

Medium disaster

100–1000 casualties
50–150 persons requiring hospitalization

Major disaster

Over 1000 casualties
Over 250 persons requiring hospitalization

The following items form the basis of any disaster plan and must be considered in its development. All of these points do not necessarily apply to all sites and situations, however, all applicable points should be established before a final plan is adopted. A broad approach should be taken to answer all possible points, as they may be found to be a necessity at a later date. In answering each question, do not use a short form, such as yes or no. This will be found to be of little value when compiling your final plan and implementation.

DISASTER PLAN

1.   Identify the goals of the plan.

_____

_____

2.   Consider the various settings.

_____

_____

3.   Consider the products used, by-products, products manufactured, products stored and internal product distribution.

_____

_____

4.   Number and location of on-site personnel.

_____

_____

5.   Location and number of on-site water lines, gas lines, hydro lines, etc.

_____

_____

6.   Location and number of on-site emergency power supplies, telephones and radio communications.

_____

_____

7.   Location of on-site emergency and equipment facilities, such as first aid posts.

_____

_____

8.   Emergency facilities available in the community and your proximity to these.

_____

_____

9.   Response time needed for community services to arrive at your site.

_____

_____

10.   The potential necessity of evacuating all employees and the orderly shutdown of all operating equipment.

_____

_____

11.   The potential necessity of evacuating residents in proximity to the site.

_____

_____

12.   Defining a reception area for casualties.

_____

_____

13.　　　　The geography of the company.

_____

_____

14.　　　　Defining a central reporting area for all community services as they arrive on-site.

_____

_____

15.　　　　Supplying and issuing identification passes to all required personnel.

_____

_____

16.　　　　The designation of an over-all coordinator.

_____

_____

17.　　　　The designation of a triage coordinator to supervise all casualties. Triage is defined as the treatment and categorizing of casualties and the process of sorting sick and wounded on the basis of urgency and types of conditions presented so that they may be properly routed to medical institutions appropriately situated and equipped (Blakiston Pocket Dictionary, 3rd ed.).

_____

_____

18.　　　　Establishment of an effective internal and external communications network, including the possibility of establishing a common frequency with local agencies.

_____

_____

19.   Establishing a list of key internal and external personnel and agencies, available for immediate use as needed.

_____

_____

20.   Establishing an effective fan-out system to notify all required personnel as quickly as possible.

_____

_____

21.   Establishing a means of effective crowd control, media liaison, family notification and control measures.

_____

_____

22.   The establishment of a permanent Central Control Centre, which can be brought into operation immediately. A security post, normally manned on a 24-hour basis, could be designated for this function.

_____

_____

23.   Identifying the appropriate senior personnel to declare a disaster.

_____

_____

24.   Establishing a job description for every disaster and the chain of command.

_____

_____

25.   Identification of high risk areas.

        _____

        _____

26.   Training and maintaining the appropriate list of
        a large number of internal personnel properly
        trained in first aid, C.P.R., disaster procedures
        and the necessity of accurate documentation.

        _____

        _____

27.   Development of casualty (trauma) sheets and
        tags and instructing personnel in their use.

        _____

        _____

28.   Establishing a plan for food and rest areas for
        personnel.

        _____

        _____

29.   Development of a contingency plan for quiet
        periods, such as weekends.

        _____

        _____

30.   Appointing and training personnel in rescue
        and search techniques.

        _____

        _____

31.   Identifying valuable and important documents
        and their location.

        _____

        _____

32.   Identifying emergency repair crews.

_____

_____

33.   Identifying the legal aspects (insurance, poten-
           tial law suits, etc.)

_____

_____

34.   Establishing a notification list of neighbouring
           industries.

_____

_____

35.   Identifying the appropriate senior personnel to
           re-assess the disaster.

_____

_____

36.   Identification and marking of safe, efficient
           evacuation routes.

_____

_____

37.   Development of mock disaster to ascertain the
           feasibility of your plan.

_____

_____

38.   Follow-up discussion and further planning in-
           volving all individuals who participted in the
           mock disaster.

_____

_____

Once the disaster plan has been designed, all internal

and external personnel and agencies affected should be given a copy, with their particular duties highlighted in some fashion, such as placing the appropriate page on top of the report.

In every type of disaster, there are a number of persons and organizations who must be notified immediately. Their response will depend on which category the disaster falls into, however, even if the disaster is considered minor, they must be made aware of the happening and requested, as a minimum, to be on a stand-by basis. While the following list may be amended to suit your particular needs, all these groups should receive consideration. These are not listed in any order of priority.

—Fire Department
—Police
—Ambulance service
—Hospital(s)
—Search and Rescue service
—Emergency Measures Organization
—Senior management and local government officials
—Social services
—National defence
—News media
—Medical personnel

Immediate factors which must be ascertained and re-layed to the above personnel should include the following:

—Radius of the area involved
—Location of the disaster
—Ease of access to the site
—Type of disaster (fire, air crash, etc.)

Of immediate concern in any disaster, is the safe and orderly evacuation of all employees in the affected area. The safety of the individual is of the utmost concern and must take priority over any other function. Once the area has been evacuated, a physical count should be taken in order to establish if any employees are missing. If all employees cannot be accounted for, an immediate search, if physically possible, should be conducted. Supervisors must be trained in search methodology; however, no search should be conducted when there is a physical danger to the searchers themselves.

When all personnel have been accounted for, immediate action should be taken to shut down any equipment which would further contribute to the disaster, such as natural gas supplies to an area where there is a fire. Certain employees should be delegated, prior to any disaster, to handle this type of function. They should be under strict supervision and instructed not to take any action until directed to do so. In many instances, it is possible to shut off supplies from an external source where there would be no danger to the individual. Under no circumtance should a person be instructed to go to a hazardous area to perform a duty that would endanger his well-being.

2. CLASSIFICATION METHOD OF CASUALTIES

A triage, or casualty, tag is a method of identifying and classifying injured personnel according to the degree of injury, including death.

The tag denotes the degree of urgency required to treat the injury effectively. The best system to use is one which is colour-coded, with the various colours denoting the extent of the injury. Vivid colours are more readily identifiable than mere handwriting on a form. The tag should contain sections listing such things as name, age, allergies, severity of injury and treatment received so far, and time of treatment or death. The tag should contain a tear-off section to enable the coordinator to keep one for his records and eventual follow-up as required.

The tag should be placed on the same part of the body for each person if at all possible and should only be issued by the triage coordinator or his designate. By utilizing this system, all individuals requiring immediate treatment should receive it quicker than those who are suffering from minor injuries only, hopefully saving lives.

3. BOMB THREATS

Unfortunately, bomb threats are becoming more common and posing more of a threat to the security of businesses, especially those dealing in areas seen by the general public as being defence related. All personnel involved in answering telephone calls on behalf of the company should be aware of the very real threat of a bomb attack and instructed closely on how to react. Each situation will differ somewhat; however, the following points will apply to virtually all telephone calls received. The recipient of a bomb threat must treat each such call received as being genuine. Indifference could result in major loss of life and property.

As a bomb threat is a form of a disaster and may actually become one, it must be considered in the same light as any other disaster and the preceding check list should be completed accordingly. One very important element which must be decided and made known to all recipients of telephone calls is the identity of the individual who will receive the information of the threat.

He must be given the authority to respond immediately and take any action which he feels is appropriate. This may well involve the total evacuation and shut-down of the entire company. He would also bear the responsibility for the eventual callback of all employees when he feels the area is no longer in danger. The information received over the telephone will assist him greatly in arriving at the appropriate decision.

Should the caller indicate a familiarity with the company or describe a particular area in any detail, it is quite likely the bomb will be in that location. At the very least, this will give an area for immediate focus for any potential search.

If the caller indicates a particular time span before the bomb will be activated, it may be feasible to initiate an immediate search to locate the bomb. It must always be borne in mind that the safety of the individual must come first, and no action should be taken that would jeopardize any person.

A location must be designated as the Headquarters and report-in centre for any search. The security gatehouse is quite feasibly the ideal location, as it is not located within any other premise and as such is unlikely to be in immediate danger.

Search teams for all areas of the site should be formed in advance and fully briefed on their duties. The composition of the team is quite important. Where possible the team should consist of employees familiar with the area they are to search. This will cut down on wasted time trying to acquaint the individuals with the particular part of the site. Teams should be relatively small in number and under the direction of a team leader, who in turn would be in direct contact with an over-all Supervisor. As each team member completes his search, the team leader would advise the supervisor of the results. Once all team members have reported, they should evacuate the area until they receive a signal to return.

Should the decision be made to evacuate the entire area, the teams would assist in this duty as well. They must be properly trained in all aspects of safety and instructed not to show any signs of panic. If people begin to panic, injuries may well result. If an evacuation is done in an orderly manner, it can be completed quicker and much more safely. The security staff can assist in both the search and evacuation, however they are limited in number, and, as such, the main responsibility of evacuation must rest with the teams.

Teams should be aware of the location to which evacuees are to be taken, an area well removed from the affected site, but not too distant that they cannot reach it quickly. If the personnel are to be recalled once the area has been declared safe, it would be virtually impossible to bring them back if they are a long distance away. One aspect that should be remembered is the weather. If it is winter time, for example, obviously an open parking lot is not an acceptable area as most of the employees would not have had the opportunity to gather their coats.

Local agencies such as the public police and fire departments and the Emergency Measures Organization should be advised of the threat immediately. They are often in the position of being able to provide needed equipment such as dogs and metal detectors, as well as additional manpower.

A check list, containing the following points, should be given to all telephone operators. The usage of such a form will enable them to accurately receive all possible information as well as enabling the Security Director to review the information received quickly, as it will always be in the same order.

4. INSTRUCTIONS TO RECIPIENTS OF BOMB THREATS

WHEN A BOMB THREAT IS RECEIVED:

—Listen carefully
—Be calm and courteous
—Do not interrupt the caller
—Obtain as much information as possible
—Initiate trace action (where possible)
—Notify the appropriate in-house authority
   by pre-arranged signal while the
   caller is on the line.

THE FOLLOWING QUESTIONS MUST BE ANSWERED AS COMPLETELY AS POSSIBLE:

1.   What time will the bomb explode?
   _____
   _____

2.   Where is it located?
   _____
   _____

3.   Why did you place the bomb?
   _____
   _____

4.   What does the bomb look like?
   _____
   _____

5.   Where are you calling from?
   _____
   _____

6.   What is your name?

         _____

         _____

7.   Exact wording of threat (word by word if possible, including offensive language).

         _____

         _____

8.   Sex and estimated age.

         _____

         _____

9.   Accent or ethnic background.

         _____

         _____

10.   Voice (soft, loud, fast, slow).

         _____

         _____

11.   Diction and manner of speech.

         _____

         _____

12.   Background noises (e.g., baby crying, other voices).

         _____

         _____

13.   Was the voice familiar?

         _____

         _____

14.   Was the caller familiar with the area of the company?

         _____

         _____

15.　　　　Date, time and duration of call.

16.　　　　Recipient's name, department and telephone number.

Because of their nature, both disasters and bomb threats are unpredictable and difficult to plan for. The full co-operation of both management and all employees must be received in order to avoid the ever-present risk of death, injury and property damage. All levels of employees and management should be involved in the initial planning stages and made aware of their particular responsibility in the event of a misfortune. Periodic reminders should be sent to all personnel and, if possible, practice sessions should be held.

21

Surveillance

Surveillance can be best described as the systematic art of following or watching an individual or specific location. It is an integral part of security work, especially for contract security, who may be called upon to perform it in cases as diverse as fraudulent insurance claims or divorce settlements.

For instance, observing a subject playing a mean game of tennis every week when he has submitted an insurance claim for severe back injuries may well negate any claim he might have.

There are three distinct types of surveillance:

Fixed—where surveillance is done from one location, such as a room directly across from a suspect location,

Overt—where a prominent individual is watched closely to protect him from harm or embarrassment,

Covert—the most difficult type of surveillance, where an individual is watched and followed without him being aware of the act.

Fixed surveillance requires careful planning before it can be properly executed. The proper location must be found, which will allow for a clear view of the location to be viewed, as well as allowing easy access at all hours. Because the continual viewing of a fixed spot can be extremely demanding, relief operatives must be supplied after relatively short shifts. If it is impossible to enter premises during odd hours, problems will be compounded.

The location must be supplied with all needed equipment, such as cameras, binoculars and communication equipment—consisting of radios to contact other surveillance team members and a telephone to contact a central location if needed. There must be the amenities of life, such as food, water and washroom facilities. An item such as a radio or television should also be provided, to cover any noise from the portable radio through what may be paper-thin walls.

Quite often a suitable location cannot be located. When this is the case, the use of a van may be considered. A discreet vehicle, parked on a street for long periods of time, will not draw undue attention. If equipped with one-way glass so no one can see in, the operative can perform his duties with little chance of detection. The vehicle should be driven to the area by another team member, who will park it and walk away. The same member can return later and drive it away with little chance of raising suspicion.

Overt surveillance is not a true type of surveillance, but is often described as such. This duty can be performed by both uniformed and plainclothes personnel. The primary function is to protect the individual or location being watched from any risk or danger. For instance, the president of a major company which has recently announced an unpopular decision may be the target of egg-throwing demonstrators. By being on the watch for this, possibly an alternate route or accelerated road caravan, will eliminate the risk of embarrassment.

Covert surveillance, as mentioned, is by far the most difficult to carry out and requires careful preparation and planning. Individuals chosen for surveillance duties should, wherever possible, be the type of person who will blend into the background with little chance of being noticed. For example, someone looking like a member of a motorcycle gang would not fit into a classy restaurant, whereas a person closely resembling an accountant would look out of place in a hangout for teenagers.

Dress for members of a surveillance team is also important, for the same reason. Clothing should be chosen with care, bearing in mind where a subject is likely to go during the period he is being watched. Clothing should be nondescript and neutral. Flashy colours and dress styles should be avoided, as they will call attention to the individual. For example, if the subject sees someone wearing a pink shirt and purple pants and sees the same outfit later in the day, he is going to suspect something is wrong. Probably one of the best outfits for men is a pair of slacks in a neutral shade, a plain coloured shirt and soft-soled shoes. With the addition of a jacket and tie the person is set to go almost anywhere. The jacket and tie can be stored in the surveillance vehicle when not needed.

Women can be particularly useful in a surveillance operation because of their ability to so easily change their appearance. By simply putting their hair up or down and adding makeup, they can drastically change how they look. The situation is similar with clothing. A pair of slacks and blouse is quite ideal. By pulling on a skirt, removing the slacks, and possibly adding a blazer or scarf, the female operative can go into almost any given location.

Surveillance teams should always consist of at least two persons, with a male/female team being preferred. If the subject should enter a restaurant or theatre, a couple can easily blend in, whereas two males or two females will often draw attention to themselves. Similarly, if parked on a quiet street at night, people will tend to ignore a couple, where they will quickly take note of two members of the same sex.

Individuals chosen for surveillance duties should be capable of acting independently, as it is often difficult to contact another team member. They must also exhibit a large amount of patience, as surveillance can be long and often monotonous. A team may not move from a location for long periods of time, but must still stay alert for that sudden move.

Every member of the team should be provided with communications equipment. Portable radios can be normally hidden under jackets, in rolled-up newspapers or in women's purses. However, as radios cannot always be carried (such as in hot weather) or will not work because of interference from the surroundings, a simple system of hand signals should be devised and rehearsed by the whole team.

These must be of a type which would not be obvious to anyone else and would look like a normal action to the casual passerby. Signals should cover such potential actions as a left or right turn, where is the subject, I think he's seen me and subject has stopped directly ahead.

Every surveillance member should be in possession of money in small denominations as well as change. Should the subject enter a restaurant, the team member must be in a position to pay his bill quickly if the subject suddenly leaves. If the member has to wait for change, the subject may be long gone and never be seen again. Change is also needed for the quick telephone call if other forms of communication are not working.

Surveillance vehicles must also be chosen with great care. Something that resembles a police car, for instance (small hubcaps, no chrome), will be quickly spotted. Similarly, a flashy sports car will have the same effect. Normally the most practical type of vehicle is the family sedan. There are many of these on the road and, if a neutral colour, they will not be easily spotted. Vehicles should be changed as frequently as the operation demands.

Sometimes, though, particular vehicles are best utilized. If the operation is in an exclusive area of the city, expensive vehicles would probably be the least conspicuous, similarly if the operation is in a rural area trucks or vans may best suit the purpose.

Vehicles should be as normal looking as possible. Radios should be hidden and care should be taken with both the interior and exterior appearance. If it has been raining and the roads are muddy, a clean, freshly-washed vehicle will draw attention. Similarly, an unwashed vehicle when the weather has been sunny for a long period will also be quite noticeable.

The interior of the vehicle should be kept as clean as possible at all times. Not only are team members required to live in the vehicle for long periods (who wants to live in garbage?), but anyone looking in the vehicle would wonder why the car is so dirty.

Items such as coffee cups and hamburger containers should never be placed on the dash. Take a look the next time you're on the street and see how many vehicles have such articles placed there. Chances are the only ones you will observe are taxis, whose members also spend a great deal of time in their cars. Also, items hanging from the rear-view mirror or bumper stickers should not be on the surveillance vehicle. They will draw attention to you.

Vehicles should be fully gassed and in good repair before any surveillance operation is undertaken. A noisy muffler will draw attention to you in a quiet area or late at night. If the vehicle runs out of gas, the subject will be long gone before you can obtain additional fuel. A good rule-of-thumb to follow is never let the gas tank get below half full. It is rare when there isn't a break in surveillance that will allow a vehicle to be repaired or gassed up.

Surveillance is best performed by a minimum of three separate teams, each team consisting of at least two members, allowing teams to rotate when following a subject, thus reducing the chance of detection.

All members of each team must be fully briefed as to the operation and their particular role. The team must be familiar with the subject and all habits and peculiarities that can be determined in advance. They should be shown photographs of the subject and supplied with a detailed description, including such items as height, weight, hair colour, normal style of dress, usual associates and hangouts, etc.

Diagram 1 shows a basic pattern for conducting surveillance while on foot. Two surveillants follow the subject on the opposite side of the street, one acting as a back-up should the member having control (having the best view) have to leave the scene. The other surveillant follows the individual at a discreet distance and will be able to observe any small operation, such as the dropping of a piece of paper by the subject.

Should the subject turn at the next intersection, the team members can simply change positions, making it more difficult for the subject to notice them. In the diagram, for instance, should the subject turn east, the support man would cross the street and become the control, the control would also cross and become the back-up man, and the back-up would now become the support man. This pattern could be alternated as often as required, with the surveillance team themselves changing at intersections by crossing the street. Diagram 2 illustrates quite clearly how this can be accomplished.

The control man always has precedence in decisions. He has absolute priority on any radio time and the other two operatives will watch him quite closely for any hand signals.

The distance the control man is away from the subject will be determined largely by the activity in the area. If the streets are crowded, the distance would not be very great for either the controller or the support man. In a residential area, no more than one surveillant should be in the same block as the subject, and he should always be on the other side of the street.

Should the subject enter a building, all exists should be watched closely. He may simply be using the premises for a shortcut. If the building is a house or small business, it may be impossible for the surveillance team to enter. In this instance, obtaining the address and description of anyone inside will aid in further investigation at a later date.

If the building is a department store or large office building, the subject can safely be followed inside. If the subject gets on an elevator, note what floor he has gone to and follow him accordingly. If it is possible to enter the elevator with him, do not get off at the same floor. There may be only one office there and you will be caught without a decent cover story for your action. Take the elevator to the next floor and descend via the stairs.

Vehicle surveillance presents its own unique problems. Team members should be familiar with the particular terrain, especially one-way streets, traffic lights, stop signs and any road construction.

All vehicles should be equipped with two-way radios and identical maps. The maps are particularly useful should the vehicle, because of traffic lights or construction, fall behind the operation. If radio communications are weak, the team may not be able to clearly hear where the subject currently is. However, if grid markings, such as K5, are repeated, the team is likely to hear this. When they get near the area, they can call and be given more specific directions.

Diagram 4 shows vehicle surveillance being done in a pattern commonly referred to as paralleling. In this method, the control car follows the subject whereas the other vehicles parallel on a side street. Should the subject turn a corner, the vehicles can easily change position, as indicated in the diagram. If you have a fourth vehicle involved in the surveillance, this vehicle would precede the subject. Rarely would a subject suspect he is being watched from the front.

It is extremely important that the control vehicle (the one behind the subject) have full control of all radio broadcasts. If he is not able to give direction, the subject is liable to make any number of turns before the other vehicles can be notified. Parallel vehicles should restrict their conversation to specific statements only, such as calling if they are stopped by a traffic light.

The control vehicle should keep conversations as short as possible, while giving full information to the other vehicles. Remember, the other vehicles cannot see the subject and do not know what is happening. The controller should radio at every intersection the subject goes through and every stop he makes, thereby enabling the other teams to correct their speed and location accordingly. If street signs are not readily visible, a landmark, such as a particular restaurant, may suffice.

The control car should not signify the subject has passed through an intersection until he has actually done so. The subject may suddenly turn, leave the paralleling vehicles out of position and unable to take the correct action.

The actual distance the control vehicle will follow the subject is dictated by local conditions. If the traffic is heavy, the distance would be quite short, possibly with only one neutral vehicle in between, whereas in a quiet neighbourhood the distance may well be one or two blocks behind.

All teams must be immediately notified of any change to the subject, such as another person entering/exiting the vehicle or the donning of a hat and sunglasses. The paralleling vehicles, who may not have seen the subject for some time, may not recognize him later.

The most important item to remember for surveillance is discretion. Always attempt to blend into the background fully and not do anything which will attract attention to the team or its members.

It is no disgrace to be observed by the subject. This can happen in the most controlled cases. What does create a large problem is when the team member refuses to acknowledge he has been 'blown'. His continued association with the rest of the team may well jeopardize the whole operation, but if he leaves the scene quietly, the subject may feel he is quite safe and the operation can continue to a successful conclusion.

1. SURVEILLANCE REPORTS AND NOTEMAKING

Notes should be made by all surveillance team members as soon after the particular happening as is feasible. Times and actual action must be carefully noted. Personal opinions of team members, while of invaluable importance, must be noted as being exactly that—opinions.

Only one report should be submitted for each individual shift. If each team member submitted his own report, it would be very difficult for anyone to decipher. In the sample report shown, for example, team member 2 would only be submitting a report for an action at 9:23 a.m. and 9:32 p.m. The person reading the report would have no idea of what happened during the interm.

The sample report indicates when something happened and who observed the happening. Item 9:20 a.m., for instance, shows that team members 3 and 4 observed the subject leave his residence and drive to Joe's Diner. Should there be any reason to clarify this information, the person requesting the clarification would only have to contact members 3 and 4, rather than the whole team. The team member's names may be shown in place of a number, but if the report is lengthy, it may save a lot of time to show the number rather than the name.

The use of the word "COMMENT" clearly indicates what follows is an opinion, rather than fact. If further information was needed as to exactly how the subject was acting at 9:32 p.m., team members 1 and 2 would be able to elaborate.

The use of U.M. is merely a short form for Unidentified Male and as this term as well as U.F. (Unidentified Female) are used often, the abbreviation is recommended.

In the same report, no mention is made of times when nothing has happened. Reference the time between 2:45

p.m. and 9:32 p.m. As nothing is mentioned, the assumption is automatically made that nothing happened and the team members were on location waiting. If all time was mentioned individually, the report would be quite lengthy and very difficult to comprehend.

As numbers were used for team members rather than their names, the names must be mentioned somewhere in the report. This may be done at either the beginning or the end.

The sample report does not indicate what action was taken as a result of the money and package, probably containing drugs, changing hands. This is quite true in many surveillance operations. It can be assumed in this case that follow-up action is to be taken. Perhaps the operative in charge of the case wishes to learn more of the subject's habits, or who he may be selling to. This operation may well continue for a longer period in order to obtain more evidence, or perhaps the subject is an informer and the operative only wished to offer him full protection in the event of any mishap. For operational reasons, quite often the surveillance team is not given more detail than is absolutely necessary. Their job is simply to observe and note any happenings, which they have done in their report. Further action would be dictated by the operative in charge of the case.

SURVEILLANCE CHECK LIST

As with any investigational activity, a check list is always handy, however, with surveillance it becomes a necessity. Surveillance teams cannot leave their duty to return to the office to obtain any equipment that may have been forgotten and without which their task is that much more difficult.

The following check lists can be adapted to fit almost any need.

Fixed Surveillance

1. Has an observation post been located? What is the address?
2. What are the limitations on accessibility?
3. Who has the key?
4. Who will be working in the post and do they know how to gain access?
5. Do the team members have a suitable 'cover' story?
6. What is it and what is required to offer authentication?
7. Have the team members been briefed on the operation?
8. Have the team members been supplied with a list of members performing mobile surveillance?
9. Is there a telephone in the observation post? What is the number?
10. Has the team been issued with portable radios?
11. Is there food and water available?
12. Are there washroom facilities?
13. Has the team been supplied with a photograph and description of the subject?
14. Has the team been issued with technical equipment (cameras, film, binoculars, etc.)?
15. Does the team have a map identical to the mobile team members?
16. What is the general locale of the observation post (residential, business, etc.)?

17. What style of dress should be worn by the team members (business suits, casual, etc.)?
18. Has the team been supplied with adequate materials for recording data (pens, pencils, paper, tape recorders, etc.)?
19. Have relief teams been briefed on arrival time and method of entry?
20. Are there any particular problems which may be encountered?

Mobile Surveillance

1. What type of vehicles are required (new, old, cars, trucks, colors, etc.)?
2. Have they been obtained and where can the team members get them from?
3. Are all vehicles equipped with radios?
4. Have all vehicles been checked for mechanical condition, general appearance and gas?
5. Has each vehicle been supplied with all necessary technical equipment (cameras, binoculars, tape recorders, etc.)?
6. Have all vehicles been supplied with identical maps?
7. Have all team members been supplied with a photograph and/or description of the subject?
8. Do all team members know the type of area they will be working in?
9. Have they been advised of any particular problems with this particular area (parking restrictions, traffic flow, etc.)?
10. What style of clothing will be required by team members and have they been instructed to dress accordingly?

11. Are all team members familiar with the hand signals to be used?
12. Are all team members aware of their work schedule and where they are to report?
13. Are all team members aware of a central telephone number to be used for emergencies?
14. Have all foot surveillance members been supplied with radios? What is their range?
15. Have all foot surveillance members been supplied with expense money, including small change?
16. Do all team members know the type of vehicle driven by the subject, including licence number?
17. What is the anticipated traffic flow in the area (light, medium, heavy)?
18. Are all team members aware of the observation post, its location and how to make contact?
19. Have all team members been supplied with a 'cover' story? What are they?
20. Are all team members aware of when their reports are required? When are they required?
21. Are all team members aware of who to contact in an emergency? Who do they contact?
22. Are all team members aware of who is in charge and who will assume responsibility for any decisions?
23. Is there a possibility of counter-surveillance and are team members aware of this?
24. Have all team members been fully briefed on the case?
25. What provision has been made to provide team members with any new information that may be obtained?

SURVEILLANCE REPORT

8:30 a.m. (team)	Surveillance commenced at the residence of subject, 101-A St. Subject's vehicle, a

1985 Ford sedan, blue colour, Ontario licence ABC 123, observed parked in the driveway. No sign of activity.

9:20 a.m.
(3, 4)

Subject leaves his residence and enters his vehicle. He drives directly to Joe's Diner, 721-D St., and enters.

COMMENT: Subject is described as approx. 180 cm., 77 kg., brown hair, blue eyes, 24–25 yrs., wearing a black leather jacket, blue jeans, red shirt and green baseball hat.

9:23 a.m.
(2)

Subject is observed sitting with U.M. #1 in a back booth. They appear to be in casual conversation. Subject is drinking coffee.

COMMENT: U.M. #1 is described as 40–45 yrs., 170 cm., 86 kg., dark hair, dirty white T-shirt, faded blue jeans and jean jacket. He has a dirty appearance. Subject and U.M. # appear to be well acquainted.

10:17 a.m.
(5, 6)

Subject leaves the restaurant with U.M. #1 and enters his vehicle. U.M. #1 enters a 1978 Chevy half-ton truck, red colour, Man. licence DE456. Both depart in different directions.

10:19 a.m.
(team)

Subject departs the parking lot at Joe's Diner and proceeds directly to Bill's Billiards, 123-B St., and enters, parking his car directly in front.

10:21 a.m.   Subject is noted in an animated conver-
(1, 4)   sation with U.M. #2. After what appears
             to be an argument, subject is observed to
             pass U.M. #2 a large quantity of money.

             COMMENT: U.M. #2 is described as
             30–32 yrs., 175 cm., 68 kg., dark hair
             and mustache, grey suit, white shirt, red
             tie. Very neat appearance.

2:45 p.m.   Subject departs Bill's Billiards, enters
(team)   his vehicle, drives directly to his residence
             and enters at 2:51 P.M.

9:32 p.m.   Subject leaves his residence, wearing the
(1, 2)   identical clothing shown at 9:20 A.M. He
             walks north on A st. to the intersection of
             R Ave., turns west and enters a back alley
             between B and C St.

             COMMENT: Subject is acting in a furtive
             manner and appears to be looking for any
             surveillance.

9:39 p.m.   Subject exits the alley carrying a package
(4, 6)   wrapped in brown paper, approx. 30 cm.
             square by 5 cm. deep, walks directly to
             his residence and enters.

9:43 p.m.   U.M. #2, described at 10:21 A.M. leaves
(3)   the back alley after subject, enters a 1986
             grey Cadillac sedan, Ontario licence JKL
             789 and departs the area.

COMMENT: JKL 789 is registered to U.R. Crazy, a known drug dealer. The description of U.M. #2 is identical to that of Crazy.

11:00 p.m.   All lights go out in subject's residence.
(5, 6)

11:30 p.m.   Surveillance discontinued.

Team members:

        #1—J. Doe
        #2—W. Brown
        #3—B. Smith
        #4—R. Brown
        #5—K. Jones
        #6—T. Lee

Diagram 1

SUSPECT PROCEEDING STRAIGHT

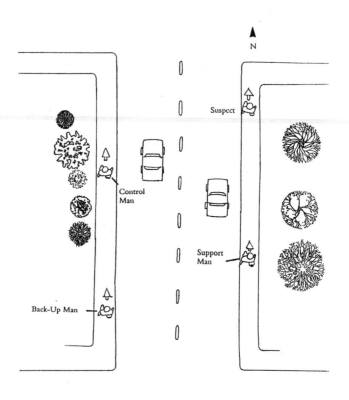

Diagram 2

SUSPECT CROSSES STREET

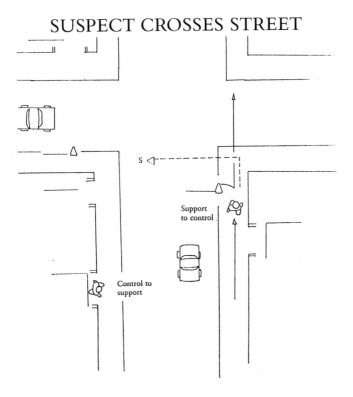

Diagram 3

SUSPECT STOPS AND U-TURNS

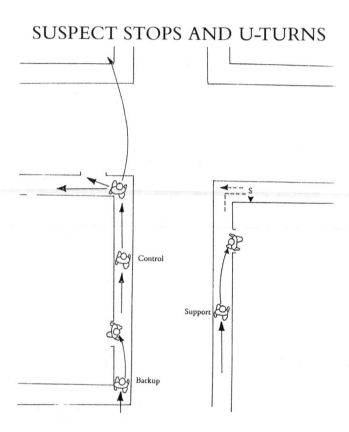

Diagram 4

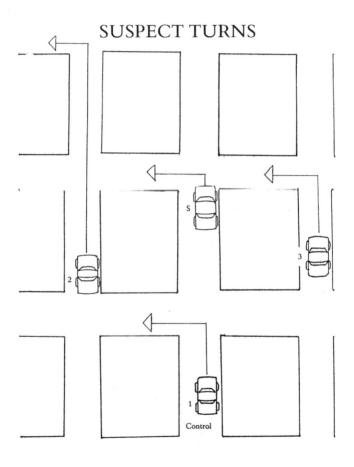

SUSPECT TURNS

22

Drug Awareness

In the field of private security, it is rare that an investigator would be involved in drug enforcement; however, a good working knowledge will provide some form of awareness to the problems that may be encountered in every day dealings with employees and the public. This awareness may provide the tools necessary to spot employees or the public who are experiencing trouble with drugs. Actions may prevent future injury to yourself, fellow workers and the drug abuser himself. Industry has many programs in place to deal with the employee who is having trouble with drug abuse and the employee is encouraged, without penalty, to seek assistance.

The first drug, and the most common drug that society is familiar with, is alcohol.

1. ALCOHOL

(a) What is Known About Alcohol?

Ethyl alcohol or ethanol is the alcohol people drink. This drug can be manufactured, or it can be produced naturally by fermentation of fruits, vegetables, or grains.

In Canada, beer contains five per cent alcohol and most table wine ten to fourteen per cent. Fortified wines such as sherry, port, and vermouth contain sixteen to twenty per cent alcohol. Distilled spirits such as whisky, rum, gin, etc., contain 40 per cent alcohol. A twelve-ounce bottle of beer contains the same amount of alcohol as a drink containing one and one-half ounces of spirits. About the same amount of alcohol is found in a five-ounce glass of table wine or a three-ounce glass of fortified wine.

(b) Short Term Effects

Alcohol decreases the activity of parts of the brain—in proportion to the amount of alcohol in the blood stream. This, in turn, depends in general on the amount consumed, rate of drinking, amount and kind of food in the stomach, and the drinker's body weight. After one or two drinks most people talk and act more freely than usual. Generally, there is a feeling of cheerfulness and well-being. However, the emotions expressed depend on how the person feels at the time. When an average-sized person has in his body an amont of alcohol equivalent to three or four drinks, he usually becomes dizzy and poorly co-ordinated, and his behavior changes. With six to eight drinks inside him there is staggering, double vision, and loss of balance. Extremely large doses can kill by knocking out the brain's control over breathing. This rarely happens, since a person would usually become unconscious before a fatal dose can be taken.

(c) The Hazards of Alcohol

When affected even slightly by alcohol, most people

say or do things they might ordinarily think unwise. Combining alcohol with tranquillizers, antihistamines, or barbiturates (or other sleeping pills) can be dangerous. Alcohol can intensify the effects of these drugs and vice versa. Many accidental deaths have been attributed to barbiturates and alcohol combined. Some alcohol-dependent people who are subject to regular heavy drinking have their lives and careers severely disturbed by uncontrolled drinking. Warning signs of such a problem include loss of interest in work, family or hobbies, frequent hangovers, blackouts (periods the drinker cannot remember), and alcohol-related accidents.

(d) Who Uses Alcohol? Why?

In general, people drink to celebrate, to enjoy a "high" feeling, or to overcome a "low" feeling. They also drink to relax and promote sleep, to relieve social or physical discomforts, to quench thirst, to increase appetite, to make a get-together more enjoyable, or as a part of social or religious ritual. Other reasons include curiosity, boredom, and "going along" with a group in which alcohol is frequently used.

The next area of abuse is the use of solvents.

2. SOLVENTS

(a) What is Known About Solvents?

Solvents commonly encountered as drugs of abuse include polystyrene cements (especially "airplane glue"), nail-polish remover, lighter fluid, cleaning fluids, anesthetics, and gasoline.

(b) What Are the Active Ingredients?

The intoxicants in these substances include such volatile hydrocarbons as hexane, cyclohexane, benzene, and naphtha (all of petroleum origin), as well as acetone, ethylacetate, carbon tetrachloride, and toluene. The principal intoxicant in model airplane cement is toluene (some substances also contain alcohol). The volatile hydrocarbons are lipid soluble—that is, they readily form solutions with fats but not water.

(c) What Are the Methods of Use?

Users inhale fumes in as concentrated a form as possible, frequently by holding a bag or cloth containing a solvent over the face. Solvents are occasionally mixed with carbonated beverages for drinking.

(d) What Are the Effects of Solvent Abuse?

The effects can range from mild intoxication to exhilaration and disorientation. Within a few minutes, most sniffers experience confusion, slurred speech, dizziness, and euphoria (a sense of well-being). There will also be distortions of perception, visual and auditory hallucinations, and delusional ideas. As the concentration of an intoxicant in the brain cell increases, the user becomes drowsy and finally unconscious. Excessive nasal secretions, watering eyes, and poor muscular control are also symptoms of solvent abuse. Inhaling of solvents has been known to induce aggressive behaviour—for example, fighting and setting fires—and dangerous actions, such as trying to fly from a roof. Explosions causing death have resulted from smoking and inhaling gasoline fumes at the same time.

(e) How Long Does the Effect of Solvent Abuse Last?

This depends on the extent of inhalation and will usually range from five minutes to half an hour. However, a sniffer who remains with his supply and inhales from time to time may stay intoxicated for many hours.

(f) Who Abuses Solvents? Why?

Solvents are mainly abused by children, however anyone can select this type of abuse. People who are solvent sniffers are usually seeking to reduce mental stress or to achieve feelings of well-being and new sensory experiences such as hallucinations.

(Information can be obtained from the Addiction Research Foundation of Ontario.)

CHRONOLOGY OF DRUG ABUSE

 700 B.C. Opium Poppy cultivated
2700 B.C. Cannabis being used medically in China
1500 B.C. Opium being used by the Egyptians
1000 B.C. Incas of South America using coca leaf
 900 B.C. Homer's *Odyssey*—tells of opium
 900 A.D. Arabs are thought to have taken opium from China to India
1500 A.D. paracelsus—a German doctor prepares laudanum, a potent alcoholic mixture of opium
1600 A.D. Opium being smoked in China
1656 A.D. Sir Christopher Wren suggests the intravenous injection of drugs

1729 A.D. Two-hundred opium chests (each chest contained 140 pounds of opium) imported annually into China

1800 A.D. Opium preparations were being widely used in many parts of the world for the same conditions as today

1790 A.D. Four-thousand opium chests imported annually into China

1805 A.D. Morphine, the first alkaloid isolated from a plant—opium poppy

1830 A.D. Sixteen thousand, eight hundred and seventy-seven opium chests imported into China this year

1832 A.D. Codeine (methylmorphine), another opium alkaloid, isolated

1839–1842 A.D. First Chinese Opium War—Hong Kong

1839–1853 A.D. Hydpodermic needle and syringe perfected and commonly used

1856–1860 A.D. Second Chinese Opium War—Kowloon

1858 A.D. Seventy-thousand opium chests imported into China

1860–1865 A.D. U.S. Civil War—narcotics used for relief of pain and suffering

1882 A.D. Barbituric acid discovered

1898 A.D. Diacetylmorphine (heroin) discovered

1900 A.D. The Canadian federal government shows concern about opium on the west coast of Canada

1908 A.D. Canada brings into law the Opium Act (importation and manufacturing)

1920 A.D. Opium and Drug Act renamed Opium and Narcotic Drug Act

1923 A.D. Cannabis added to Opium and Narcotic Drug Act

1938 A.D. Cultivation of opium and cannabis prohibited

1961 A.D. Narcotic Control Act (September 15) replaces Opium and Narcotic Drug Act

1969 A.D. Food and Druges Act, Part IV, Schedule H, Part (j) enacted, limiting LSD (Lysergic acid diethylamide) and other hallucinogenic drugs to scientific use only, with a penalty of illegal possession

Canada is obligated to ensure that narcotic and controlled drugs are available in the country for medical and scientific purposes.

The Royal Canadian Mounted Police are charged with the enforcement of the Narcotic Control Act and Parts III and IV of the Food and Drugs Act.

The prime responsibility for enforcement rests with the Royal Canadian Mounted Police. Local, municipal, and Provincial police have a duty and the right to enforce these laws as well.

3. THE NARCOTIC CONTROL ACT

(a) Definitions

Narcotic —Any substance included in the schedule to the Narcotic Control Act (section 2(e)).

Possession —Possession means possession as defined in the Criminal Code (section 2 of the Narcotic Control Act), and section 4(3) of the Criminal Code is as follows:

(a) A person has anything in possession when he has it in his possession or knowingly

(i) has it in the actual possession or

custody of another person, or

(ii) has it in any place, whether or not that place belongs to or is occupied by him, for the use or benefit of himself or of another person; and

(b) where one of two or more persons, with the knowledge and consent of the rest, has anything in his custody or possession, it shall be deemed to be in the custody and possession of each and all of them.

Trafficking —(a) to manufacture, sell, give, administer, transport, send, deliver or distribute, or

(b) offer to do anything mentioned in paragraph (a) otherwise than under the authority of this Act or the regulations (section 2 of the Narcotic Control Act).

(b) Offences

Section 3(1) of the Narcotic Control Act—Possession charges may be laid by the police when a narcotic is found in the possession of a person. The security member may use this section in the circumstance where an employee may be acting strangely at his worksite and the foreman or supervisor has notified security. In conversation with the employee a bag of substance the security employee believes to be a narcotic falls on the ground in front of his view. The employee denies it is his and does not want it back. In this instance the security investigator must seize this exhibit and properly mark and identify it, and then would immediately call the public police and the Director of Security. The notes that he made at the scene would be relayed to the responding public police member as well as the Director of Security. A full report would follow. The public police having jurisdiction may wish to lay an information and proceed with charges or proceed by way of found drugs where no owner can be established.

Section 4(1) of the Narcotic Control Act—Trafficking. This section deals mainly with the purchase by an undercover policeman from a drug trafficker and would not apply in normal duties.

Section 4(2) of the Narcotic Control Act—Possession for the purpose of trafficking. This section deals with insufficient evidence of trafficking where the quantities of the drugs seized, and perhaps the existence of other evidence, suggests the only conclusion is that the person had the drug for trafficking. In this instance the security employee may encounter an employee sitting next to a bag and he denies ownership. The bag is seized and the security member looks inside in an attempt to identify an owner and return whatever might be inside. Upon looking inside, the security member finds ten bags containing green plant material believed to be cannabis marihuana. Enquiries are then conducted and contact made with the Director of Security and public police having jurisdiction. The exhibit is to be properly marked, but nothing inside should be touched if at all possible. The police responding may examine the bag and through their investigation find a fingerprint on one of the bags and match the fingerprint with a suspect. The suspect may be the employee who was sitting next to the bag in the first instance. This case may be proceeded with as possession of a narcotic for the purpose of trafficking acting on your evidence and notes taken at the time.

4. FOOD AND DRUGS ACT, PART III
—CONTROLLED DRUGS—SCHEDULE "G"

(a) Definitions

Controlled
Drug
—Any drug or other substance included in Schedule "G"

e.g., Amphetamine and its salts
Barbituric acid and its salts and derivatives
Benzphetamine and its salts
Methamphetamine and its salts
(and many others)

Possession
—Possession as defined by the Criminal Code

Traffic
—To manufacture, sell, export from or import into Canada, transport or deliver, otherwise than under the authority of this Part of the Regulations.

(b) Offences

Section 39(1) of the Food and Drugs Act—Trafficking in controlled drugs. This trafficking section would basically not apply to your normal duties as security members.

Section 39(2) of the Food and Drugs Act—Possession for the purpose of trafficking. The same prosecution policy would be available to the public police relevant to the Narcotic Control Act can be applied under the Food and Drugs Act, but with the following limitations:

1. possession of controlled drugs is not an offence;

2. importing of controlled drugs is an offence of trafficking by an individual;
3. legal authority for possession is not a bar to prosecution under section 39(2);
4. "giving" controlled drugs does not constitute trafficking.

With the foregoing in mind we will relate this to your job as security members. Should you find an employee sitting next to a jar containing 100 white pills and these pills belong to another employee who left and forgot them, you would seize the jar containing the pills. On inspection they are found to be a name brand of diet pill. The police in this instance would not have to be contacted as possession of a controlled substance such as these would not be a violation.

5. FOOD AND DRUGS ACT, PART IV —RESTRICTED DRUGS—SCHEDULE "H"

(a) Definition

Restricted Drugs—those drugs included in Schedule "H" and controlled under Part IV of the Food and Drugs Act. Restricted drugs are referred to as the hallucinogenic or psychedelic drugs. Most hallucinogenic drugs in illicit channels of distribution are manufactured in clandestine laboratories. Legitimate chemical manufacturers in foreign countries do produce some hallucinogenic drugs, but only for investigative or chemical purposes.

> One common example is Lysergic acid
> diethylamide (L.S.D.) (and many
> others are listed).

(b) Offences

Section 47(1) of the Food and Drugs Act—Possession of a restricted drug.

Section 48(1) of the Food and Drugs Act—Trafficking in restricted drug.

Section 48(2) of the Food and Drugs Act—Possession for trafficking.

The same prosecution policy relevant to controlled drugs can be applied except that possession is an offence.

6. FOOD AND DRUGS ACT—SCHEDULE "F" DRUGS

Schedule "F" drugs are controlled by Regulation c.01.041, which prohibits sale without a prescription. Examples of Schedule "F" drugs are Chlordiazepoxide and its salts (Librium), and Diazepam and its salts (Valium) (many more are listed). Schedule "F" drugs are those included in the Food and Drugs Act not intended for self-medication and for which physician's prescriptions are required. Basically they are defined as drugs which alter mood.

The following are examples of the more common drugs that may be abused:

MORPHINE—An active element of and is derived from opium by a chemical process.

Often-prescribed brand name—Morphine.

Description—The pure alkaloid appears as a white

crystalline powder, and may feel like chalk.

Medical uses—Analgesic.

Physical dependence—High.

Potential psychological dependence—High.

Tolerance—Yes (tolerance refers to the more the drug is abused the more the body adjusts to its affects and thus the more the drug is abused the quantity must be increased to achieve the same state of euphoria).

Duration of effect—Three to six hours.

Usual method of administration—Smoked or injected.

Possible effects—Euphoria, drowsiness, respiratory depression, constructed pupils, nausea.

Effects of overdose—Slow and shallow breathing, clammy skin, convulsions, coma, possible death.

Withdrawal syndrome—Watery eyes, runny nose, yawning, loss of appetite, irritability, tremors, panic, chills and sweating, cramps, nausea.

CODEINE—Codeine occurs naturally in opium but is produced from morphine.

Often-prescribed brand name—Codeine.

Description—It may be encountered as odourless white crystals, crystalline powder, tablets, capsules, or in solution, as in cough medicines.

Medical uses—Analgesic, antitussive.

Physical dependence—Moderate.

Potential psychological dependence—Moderate.

Tolerance—Yes.

Duration of effects—Three to six hours.

Usual methods of administration—Oral, injected.

Possible effects—Similar to morphine.

Effects of overdose—Similar to morphine.

Withdrawal syndrome—Similar to morphine.

MEPERIDINE (PENTHIDINE)—May be encountered in white powder, white tablets of varied sizes or in a sterile solution. They are all odourless. This was the first synthetic narcotic created.
Medical uses—Analgesic.
Physical dependence—High.
Potential psychological dependence—High.
Tolerance—Yes.
Duration in effect—Three to six hours.
Usual method of administration—Oral, injected.
Possible effects—Similar to morphine and codeine.
Effects of overdue—Similar to morphine and codeine.
Withdrawal syndrome—Similar to morphine and codeine.

BARBITURATES—Barbiturates are known as sleeping pills. They are sedatives and are prescribed by physicians.
Prescribed brand names—amytal, butisol, nembutal, phenobarbital, seconal, tuinal.
Description—Barbiturates drugs are usually marketed in tablet or capsule form. Tablets are usually round with no scoring or a single score. They may be sugar coated or uncoated in a variety of shapes with or without markings. Capsules are coloured or bi-coloured depending upon the manufacturer. They range widely in size and are usually filled with powder and occasionally time disintegration beads. The pure drug appears as a white crystalline powder. Specific types of barbiturates are often named after their colour, shape, or trade names.
Medical uses —Anesthetic, anti-convulsant, sedation, sleep. Barbiturates are among the most versatile depressant drugs available.

Physical dependence—High.

Potential psychological dependence—High.

Tolerance—Yes.

Duration of effect—One to sixteen hours.

Usual methods of administration—Oral, injected.

Possible effects—Slurred speech, disorientation, drunken behaviour without odour of alcohol.

Effects of overdose—Shallow respiration, cold and clammy skin, dilated pupils, weak and rapid pulse, coma, possible death.

Withdrawal syndrome—Anxiety, innsomnia, tremors, delirium, convulsions, possible death.

TRANQUILLIZERS—The tranquillizer is similar in effect to the barbiturates, but is not as habituating, therefore the same type of controls are not required.

Often-prescribed brand names—Equanil, librium, miltown, serax, tranxene, valmid.

Description—Drugs in this class are sold in tablet or capsules of various sizes, shapes, and colours. They are also available as spansules (sustained - release capsules), syrups, suppositories, or in solution (for injection).

Medical uses—Anti-anxiety, muscle relaxant, sedation. Used medically, these drugs counteract tension and insomnia as well without depressing the central nervous system to the extent that barbiturates do.

Physical dependence—Moderate.

Potential psychological dependence—Moderate.

Tolerance—Yes.

Duration of effect—Four to eight hours.

Usual methods of administration—Oral.

Possible effects—Similar to barbiturates.

Effects of overdose—Similar to barbiturates.

Withdrawal syndrome—Similar to barbiturates.

COCAINE—Cocaine is obtained from the leaves of the coca bush found in certain South American countries. It is an odourless, white crystalline powder with a bitter taste, producing numbness of the tongue.

Medical uses—Cocaine was once widely used as a local anesthetic. Its place in medicine, however, has been largely taken by newer, less toxic drugs.

Physical dependence—Possible.

Potential psychological dependence—High.

Tolerance—Yes.

Duration of effect—Two hours.

Usual methods of administration—Injected, sniffed.

Possible effects—Increased alertness, excitation, euphoria, dilated pupils, increased pulse rate and blood pressure, insomnia, loss of appetite.

Effects of overdose—Agitation, increase in body temperature, hallucinations, convulsions, possible death.

Withdrawal syndrome—Apathy, long periods of sleep, irritability, depression, disorientation.

Lysergic Acid Diethylamide (LSD)—LSD was first discovered in 1938 by a Swiss chemist, Dr. Albert Hoffman, who was experimenting with various derivatives of lysergic acid in an attempt to find something to alleviate migraine headaches. LSD is a component of a fungus called ergot, which attacks certain plants, especially rye. By changing the molecular structure of the acid, he hoped to find the means of alleviating headaches. In 1943 Hoffman accidentally inhaled some of this colourless, odourless substance and stumbled onto a hallucinogenic drug.

Description—Legitimate chemical manufacturers in foreign countries do produce some hallucinogenic drugs, but only for investigational or chemical purposes. On the drug market there are no standards for manufacture, unknown dosage forms nor markings which make visual identification possible.

Medical uses—LSD has been reported to be useful in the rehabilitation of criminals, treatment of sexual disorders, and treatment of mentally retarded and schizophrenic children and also the treatment of psychotic adults, to relieve intolerable pain in terminal cancer patients, drug addicts, adolescent behavioural problems in boys, character disorders, sociopathic personality disorders, and treatment of alcoholism.

Physical dependence—None.

Potential psychological dependence—Degree unknown.

Tolerance—Yes. Tolerance to the behavioural effects of LSD may develop with several days of continued use.

Duration of effect—Variable.

Usual method of administration—Oral.

Possible effects—Illusions and hallucinations, poor perception of time and distance.

Effects of overdose—Longer, more intense "trip" episodes, psychosis, possible death.

Withdrawal syndrome—Not reported.

PHENCYCLIDINE(PCP)—This is a chemical which has an application in veterinary medicine.

Often-prescribed brand name—Sernylan.

Description—PCP comes in a powder form when first produced.

Medical uses—Veterinary anesthetic.

Physical dependence—None.

Potential psychological dependence—Degree unknown.

Tolerance—Yes.

Duration of effect—Variable.

Usual method of administration—Oral, injected, smoked.

Possible effects—In animals it acts as an anesthetic but in humans it produces very irrational, unpredictable and aggressive behaviour. It can also cause hallucinations and poor perception of time and distance.

Effects of overdose—Longer more intense "trip" episodes, psychosis, possible death.

Withdrawal syndrome—Not reported.

7. CANNABIS

Marihuana and hashish come from Cannabis Sativa L., an herbaceous annual plant often called "Indian hemp", which readily grows wild or is cultivated in most tropical and temperate areas of the world including Canada. The plant may grow from three to sixteen feet in height.

MARIHUANA—in its early stages a green cannibis plant that resembles a tomato plant. Its colour varies from a light green in young plants to dark green in the mature plant. When marihuana is grown on soil in other countries the colour may range from green to brown to red depending on the soil and other factors. Its most identifiable characteristic, regardless of where it is grown, is its leaf, which is formed by an odd number of leaflets, usually five or seven. Each leaflet is long and slender, has a serrated or saw-toothed edge and is pointed at both ends. The first leaflet on each side of the stem is considerably smaller than the others. The seed is egg-shaped, about one-eighth inch in diameter.

HASHISH—The leaves and flowering tops of the hemp plant (Cannabis sativa) produce a resin which, in relatively pure form, is called hashish in the West and much of the Middle East, and is called charas in India.

Hashish is usually prepared by shaking, pressing, or scraping the amber resin from the plant, although solvent techniques might be used. In general, hashish is several times as potent on a weight basis as marihuna, although this is not always the case.

Hashish is commonly compressed into varying shapes and sizes or may be formed into a powder.

Hashish ranges in colour from light brown to brown to dark brown to very dark green to black.

HASHISH OIL—This substance is obtained from the finely ground Cannabis leaves or from actual hashish. There are a number of methods by which it is obtained, the most common being one of ethyl alcohol extraction.

Hashish oil, or liquid hash as it is sometimes referred to, has been reported in numerous colours ranging from a pale yellow highly fluid substance resembling gasoline and through increasingly darker and more viscous states to a very dark brown semi-solid paste resembling grease.

Hashish Oil is usually sold on the street in glass millilitre vials.

The following applies to marihuana, hashish and hashish oil:
Physical dependence—Degree unknown.
Potential psychological dependence—Moderate.
Tolerance—Yes.

Duration of effects—Two to four hours.

Usual methods of administration—Oral, smoked.

Possible effects—Euphoria, relaxed inhibitions, increased appetite, disoriented behaviour.

Effects of overdose—Fatigue, paranoia, possible psychosis.

Withdrawal syndrome—Insomnia, hyper-activity, and decreased appetite reported in a limited number of individuals.

As information indicates, there are many forms of drugs on the market today. Some take the form of illegal drugs and some are drugs readily obtained from a drug store and/or by prescription.

In the security field, the security employee may come in contact with the drug abuse problem.

It is difficult, if not impossible, in most instances to ascertain if a person has abused a drug. In dealing with the same employees on a day to day basis, changes in personality or behaviour of a given individual may be observed. There may be a specific reason for this behaviour, however, always bear in mind that drug abuse may be a factor.

Some forms of drug abuse will be obvious, depending on the drug abused. For instance, should a person be found lying on the floor, and security is notified, the security employee may find the person relating to wild colors and machinery that moves and talks to him. In all likelihood this person has abused some form of hallucinogen. Extreme caution should be used in this case.

NEVER TASTE A SUBSTANCE IN AN ATTEMPT TO DETERMINE WHAT IT MAY BE.

HANDS SHOULD ALWAYS BE WASHED AFTER HANDLING A SUBSTANCE BELIEVED TO BE A DRUG.

Should a substance be seized that is believed to be a drug, it must be carefully preserved as it is evidence. Seal it and place your initials, time and date on the package. Notify the Director of Security and the police department responsible for disposition.

23

Transportation and Regulation of Dangerous Goods

In this chapter we will discuss the transportation and handling of dangerous goods and commodities. As you are aware, in today's modern times many, if not all facets of industry and the retail sector are in some way affected by this subject. Whether you are the shipper or manufacturer, truck driver or stock person you may come in contact with dangerous goods in one form or another. Recent history has shown the need for such regulations as you are all aware and both the federal and provincial governments have taken necessary steps to regulate the proper handling of such goods.

Before going into detail with the items listed in the introduction it is necessary to cover the Federal Transportation of Dangerous Goods Regulations briefly, in order to form your basis of understanding. Should you be charged with establishing policy or guidelines for your company the regulations will have to be studied carefully in full detail.

The Transportation of Dangerous Goods Regulations cover the following:

Interpretation— Part I	A definition of words and terms in the Act and Regulations; (mostly definitions).
Application— Part II	Where and under what circumstances the Act does and does not apply (what the Regulations apply to and also exceptions).
Classification— Part III	Characteristics of the nine classes of dangerous goods identified in the Act (description of the nine classes of goods and how they are determined).
Documentation— Part IV	Information required in shipping documents (format of documents, exceptions, alternatives, and additional documents).
Safety Marks— Part V	Requirements for placards, labels, signs and other marks (also how and when to apply for the above and other examples of safety marking).
Safety— Standards Part VI	Specifications for packaging (this section has not been completed at the time of writing and further information is to be written in the future).
Safety— Requirements Part VII	For the handling or offering for transport of dangerous goods (limited quantities and consumer commodities, incompatible dangerous goods, emergency response plans).

Safety— Requirements Part VIII	For the transport of dangerous goods (not complete at this time).
Safety— Requirements Part IX	For reporting dangerous occurrences, for the training of persons (training of staff, registration, notification of lost goods, stolen, etc., delay of receiving explosives and reporting of occurrences).
Direction— Part X	The requirements for starting and administrating a protective direction to protect the public, property or the environment (the Minister can direct the handling of a material in some way other than that specified in the regulations).
Permits— Part XI	The procedures for application and issuance of a Permit for Equivalent Level of Safety and a Permit for exceptions (self-explanatory).
Appointments— of Agents Part XII	Requirement for non-residents to be represented by Canadian agent when shipping dangerous goods within Canada (persons outside Canada must appoint a Canadian agent for certain classes of shipments).
Inspectors— Part XIII	Procedures for appointing inspectors; their duties and powers (their certification and method of performance of duties, etc.).

The regulations were published in February, 1985, and were made effective in stages, culminating with the final effective date of July 1, 1985. They are now in effect. The provincial governments subsequently created their own acts, most of which, accept the federal Act and Regulations, as written, although some have added additional rules. Individuals should consult their respective provincial acts.

The following areas of the Regulations are in the process of being developed and will be amended in the future;

Safety Standards—	Part VI
Safety Requirements—	Part VII
Safety Requirements—	Part VIII*

*The above information was obtained from the handout titled "Transporting Dangerous Goods—Know the Rules", produced in cooperation with the federal, provincial and territorial governments in Canada.

The next area that we will cover (very briefly) is the Transportation of Dangerous Goods Act. You must remember that this is a brief outline and only offers highlights of the Act. If you are required to establish policy and/or procedures you will have to acquire a copy of the Act and read it carefully in its entirety.

The Transportation of Dangerous Goods Act covers the following:

Section 1 — Short Title
Section 2 — Definitions
Section 3 — Application of The Act

3.(1) Subject to subsections (3) to (6), this Act applies to all handling, offering for transport and transporting of dangerous goods, by any means of transport, whether or not for hire or reward and whether or not the goods originate from or are destined for any place or places in Canada.

Sections 4, 5, 6, 7, 8 — Offence Sections

4. No person shall handle, offer for transport or transport any dangerous goods, unless

    (*a*) all applicable prescribed safety requirements are complied with; and

    (*b*) all containers, packaging and means of transport comply with all applicable prescribed safety standards and display all applicable prescribed safety marks.

5. No person shall

    (*a*) put any prescribed safety mark on any container, packaging or means of transport used or intended for use in handling or transporting dangerous goods, or

    (*b*) sell, offer for sale, deliver or distribute any container, packaging or means of transport used or intended for use in handling or transporting dangerous goods, on which any prescribed safety mark is displayed,

unless the container, packaging or means of transport complies with all applicable prescribed safety standards.

6.(1) Every person who contravenes or fails to comply with section 4 or 5, or a direction under section 28 of which he has been notified in accordance with the regulations, is guilty of an offence and is liable

    (*a*) on summary conviction, to a fine not ex-

ceeding fifty thousand dollars for a first offence, and not exceeding one hundred
thousand dollars for each subsequent offence; or

(b) on conviction on indictment, to imprisonment for a term not exceeding two years.

(2) Every person who contravenes or fails to comply
with any provision of this Act or the regulations for
which no other punishment is provided is guilty of
an offence and is liable

(a) on summary conviction to a fine not exceeding ten thousand dollars; or

(b) on conviction on indictment, to imprisonment for a term not exceeding one year.

8. No person is guilty of an offence under this Act
if he establishes that he took all reasonable measures
to comply with this Act and the regulations.

Sections 10 to 16 Inclusive — Enforcement Sections

10. In any prosecution for an offence under this Act,
it is sufficient proof of the offence to establish that it
was committed by an employee or agent of the accused whether or not the employee or agent is identified or has been prosecuted for the offence, unless
the accused establishes that the offence was committed without his knowledge or consent and that he
took all reasonable measures to prevent its commission.

11. . . . any officer, director or agent of the corporation who directed, authorized, assented to, ac-

quiesced in or participated in the commission of an offence is a party to and guilty of the offence . . .

13.(2) The Minister shall furnish every inspector with a certificate . . . an inspector shall, if so required, produce the certificate to the person in charge thereof.

14.(1) . . . an inspector may, at any time, enter and inspect any building or place . . . and request the opening and inspection of or open and inspect any container, packaging or means of transport . . .

14.(2)(a) for the purpose of analysis, take samples of anything found therein . . .

  (b) . . . examine and make copies of and extracts from any books, records, shipping documents or other documents or papers that he believes on reasonable grounds contain any information relevant to the administration or enforcement of this Act and the regulations.

. . .

(5) The owner or person who has the charge, management or control . . . shall give an inspector all reasonable assistance in his power to enable the inspector to carry out his duties and functions under this Act.

(6) No person shall . . .

  (a) fail to comply with any reasonable request of the inspector;

  (b) knowingly make any false or misleading statement either verbally or in writing to the inspector;

(c) . . . remove, alter or interfere in any way
with anything seized or removed by the inspector; or
(d) otherwise obstruct or hinder the inspector.

15.(1) Where an inspector believes on reasonable
grounds that

(a) there is occurring or has occurred a discharge, an emission or an escape of dangerous goods or an emission of ionizing radia-
tion exceeding levels or quantities prescribed pursuant to the *Atomic Energy Control Act* from any container, packaging or
means of transport by means of which the
goods are being handled or transported, . . . the inspector may, where he
considers it necessary to do so in order to
prevent or reduce any serious and imminent
danger to life, health, property or environment,

. . .

(d) seize any dangerous goods, container, packaging or means of transport . . .
(e) remove or direct the removal of the seized
goods, container, packaging or means of
transport to an appropriate place, and
(f) take such other measures as are practicable
to protect persons and property.

Sections 17 to 20 Inclusive—Dangerous Occurrences Reports and Remedial Measures

17.(1) Where there occurs an event referred to in
paragraph 15(1)(a), any person who at the time has
the charge, management or control of the dangerous
goods, shall, . . . report the discharge, emission or
escape to an inspector or to such person as is prescribed.

(2) Every person required to make a report under
subsection (1) shall . . . take all reasonable
emergency measures consistent with public safety to

repair or remedy any dangerous condition or reduce or mitigate any danger to life, health, property or the environment . . .

(3) . . . an inspector . . . may request that any such measures be taken by any person the inspector considers qualified to do so or take them himself.

(4) Any inspector or other person required, requested or authorized to take reasonable emergency measures . . . may enter and have access to any place or property and may do all reasonable things in order to comply . . .

(5) Any person requested to act under subsection (3) is not personally liable . . .

Section 31—Inconsistent Provisions

31. In the event of any inconsistency between the regulations made pursuant to this Act and any orders, rules or regulations made pursuant to any other Act of Parliament, the regulations made pursuant to this Act prevail to the extent of the inconsistency.

The Act prescribes nine classifications that are further broken down into divisions by the regulations, as outlined below.

Class 1   Explosives, including explosives within the meaning of the Explosives Act.
This classification has 5 divisions depending on the nature of the explosive effect.

Class 2   Gases: compressed, deeply refrigerated, liquified or dissolved under pressure
2.1 Flammable
2.2 Compressed gas not otherwise specified
2.3 Poison Gas
2.4 Corrosive Gas

Class 3   Flammable and combustible liquids.
This class had 3 divisions depending on the flash point.

Class 4   Flammable solids; substances liable to spontane-
             ous combustion; substances that on contact
             with water emit flammable gases.
             4.1 Flammable solids
             4.2 Substances liable to spontaneous combus-
             tion
             4.3 Substances that emit flammmable gases in
                 contact with water

Class 5   5.1 Oxidizing substances
             5.2 Organic substances containing the bivalent
                 "–0–" structure

Class 6   Poisonous (toxic) and infectious substances.
             6.1 Poisonous
             6.2 Infectious

Class 7   Radioactive materials and prescribed substances
             within the meaning of the Atomic Energy Con-
             trol Act.

Class 8   Corrosive.

Class 9   Miscellaneous products, substances or or-
             ganisms considered by the Governor in Council
             to be dangerous to life, health, property or the
             environment when handled, offered for trans-
             port or transported and prescribed to be in-
             cluded in this class.
             9.1 Miscellaneous goods
             9.2 Hazards to the environment
             9.3 Dangerous wastes

        The above information was obtained from the Transportation of Dangerous Goods Act (S.C. 1980–81–82–83, c. 36, assented to July 17, 1980).

To this point in the chapter we have dealt with the regulations and Act as it applies to the transportion and handling of dangerous goods and commodities. At this point in the chapter we will deal with the regulations and introduce you to classification, packaging, safety marking, documentation, and reporting.

1. CLASSIFICATION

Dangerous goods are divided into nine classifications. These classifications indicate the type of hazard by the goods in question. These nine classes are further divided into divisions in order to further define the nature of the hazard or to identify the degree of the hazard. Every material defined as dangerous will fit into one or more of these classifications.

In the case of a material which has more than one dangerous property, there may be a primary classification (primary danger) and a subsidiary classification (the secondary danger). For example, nitric acid is both corrosive and hazardous to the environment. Thus its primary classification is 8, because it is corrosive, and its sub-classification is 9.2, because it is dangerous to the environment. Each classification number provides important information about the appropriate safety measures to be taken when handling the material.

(a) How to Classify Goods

(i) *Goods received from a manufacturer*

The manufacturer of a dangerous material is responsible for its classification. Materials which have been received previously should have been classified by the manufacturer at the time of their original shipment. For this reason, it is important to keep copies of shipping documents relating to dangerous goods. All the information required to properly identify and classify the goods for re-shipment is contained on that document.

(ii) *Goods generated by your company*

As stated in the preceding paragraph, the manufacturer of a material is responsible for the proper classification of that material under the Regulations. The governing section is section 3. If you have reason to believe that a material may be dangerous, it is necessary to first determine if it is listed in Schedule 2 as a fully specified dangerous good. If it is not listed, you must evaluate it using the criteria in section 3 to determine if it is regulated. Laboratory testing may be necessary.

(b) Information Required for Classification

The following information must be available to identify each dangerous shipment properly:

(i) *Proper shipping name*

The proper shipping name is often not the same as the common name of the material. For example, some liquid drain cleaners are properly described as Corrosive Liquids N.O.S. (Not Otherwise Specified.) Care must be taken to ensure that the proper shipping name is used.

(ii) *PIN/UN number*

The PIN (Product Identification Number) or UN (United Nations) number is a four-digit number which is recognized worldwide as describing a certain specific material or class of material. For example "Flammable Liquids N.O.S." is PIN 1993. In addition to PIN and UN, the prefixes NIP (Numéro d'Identification de Produit) or NA may apply.

(iii) *Classification and division*

The classification/division will be expressed as either one number in the case of class 7 or 8 or two numbers separated by a decimal point (such as 3.2) in all other cases. The first number is the classification, the second the division. The number 3.2 represents a flammable liquid (indicated by the 3) of moderate danger (indicated by the 2).

(iv) *Sub-classification*

The sub-classification (if any) gives information on secondary dangerous properties.

(v) *Packing group*

The packing group gives information on the level of danger. Packing group I is the most dangerous and III is the least. Packing group X means that the method of packing is the most dangerous property. This is often found with compressed gas cylinders.

When all of the information listed above is known, the goods may be considered classified. If aspects remain unknown it will be necessary to seek advice or consult the Regulations.

(c) Packing Requirements

The segment of the regulations which pertains to packing has not yet been completed. Therefore a large measure of common sense must be applied to this area.

(d) Safety Markings

There are basically four types of safety markings. These are placards, labels, signs and other safety marks. Labels are used on small packages or containers and placards are used on large transport containers or vehicles. Labels are for the most part very similar to the larger placards.

Small packages should have two labels placed on opposite sides (not the top or bottom) of the package to indicate the primary classification. The exception is with compressed gas cylinders. In this case one label is affixed to the shoulder. If the material has a subsidiary classification, that label should be placed to the right and below or immediately to the right of the primary label.

It is frequently not required to have the sub-class label. If the goods in question have a sub-class, contact your company shipping department who should have trained employees in this area as they deal with the problem on a regular basis.

Certain special labels are required in special cases. Any magnetized material being spent by air must have a special label attached. P.C.B.'s also require a special label. Lastly, all packages containing a dangerous liquid must have package orientation labels (this-side-up arrows) applied.

Two signs are available for the use with containers which present dangers from oxygen depletion or fumigation. These would normally be placed on large containers where entry into the container by personnel would present one of these dangers.

Most shipments require other safety marks. These include commodity notations on tank cars, the noting of the proper shipping name and PIN on packages and the use of self-identifying symbols on tanks. The Regulations should be consulted for the application of the safety marks.

(e) Documentation

The Regulations require that certain specific information be provided on the bill of lading for shipments of dangerous goods. This is so emergency crews will have all the information that they require available to them if an accident happens. Fire or police authorities must know exactly what they are dealing with before they can take the appropriate action. The following documentation form is suggested to assist you in making out bills of lading. When completing the form remember that all information between lines five and seventeen must be in the exact order shown.

You must also note that empty containers which were used for dangerous goods require the exact same information as for full containers, plus the words "Empty, Last Contained - - - - ".

Shipments containing both dangerous and non-dangerous goods *may* be listed on one shipping document if necessary. The Regulations provide specific requirements for this in section 4.6.

2. DANGEROUS GOODS DOCUMENTATION

1. Name and address of consignor (shipper).
2. Name and address of consignee.
3. Name of first carrier.
4. For rail cars, the car number.
5. The proper shipping name.
6. The word "CLASS", followed by the classification number.
7. The sub-class number in brackets if applicable.
8. The letters "PIN", "NIP", "UN", or "NA" as applicable, followed by the product identification number.
9. The letter E or I in brackets if listed in Column III of List II to Schedule II.
10. The words "Packing Group" followed by Roman numerical I, II, or III. Note Packing Group X need not be shown.
11. Where the goods are to be shipped by rail and special provision 102 is listed in Column IV of List I Schedule II or List II of Schedule II, the words "Special Commodity" must be shown.
12. The words "Summary of Emergency Response Plan", followed by the appropriate number, must be shown if the goods are listed in Schedule XII and they are shipped in quantities indicated in Section 7.18 of the Regulations.
13. If number (12), include the words "Activate by Calling - - - - " and the phone number provided. This is usually a 24-hour phone number that is constantly manned, usually by a security department who would have the response procedures available.
14. Total weight or volume.
15. Any special insructions.
16. The words "24-Hour Emergency Phone". Usually

same number as indicated in item (13).

17. The type and number of placards required, if any (for example, "4, Class 8 Placards Required").

18. The shipper's signature and company name.

19. Each document must have a Unique Number assigned to it.

3. REPORTING

Any dangerous occurrence involving the transportation of dangerous goods must be reported to the authorities. A dangerous occurrence can include spills, leaks, fires, or explosions involving the transportation of dangerous goods.

In the event of an emergency, the person who has the care and control of the dangerous goods must report the occurrence to the authorities if it meets the criteria as a reportable occurrence. One way of facilitating such a report is to funnel it through your 24-hour emergency phone number if your company uses an internal number. It is suggested that the person involved report the following:

1. his name, company department and his phone number;

2. location of the occurrence;

3. nature of the occurrence. (spill, leak, etc.);

4. a complete description of the dangerous goods, including shipping name, PIN or UN number, Class and Sub-Class;

5. total quantity of the shipment and quantity involved. (for example, a shipment of 14, 100L pressure cylinders, one leaking);

6. emergency phone number from the bill of lading, if applicable;

7. shipper's name and address, if applicable;

8. any special instructions listed on the bill of lading;
9. carrier's name.

The person receiving the call (normally the security department), would collect the informatin (as shown under the caption Receiving Information) and relay it to a coordinator, whose job it is to determine if the incident is reportable and initiate the report if required.

When reporting an occurrence involving the transportation of dangerous goods, remember that safety comes first and you must make the call from a safe and secure location.

4. THE DRIVER'S RESPONSIBILITIES

Anyone operating a vehicle being used to transport dangerous goods has a number of responsibilities. These are outlined below.

1. The vehicle operator must ensure that he received one copy of a properly completed shipping document for all dangerous goods.
2. These documents will remain within reach while the goods are in transit. Should the driver leave the vehicle for any reason, the documents are left on the driver's seat or in a pocket in the driver's door.
3. The driver must ensure that packages containing dangerous goods are properly labeled, and that the vehicle is placarded if necessary.
4. Upon arriving at his destination, the driver will present one set of documents to the receiver. Copies should be retained by the driver's employer for filing. If the trailer is left parked in a supervised parking area, without the

power unit attached, the documents should be left with the person in charge of the area.

5. The driver must be familiar with the reporting procedures outlined previously and must report all dangerous occurrences as soon as is practically possible.

5. RECEIVING INFORMATION

The following is a sample form that may be used in collecting the information required should you receive a call from an in-plant location, or from an outside agency if a shipment originating from your company is involved in an occurrence under the Transportation of Dangerous Goods Act.

The call would be made by the person reporting the occurrence and the number would be noted on the bill of lading.

It is suggested that the 24-hour emergency phone number be manned by your security department who would have this suggested form on hand. The calls may be received from an in-plant location, company satellite or from an outside agency if a shipment originated by your plant is involved.

SECURITY

1. Person reporting   _____
                              _____

2. Department or   _____
   organization   _____

3. Phone number   _____
                              _____

4. Location of occurrence   _____

_____

5. Nature of occurrence   _____

_____

6. Company department
   responsible for
   shipment   _____

_____

7. Shipping name of goods   _____

_____

8. PIN or UN number   _____

_____

9. Classification and
   sub-class   _____

_____

10. Total quantity of
    shipment   _____

_____

11. Quantity involved   _____

_____

12. Emergency phone no.   _____

_____

13. Shipper's name   _____

_____

14. Consignee's name   _____

_____

15. Special instructions   _____

_____

16. Carrier's name   _____

    _____

17. Information or   _____
    assistance requested   _____

The following will explain the above form and should clarify any questions involving each of the divisions.

1. Person reporting—This item is largely self-explanatory, however on occasion the person may be someone other than the individual involved, for example in the case of a vehicle accident where the driver is unable to leave his vehicle.

2. Department or organization—In the case of employees from your company, the employee should indicate what department he or she works in. If calls are received from outside agencies the name of the agency (R.J. Shipping Company, or the Ministry of Transportation and Communications) should be recorded.

3. Phone number—The phone number to be collected is the number where the caller can be reached for further information if necessary.

4. Location of occurrence—This should be as specific as possible. For example, if the material is located in a company warehouse, obtain the street name if applicable, location in the building, nearest door or unloading dock, etc.

5. Nature of occurrence—Again the description should be specific. It is important that the coordinator know exactly what is happening. For example, if the truck is on fire—is the load on fire? If the drums are leaking, are they leaking into a river, on the road and so on.

6. Company department responsible for shipment—This

information will govern the selection of coordinators. You should have possibly established several coordinators depending on the size of your company and the varied products. It would also depend on whether or not your company has off-plant satellites that come under your direction.

7. Shipping name of goods—This is the material name as listed in the regulations. Frequently, this may be quite different from the common name. For example, liquid drain cleaner might be listed as "Corrosive Liquids N.O.S. (Sulphuric Acid)". Some materials, on the other hand, are quite recognizable (for example, Chlorine).

8. PIN, NIP, NA or UN number—This is a four-digit number and may be listed as a PIN or as a UN number. It specifically indicates the product and is vital to emergency crews. The following are some examples: Chlorine PIN 1017; Flammable Liquids N.O.S. PIN 1993; Explosives, Blasting, Type A UN 0081.

9. Classification and sub-class—The classification is a number which indicates the type of danger involved. It is usually written as a decimal such as 2.1. This first number (from 1 to 9) indicates the type of danger (in this case a compressed gas), while the second indicates a more specific danger (in this case flammable). They are always written as a decimal except for class 7 and 8 which never have decimals. The classification of an explosive always includes a letter to indicate compatibility (for example, 1.1D). The sub-classification is expressed in exactly the same way but indicates a secondary danger. It is usually written in brackets following the classification (for example, Chlorine, which is 2.4(9.2)).

10. Total quantity of shipment—This should indicate the total of all dangerous goods on board, whether they

are involved with the occurrence or not (for example, fourteen 45-gal. drums).

11. This is the amount of dangerous goods actually involved with the occurrence (to use the example above, fourteen 45-gal. drums, 1 leaking).

12. Emergency phone number—This will be reported only if the goods are being received from a supplier to your company and will be the supplier contact number. If it is your company who originated the shipment, the emergency phone number will be the one that has been suggested.

13. Shipper's name—This is the name of the company originating the shipment. It may be your company in some cases or may be one of your suppliers.

14. Consignee's name—The name of the company that the goods are being shipped to.

15. Special instructions—Any instructions necessary for safety, such as a control and emergency temperature.

16. Carrier's name—Transport company name (for example, Bob's Transport Co. Ltd.), or if your company truck is involved, the truck number and/or license plate.

17. Information or assistance requested—If an inquiry is received from an outside agency about a shipment originating from your plant (for example, the carrier) he may require specific information about the characteristics of the material or may be requesting general information. The nature of his requirement must be passed on to the selected coordinator.

All of the above information will be forwarded to your company coordinator(s) as well as an identical copy to the security department manning the emergency telephone number.

Coordinators:

In-plant
1. Name one
2. Name two, etc.

Warehouse not on property
1. Name one
2. Name two, etc.

Company property in another city
1. Name one
2. Name two, etc.

Special chemicals
1. Name one
2. Name two, etc.

Remember when completing this form you must implement any other existing procedures to ensure the safety of all concerned.

After the occurrence has taken place and you have properly received and recorded the call the next question is, "What do I do with it?" You must relay all of the information to the reporting coordinators.

6. REPORTING COORDINATORS

Two distinct types of call may be received by the reporting coordinator.

Calls from employees—Calls received from employees will be for reporting purposes. When an employee has care and control of a dangerous material at the time of an occurrence he will relay all information which will enable the reporting coordinator to determine if a formal report is necessary.

Calls from outside agencies—If a shipment originating with your company and containing dangerous goods is involved in an incident while enroute, the person or agency having care and control of the goods at that time (such as the carrier or receiver) may call for further information. This does not require a report to be filed by your company and your respnsibility is merely to provide advice as requested.

Immediate reporting—Having received the information listed from the suggested reporting form that would be obtained from the 24-hour emergency phone number, it is necessary to evaluate the occurrence to determine if it is a reportable incident under the Transportation of Dangerous Goods Regulations.

These regulations do not apply in the following circumstances:

1. the goods were received in stock for consumption prior to the occurrence; or
2. the goods are not being prepared for shipment; or
3. the goods are not in transit; or
4. the goods are not in the care and control of your company employee.

If it is determined that the occurrence is transportation related, it must meet the following criteria to be reportable:

1. a discharge, emission or escape from any container,

packaging, or means of transport that contains dangerous goods,

   a) in the quantity or level set out in Table 1 (see below);

   b) that represents a danger to health, life, property or
the environment; or

2. a transportation accident in which there is damage to
the integrity of a bulk containment unit containing
dangerous goods; or

3. a transportation accident involving dangerous goods including Class 7 (Radioactive Materials); or

4. an unintentional fire or explosion involving dangerous
goods.

If the occurrence does not meet one or more of these
four criteria the law does not require the incident to be
reported.

In the event a report is required the following agencies
should be advised immediately:

1. police (see Table 2);

2. where a railway vehicle is involved, the Canadian Transport Commission;

3. where a ship is involved, the Canadian Coast Guard
and/or the port authority;

4. where an aircraft is involved, the Canadian Air Transport Administration;

5. where a road vehicle is involved, the owner, lessee, or
charterer of the vehicle;

6. the owner or consignor of the consignment of dangerous goods.

(a) 30-Day Reporting

A written report will be filed within 30 days by the

employer of the person who has management or control of the dangerous goods at the time of one of the following conditions:

1. The discovery of a dangerous occurrence;
2. An accident in which there is a release of the dangerous goods and a person is killed or is injured seriously enough to require hospitalization;
3. The discovery of damage to the integrity of any pressurized means of containment;
4. The suspicion that a container has suffered damage to its integrity resulting from impact, stress, or fatigue;
5. The discovery that all or part of a Class 1 or 7 consignment has been misplaced, lost, or stolen.

This report will be mailed to:

Transport Dangerous Goods, TDGA/T
Transport Canada
Ottawa, Ontario
K1A 0N5

7. REGISTRATION

If your company manufactures dangerous goods or offers them for transport, or imports dangerous goods in bulk quantities exceeding 500 kilograms, it must register with the Director General, Transportation of Dangerous Goods Directorate, Transport Canada, by using the form found in Schedule IX of the Regulations (Form 1). This registration must be renewed every five years or in every calendar year in which there is a change in the information previously submitted. You are exempted from the need to register if the goods are in Class 1 and you hold a licence under the Explosives Act, Class 7, and you hold a licence under the Atomic Energy Control Act or pesticides and you have registered them under the Pest Control Products Act.

8. EMERGENCY RESPONSE PLANS

Subject to the quantity limitations found in section 7.18 of the Regulations, if you ship, import, or transport by road or rail the commodities listed in Schedule XII, you may be required to file an "Emergency Response Plan" summary with the Director General. This summary basically states that you have a plan for response and outlines the capability and method of activation of that plan. The following information must be included in the summary:

1. The name and address of any agent filed pursuant to Part XII.
2. A brief description of the emergency response capability.
3. Certification that this capability exists.
4. A description of the means by which the plan is activated.
5. The name, address, phone number, function and signature of the person submitting the summary.
6. The name of the person on whose behalf the summary is filed.

Remember that your plan may involve outside agencies which have contracted with to provide response capability or may involve only your own employers if that capability exists within your company.

The Director General will assign a number to your

plan which is then required to be included on your shipping documents.

Emergency response plans are subject to review by inspectors.

As you have seen from this chapter, the government has taken steps to protect people, property and the environment by ensuring that dangerous commodities are properly recorded and transported. The penalties are severe on non-compliance and industry is co-operating fully with making this sytem work.

It is suggested that the following material be acquired if you are charged with forming your company policies and procedures with respect to the transportation of Dangerous Goods:

> The Transportation of Dangerous Goods Regulations
> The Transportation of Dangerous Goods Act·
> "Dangerous Goods Documentation—Something Worth Writing About"
> "Don't Take Chances with Dangerous Goods—Comply with Regulations"
> "Dangerous Goods—You've Got the Diamonds But Have You Got the Class?" (A simple guide to dangerous goods classification)
> "Dangerous Goods—The Marks of Safety"
> "Transporting Dangerous Goods—Know the Rules" (classification, safety marks, documentation, basic responsibilities)

All of the above publications are published by the Federal Government and are available from the Queen's Printer, Ottawa, Ontario.

The following are samples of visual labels covering the different classes of dangerous goods:

TABLE I

Quantities or Levels for Immediate Reporting

Item	Column I Class and Division	Column II Quantities or levels
1.	1	All
2.	2.1	At least 100 L★
3.	2.2	At least 100 L★
4.	2.3	All
5.	2.4	All
6.	3	At least 200 L
7.	4	At least 25 kg
8.	5.1	At least 50 kg or 50 L
9.	5.2	At least 1 kg or 1 L
10.	6.1	At least 5 kg or 5 L
11.	6.2	All
12.	7	Any discharge or a radiation level exceeding 10 mSv/h at the package surface and 200 μ Sv/h at 1 m from the package surface.
13.	8	At least 5 kg or 5 L
14.	9.1	at least 50 kg
15.	9.2	At least 1 kg
16.	9.3	At least 5 kg or 5 L

★container capacity

TABLE II

Notification to Provinces

Item	Column I Province	Column II Emergency Authority or Telephone Number
1.	Alberta	Local police
2.	British Columbia	Local police or (604) 387-5956
3.	Manitoba	Local police or fire brigade, as appropriate, or (204) 944-4888
4.	New Brunswick	Local police or Zenith 49000★
5.	Newfoundland	Local police or (709) 772-2083
6.	Northwest Territories	(403) 873-7554
7.	Nova Scotia	Local police or Zenith 49000★ or (902) 426-6030
8.	Ontario	Local police
9.	Prince Edward Island	Local police or Zenith 49000★
10.	Quebec	Local police
11.	Saskatchewan	Local police 1-800-667-3503★★
12.	Yukon Territory	(403) 667-7244

★ This telephone number is not accessible from outside the provinces of New Brunswick, Nova Scotia or Prince Edward Island

★★This telephone number is not accessible from outside Saskatchewan

■✦ Transport   Transports
   Canada   Canada

OFFICE USE ONLY

REGISTRATION - FORM 1

TRANSPORTATION OF DANGEROUS GOODS REGULATIONS
(SCHEDULE IX - SECTIONS 9.8 AND 9.9)

☐ INITIAL REGISTRATION

☐ SUBSEQUENT REGISTRATION

COMPANY NAME (PLEASE PRINT)

HEAD OFFICE ADDRESS

CITY   PRTN   POSTAL CODE

DANGEROUS GOODS INVOLVED

CHECK EACH APPLICABLE TYPE OF DANGEROUS GOODS
IN BULK OR IN PACKAGES TO WHICH THIS REGISTRATION
APPLIES

TYPE OF DANGEROUS GOODS			CLASSIFICATION	BULK	PACKAGED
(A) EXPLOSIVES			1		
(B) COMPRESSED GASES	FLAMMABLE		2 1		
	NON FLAMMABLE		2 2		
	POISONOUS		2 3		
	CORROSIVE		2 4		
(C) FLAMMABLE LIQUIDS	GASOLINE		3 1		
	OTHER (FLASHPOINT LESS THAN 18°C)		3 1		
	OTHER (FLASHPOINT NOT LESS THAN -18°C, BUT LESS THAN 23°C)		3 2		
	OTHER (FLASHPOINT NOT LESS THAN 23°C BUT LESS THAN 37.8°C)		3 3		
(D) FLAMMABLE SOLIDS			4 1		
(E) SPONTANEOUSLY COMBUSTIBLE SUBSTANCES			4 2		
(F) DANGEROUS WHEN WET SUBSTANCES			4 3		
(G) OXIDIZERS	OXYGEN		5 1		
	OTHER		5 1		
(H) ORGANIC PEROXIDES			5 2		
(I) POISONS			6 1		
(J) INFECTIOUS SUBSTANCES			6 2		
(K) RADIOACTIVE MATERIALS			7		
(L) CORROSIVES			8		
(M) MISCELLANEOUS DANGEROUS GOODS			9 1		
(N) HAZARDOUS TO THE ENVIRONMENT			9 2		
(O) DANGEROUS WASTES			9 3		

TYPE OF BUSINESS (INDICATE PROMINENT ACTIVITY ALSO WITH *)

☐ PRODUCT MANUFACTURING

☐ IMPORTING

☐ FREIGHT FORWARDING

☐ DISTRIBUTING

☐ TRANSFER FACILITY

☐ WAREHOUSING

☐ CONTAINER HANDLING FACILITY

☐ OTHER (SPECIFY)

PERSON COMPLETING THIS FORM (PLEASE PRINT)

NAME   POSITION

ADDRESS

AREA CODE   TELEPHONE NUMBER   I CERTIFY THAT THE ABOVE INFORMATION IS CORRECT TO THE BEST OF MY KNOWLEDGE

SIGNATURE   DATE

16-0018

VERSION FRANÇAISE À LA PAGE 2
FOR ENGLISH CONTINUE ON PAGE 3

Canadä

PAGE 2

Transports Transport
Canada Canada

RÉSERVE À L'USAGE DU BUREAU

INSCRIPTION - FORMULE 1

RÈGLEMENT SUR LE TRANSPORT DES MARCHANDISES DANGEREUSES
(ANNEXE IX - ART. 9.8 ET 9.9)

☐ INSCRIPTION INITIALE

☐ RÉINSCRIPTION

RAISON SOCIALE (EN CARACTÈRES D'IMPRIMERIE S.V.P.)

ADRESSE DU SIÈGE SOCIAL

VILLE | PROV. | CODE POSTAL

GENRE D'ENTREPRISE (INDIQUEZ UN ASTÉRISQUE PRÈS DE L'ACTIVITÉ PRINCIPALE)

☐ FABRICATION DE PRODUITS

☐ IMPORTATION

☐ GROUPEMENT DE FRETS

☐ DISTRIBUTION

☐ TRANSBORDEMENT

☐ ENTREPOSAGE

☐ MANUTENTION DE CONTENEURS

☐ AUTRE (PRÉCISEZ)

MARCHANDISES DANGEREUSES EN CAUSE

(COCHEZ CHAQUE TYPE DE MARCHANDISES DANGEREUSES.

EN VRAC OU EN EMBALLAGES, AUQUEL S'APPLIQUE LA PRÉSENTE INSCRIPTION)

TYPE DE MARCHANDISES DANGEREUSES		CLASSIFICATION	EN VRAC	EN EMBALLAGES
(A) EXPLOSIFS		1		
(B) GAZ COMPRIMÉS	INFLAMMABLES	2.1		
	ININFLAMMABLES	2.2		
	TOXIQUES	2.3		
	CORROSIFS	2.4		
(C) LIQUIDES INFLAMMABLES	ESSENCE	3.1		
	AUTRES (POINT D'ÉCLAIR INFÉRIEUR À – 18°C)	3.1		
	AUTRES (POINT D'ÉCLAIR ÉGAL OU SUPÉRIEUR À -18°C MAIS INFÉRIEUR À 23°C)	3.2		
	AUTRES (POINT D'ÉCLAIR ÉGAL OU SUPÉRIEUR À 23°C MAIS INFÉRIEUR À 37.8°C)	3.3		
(D) SOLIDES INFLAMMABLES		4.1		
(E) MATIÈRES SUJETTES À L'INFLAMMATION SPONTANÉE		4.2		
(F) MATIÈRES RÉAGISSANT AU CONTACT DE L'EAU		4.3		
(G) MATIÈRES COMBURANTES	OXYGÈNE	5.1		
	AUTRE	5.1		
(H) PEROXYDES ORGANIQUES		5.2		
(I) MATIÈRES TOXIQUES		6.1		
(J) MATIÈRES INFECTIEUSES		6.2		
(K) MATIÈRES RADIOACTIVES		7		
(L) MATIÈRES CORROSIVES		8		
(M) MARCHANDISES DANGEREUSES DIVERSES		9.1		
(N) MATIÈRES NOCIVES POUR L'ENVIRONNEMENT		9.2		
(O) DÉCHETS DANGEREUX		9.3		

FORMULE REMPLIE PAR: (EN CARACTÈRES D'IMPRIMERIE S.V.P.)

NOM | FONCTION

ADRESSE

CODE RÉGIONAL | Nº DE TÉLÉPHONE

J'ATTESTE (QU')AU MEILLEUR DE MA CONNAISSANCE LES RENSEIGNEMENTS DONNÉS CI-DESSUS SONT EXACTS.

SIGNATURE | DATE

FOR ENGLISH VERSION TURN TO PAGE 1

SUITE DE LA VERSION FRANÇAISE À LA PAGE 3

Canadä

PAGE 3

LIST OF ANY OTHER NAMES UNDER WHICH THE REGISTRANT DOES BUSINESS IN CANADA AND TO WHICH THE REGISTRATION APPLIES.	RAISON SOCIALE DE TOUTE AUTRE ENTREPRISE QU'EXPLOITE AU CANADA LA PERSONNE QUI S'INSCRIT ET À LAQUELLE S'APPLIQUE LA PRÉSENTE INSCRIPTION.
1	
2	
3	
4	
5	
6	
7	
8	
9	
10	

ADDRESS OF EACH PLANT LOCATION OR EACH COMPANY BRANCH OFFICE WHERE DANGEROUS GOODS ARE HANDLED. ADRESSE DES SUCCURSALES OU BÂTIMENTS DE L'ENTREPRISE OÙ DES MARCHANDISES DANGEREUSES SONT MANUTENTIONNÉES.	MEANS OF TRANSPORT USED TO SHIP DANGEROUS GOODS TO AND FROM THESE LOCATIONS MOYENS DE TRANSPORT UTILISÉS POUR TRANSPORTER LES MARCHANDISES DANGEREUSES EN PROVENANCE OU À DESTINATION DE CES LIEUX

PLEASE RETURN COMPLETED FORM TO: VEUILLEZ RETOURNER CETTE FORMULE
REMPLIE À L'ADRESSE SUIVANTE:

TRANSPORT DANGEROUS GOODS
TRANSPORT CANADA
TDGA/T
OTTAWA, ONTARIO
K1A 0N5

TRANSPORT
DES MARCHANDISES DANGEREUSES
TRANSPORTS CANADA
TDGA/T
OTTAWA, ONTARIO
K1A 0N5

SCHEDULE V — ANNEXE V
PART I — PARTIE I
Labels/Étiquettes

Domestic Consignment / Envoi intérieur	U S / Canada / États-Unis / Canada
Figure 1 — Division 1, 2 or 3 / Division 1, 2 ou 3 orange / orange — class, division and compatibility group / classe, division et groupe de compatibilité	**Figure 1a** — Division 1, 2 or 3 / Division 1, 2 ou 3 A or B / A ou B — orange / orange — class, division and compatibility group / classe, division et groupe de compatibilité
Figure 2 — Division 4 orange / orange — compatibility group / groupe de compatibilité	**Figure 2a** — Division 4 orange / orange — compatibility group / groupe de compatibilité
Figure 3 — Division 5 orange / orange	**Figure 3a** — Division 5 orange orange

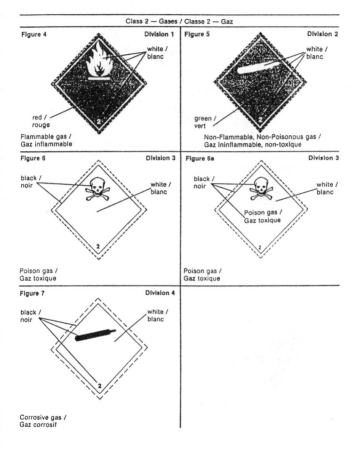

Class 2 — Gases / Classe 2 — Gaz

Figure 4	Division 1

white / blanc

red / rouge

Flammable gas / Gaz inflammable

Figure 5	Division 2

white / blanc

green / vert

Non-Flammable, Non-Poisonous gas / Gaz ininflammable, non-toxique

Figure 6	Division 3

black / noir

white / blanc

Poison gas / Gaz toxique

Figure 6a	Division 3

black / noir

white / blanc

Poison gas / Gaz toxique

Poison gas / Gaz toxique

Figure 7	Division 4

black / noir

white / blanc

Corrosive gas / Gaz corrosif

Class 3 — Flammable liquids / Classe 3 — Liquides inflammables

Class 4 — Flammable solids, substances liable to spontaneous combustion, substances that on contact with water emit flammable gases /
Classe 4 — Solides inflammables, matières sujettes à l'inflammation spontanée, matières qui, au contact de l'eau, dégagent des gaz inflammables

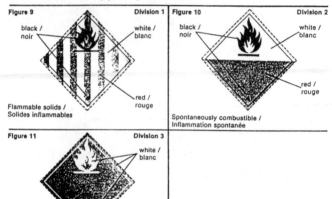

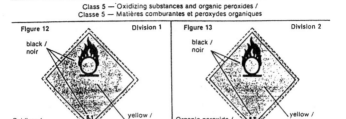

Class 5 — Oxidizing substances and organic peroxides /
Classe 5 — Matières comburantes et peroxydes organiques

Figure 12   Division 1

black /
noir

Oxidizer /
Comburant

yellow /
jaune

Figure 13   Division 2

black /
noir

Organic peroxide /
Peroxyde organique

yellow /
jaune

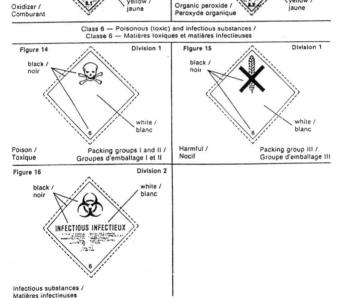

Class 6 — Poisonous (toxic) and infectious substances /
Classe 6 — Matières toxiques et matières infectieuses

Figure 14   Division 1

black /
noir

white /
blanc

Poison /
Toxique

Packing groups I and II /
Groupes d'emballage I et II

Figure 15   Division 1

black /
noir

white /
blanc

Harmful /
Nocif

Packing group III /
Groupe d'emballage III

Figure 16   Division 2

black /
noir

white /
blanc

INFECTIOUS INFECTIEUX

Infectious substances /
Matières infectieuses

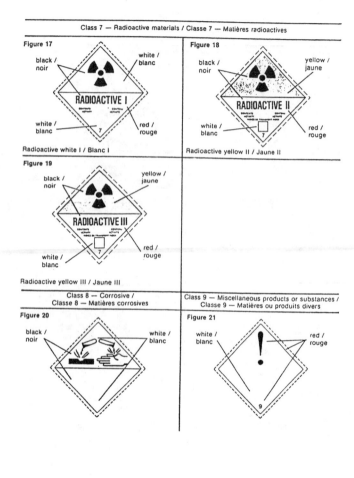

Class 7 — Radioactive materials / Classe 7 — Matières radioactives

Figure 17

black / noir — white / blanc

RADIOACTIVE I

white / blanc — red / rouge

Radioactive white I / Blanc I

Figure 18

black / noir — yellow / jaune

RADIOACTIVE II

white / blanc — red / rouge

Radioactive yellow II / Jaune II

Figure 19

black / noir — yellow / jaune

RADIOACTIVE III

white / blanc — red / rouge

Radioactive yellow III / Jaune III

Class 8 — Corrosive / Classe 8 — Matières corrosives

Figure 20

black / noir — white / blanc

Class 9 — Miscellaneous products or substances / Classe 9 — Matières ou produits divers

Figure 21

white / blanc — red / rouge

SCHEDULE V — ANNEXE V
PART IV — PARTIE IV
Special labels or placards/ Étiquettes ou plaques spéciales

Magnetized material / Matières magnétisées

Figure 1

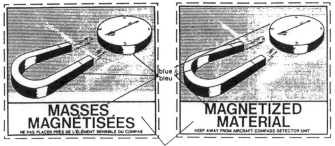

blue / bleu

white / blanc

Polychlorinated biphenyls / Diphényles polychlorés	Package orientation / Sens du colis

Figure 2

Figure 3

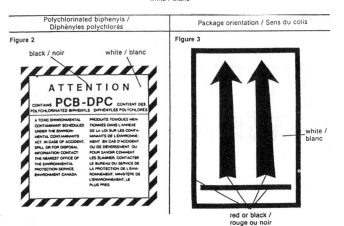

black / noir   white / blanc

white / blanc

red or black / rouge ou noir

Cargo aircraft only / Aéronef cargo seulement

Figure 4

black / noir

orange / orange

Empty sign / Écriteau « vide »

Figure 5

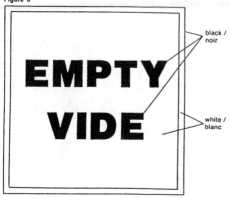

black / noir

white / blanc

Transport Transports
Canada Canada

TRANSPORTATION OF DANGEROUS GOODS

DANGEROUS OCCURRENCE REPORT
AS REQUIRED UNDER THE TRANSPORTATION OF DANGEROUS GOODS REGULATIONS
(SECTION 9.14)

TRANSPORT DES MARCHANDISES DANGEREUSES

RAPPORT SUR UN CAS DE DANGER
PRESCRIT EN VERTU DU RÈGLEMENT SUR LE TRANSPORT DES MARCHANDISES DANGEREUSES
(ARTICLE 9.14)

1. TYPE OF DANGEROUS OCCURRENCE — GENRE DE CAS DE DANGER
(CHECK ALL APPLICABLE BOXES)   (COCHEZ TOUTES LES CASES APPLICABLES)

☐ SPILL ÉPANCHEMENT   ☐ LEAK FUITE   ☐ CONTAMINATION:

☐ EXPLOSION   ☐ FIRE INCENDIE

A ☐ HUMAN DES PERSONNES   B ☐ PROPERTY DES BIENS   C ☐ ENVIRONMENT DE L'ENVIRONNEMENT

2. DATE OF DANGEROUS OCCURRENCE — DATE DU CAS DE DANGER

Y — A   M   D — J

3. TIME OF DANGEROUS OCCURRENCE (24 HR. SYSTEM)
HEURE DU CAS DE DANGER (SUR 24 HEURES)

4. LOCATION OF DANGEROUS OCCURRENCE (BE SPECIFIC)
LIEU DU CAS DE DANGER (PRÉCISEZ)

5.
☐ RESIDENTIAL AREA ZONE RÉSIDENTIELLE   ☐ COMMERCIAL AND RESIDENTIAL AREA ZONE COMMERCIALE ET RÉSIDENTIELLE

☐ URBAN CORE AREA CENTRE-VILLE   ☐ INDUSTRIAL AREA ZONE INDUSTRIELLE   ☐ RURAL AREA ZONE RURALE

6. DANGEROUS OCCURRENCE HAPPENED: — LE CAS DE DANGER S'EST PRODUIT DURANT:

☐ DURING TRANSPORT LE TRANSPORT   ☐ DURING HANDLING (SPECIFY) LA MANUTENTION (PRÉCISEZ) ....   ☐ DURING TEMPORARY STORAGE L'ENTREPOSAGE TEMPORAIRE

☐ OTHER (SPECIFY) AUTRE (PRÉCISEZ) ....

7. COMPLETE A OR B — REMPLIR A ou B

(A) DANGEROUS OCCURRENCE DURING TRANSPORT
(A) CAS DE DANGER DURANT LE TRANSPORT

OR
OU

(B) DANGEROUS OCCURRENCE DURING HANDLING OR TEMPORARY STORAGE
(B) CAS DE DANGER DURANT LA MANUTENTION OU L'ENTREPOSAGE TEMPORAIRE

(1) MODE OF TRANSPORT — MODE DE TRANSPORT

☐ ROAD ROUTIER   ☐ RAIL FERROVIAIRE

☐ AIR AÉRIEN   ☐ MARINE MARITIME

(2) TYPE OF VEHICLE — GENRE DE VÉHICULE

(3) CARRIER (NAME AND ADDRESS) — TRANSPORTEUR (NOM ET ADRESSE)

POSTAL CODE — CODE POSTAL

(1) FACILITY — INSTALLATION

TERMINAL: ☐ AIR AÉRIEN   ☐ RAIL FERROVIAIRE   ☐ ROAD ROUTIER

PORT: ☐ ON SHORE AU QUAI   ☐ ON SHIP À BORD D'UN NAVIRE

☐ WAREHOUSE ENTREPÔT   ☐ BULK STORAGE PLANT INSTALLATION D'ENTREPOSAGE EN VRAC

☐ OTHER (SPECIFY) AUTRE (PRÉCISEZ) ....

(2) FACILITY (NAME AND ADDRESS) — INSTALLATION (NOM ET ADRESSE)

POSTAL CODE — CODE POSTAL

8. CONSIGNOR — EXPÉDITEUR

NAME — NOM

ADDRESS — ADRESSE

POSTAL CODE — CODE POSTAL

9. ORIGIN OF CONSIGNMENT — POINT D'ORIGINE DE L'ENVOI

10. DESTINATION OF CONSIGNMENT — POINT DE DESTINATION DE L'ENVOI

16-0013 (2-85)

Canada

11. DANGEROUS GOODS INVOLVED IN THE OCCURRENCE WERE:
LES MARCHANDISES DANGEREUSES EN CAUSE DANS LE CAS DE DANGER ÉTAIENT:

☐ IN BULK / EN VRAC   ☐ PACKAGED / DANS DES COLIS   ☐ IN CONTAINERS / DANS DES CONTENEURS

P.I.N. NIP	CLASSI-FICATION	SHIPPING NAME — APPELLATION RÉGLEMENTAIRE	TYPE OF PACKAGE GENRE DE COLIS	TOTAL MASS OR VOLUME OF SHIPMENT MASSE OU VOLUME TOTAL DE L'ENVOI	MASS OR VOLUME OF ESTIMATED LOSS MASSE OU VOLUME DES PERTES ESTIMATIVES

12. DESCRIBE THE EVENTS LEADING TO, DURING AND RESULTING FROM THE DANGEROUS OCCURRENCE
DÉCRIVEZ LES CIRCONSTANCES AYANT CONDUIT AU CAS DE DANGER ET CELLES QUI PRÉVALAIENT DURANT ET APRÈS LE CAS DE DANGER

13. NUMBER OF DEATHS NOMBRE DE DÉCÈS	**14. NUMBER OF INJURED PERSONS REQUIRING HOSPITALIZATION** NOMBRE DE BLESSÉS QUI ONT DÛ ÊTRE HOSPITALISÉS

15. EVACUATION OF SURROUNDING AREA ÉVACUATION DES ENVIRONS
☐ YES / OUI   ☐ NO / NON

16. EMERGENCY RESPONSE PERSONNEL AT SITE OF DANGEROUS OCCURRENCE PERSONNEL D'INTERVENTION D'URGENCE SUR LES LIEUX
☐ POLICE   ☐ FIRE DEPARTMENT / SERVICE D'INCENDIE   ☐ OTHER / AUTRE

17. COMMENTS AND ADDITIONAL INFORMATION — COMMENTAIRES ET RENSEIGNEMENTS SUPPLÉMENTAIRES

18. PERSON COMPLETING THIS FORM — FORMULE REMPLIE PAR:

NAME — NOM   TITLE — TITRE

ADDRESS — ADRESSE   TELEPHONE — TÉLÉPHONE
                                                    AREA CODE / CODE RÉG. (   )

I CERTIFY THAT THIS INFORMATION IS ACCU-
RATE TO THE BEST OF MY KNOWLEDGE.
J'ATTESTE QUE LES RENSEIGNEMENTS CI-
DESSUS SONT EXACTS AU MEILLEUR DE MA
CONNAISSANCE.

SIGNATURE   DATE

SEND TO: TRANSPORT DANGEROUS GOODS, TDGA / T, TRANSPORT CANADA,
ENVOYEZ À: TRANSPORT DES MARCHANDISES DANGEREUSES, TDGA / T, TRANSPORTS CANADA,   OTTAWA, ONT. K1A 0N5

24

Human Rights

The Canadian government, as well as the provinces, have human rights legislation. The legislation may vary from province to province but basically is similar in the methods used to promote equality.

As the provinces have legislation similar to Ontario, we will not attempt to cover the similarities or differences between them or the federal government, but we will highlight the Human Rights Code as it applies to the province of Ontario.

The aim of the Human Rights Code is to create at the community level a climate of understanding and mutual respect in which all people are equal in dignity and rights with each having a contribution to make to the development and well being of the province.

The Ontario Human Rights Commission administers the Human Rights Code, 1981, and the members are appointed by the Lieutenant Governor in Council. The Commission must have at least seven Commissioners as stated in section 26 of the Ontario Human Rights Code, 1981.

The functions of the Commission are outlined in section 28 of the Human Rights Code:

28. (a) to forward the policy that the dignity and worth of every person be recognized and that equal rights and opportunities be provided without discrimination that is contrary to law;

(b) to promote understanding and acceptance of and compliance with the Human Rights Code;

(c) to recommend for consideration a special plan or program designed to meet the requirements of subsection 13(1);

(d) to develop and conduct programs of public information and education and undertake, direct and encourage research designed to eliminate discriminatory practices that infringe the rights protected by the Human Rights Code;

(e) to examine and review any statute or regulation, and any program or policy made by or under statute and make recommendations on any provision, program or policy, that in its opinion is inconsistent with the intent of the Human Rights Code;

(f) to inquire into incidents of and conditions leading or tending to lead to tension or conflict based upon identification by prohibited ground of discrimination and take appropriate action to eliminate the source of tension or conflict;

(g) to initiate investigations into problems based upon identification by a prohibited ground of discrimination that may arise in a community, and encourage and coordinate plans, programs and activities to reduce or prevent such problems;

(h) to promote, assist and encourage public, municipal or private agencies, organizations, groups or persons to engage in programs to alleviate tensions and conflicts based upon identification by a prohibited ground of discrimination;

(i) to enforce the Human Rights Code and orders of boards of inquiry; and

(j) to perform the functions assigned to it by the Code or any other Act.

The Human Rights Code, 1981, provides that every person has a right to freedom from discrimination in the areas of

1. services, goods and facilities
2. the occupancy of accommodations
3. contracts
4. employment
5. membership in vocational associations and trade unions

on the grounds of

1. race
2. ancestry
3. place of origin
4. ethnic origin
5. citizenship
6. creed
7. sex
8. handicap
9. age (18–65 years in employment; 18 years and over in the other areas)
10. marital status (includes cohabitation, widowhood, separation)
11. family status (parent-child relationship)
12. the receipt of public assistance (in accommodation only)
13. record of offences (provincial offences, pardoned federal offences—in employment only).

1. DISCRIMINATION

The Ontario Human Rights Code, 1981, prohibits the following types of discrimination:

(a) Direct Discrimination (section 8)

Direct discrimination refers to discrimination by a person acting on his or her own behalf. For example, a landlord who refuse accommodation to a person because of that person's race is discriminating directly.

(b) Indirect Discrimination (section 8)

Indirect discriminatinn is carried out through another person. For example, a landlord who instructs his or her superintendent not to take tenants of a certain race is discriminating indirectly.

(c) Discrimination because of Association (section 11)

Discrimination because of association takes place when a person who associates with a member of a particular race, colour, etc., is denied equal treatment because of that association. For example, a restaurant owner who refuses to serve a man because he has a black wife is discriminating because of association.

(d) Constructive Discrimination (section 10)

The Code prohibits not only overt discrimination, but also constructive discrimination, or practices that are not openly discriminatory but are discriminatory in their effect. For example, if an employer refuses to hire an applicant whose religion requires that he wear a beard, the employer may be found to be practising constructive discrimination, unless the exception outlined below is applicable.

Exception—The Code recognizes that there may be legitimate reasons for imposing a requirement even though that requirement has the effect of disqualifying persons who come within one of the prohibited grounds of discrimination. The person imposing the requirement must be able to show that the requirement is genuine and reasonable in the circumstances, or that the Code specifically allows such a requirement.

2. HARASSMENT

Harassment is defined by the Code as "a course of vexatious comment or conduct that is known or ought reasonably to be known to be unwelcome" (section 9 (f)). Harassment is a course of comment or cause of humiliation to a person in relation to one of the prohibited grounds.

(a) Harassment in Accommodation (section 2(2)) and Employment (section 4(2))

Landlords, people acting for landlords, and co-tenants are prohibited from harassing the occupants of a building on the ground of race, ancestry, place of origin, colour, ethnic origin, citizenship, creed, age, marital status, family status, handicap or the receipt of public assistance.

Employers, people acting for employers, and co-workers are prohibited from harassing an employee on the grounds of race, ancestry, place of origin, colour, ethnic origin, citizenship, creed, age, record of offences, marital status, family status or handicap.

(b) Sexual Harassment (section 6)

Three types of sexual harassment are prohibited by the Code:

1. The first type is "a course of vexatious comment or conduct that is known or ought reasonably to be known to be unwelcome" perpetrated by the person's landlord, someone acting for the landlord, a co-tenant, a person's employer, someone acting for the employer, or a co-worker. Examples of this type of behaviour are unwelcome sexual remarks or physical contact.
2. The second type of behaviour is a sexual advance or solicitation made by a person who is in a position to grant or deny a benefit to another. This is a contravention of the Code when the person making the solicitation or advance knows, or should know, that such behaviour is unwelcome. Unwelcome advances from a supervisor to an employee, from a landlord to a tenant, or from a professor to a student are examples of this type of behaviour.
3. The third type of prohibited behaviour occurs when a person who is in a position to grant or deny a benefit threatens or institutes a reprisal against the person who rejected his or her sexual advance. An example is the firing or demoting of an employee because the employee has refused a proposition.

(c) Responsibility for Preventing Harassment

A person who has the authority to prevent or discourage harassment may be considered responsible for failing to exercise his or her authority to do so. If a complaint of harassment goes to Board of Inquiry, the Board may find that a person, such as an employer or landlord, knew or should have known about the harassment, and could have stopped it. If the Board finds this the responsible person may be added as a party (section 38(*e*)), and if the harassment happens again, the Board may make an order against the person as well as against the harasser.

The foregoing has covered various parts of the Ontario Human Rights Code in a very general field. There are specifics in all sections and exceptions. If any areas concern you it is advisable to contact a Human Rights Officer and/or obtain literature from the Human Rights Commission.

3. PROCEDURE FOR PROCESSING COMPLAINTS

The following is in general the procedure for filing a complaint with the Human Rights Commission.

Each complaint is registered and assigned to a Human Rights officer. A copy of the complaint, outlining the complainant's allegations, is provided to all parties against whom the complaint is made (the respondents).

In order to assist the Commission in making a quick determination of the issues, the respondent is often invited to reply in writing to the complainant's allegations. Where this is done, the reply will be made known to the complainant before the case proceeds further.

(a) Fact-Finding Conference

A fact-finding conference is usually—but not always—held shortly after the complaint has been served and the respondent has had an opportunity to reply. The Human Rights Officer to whom the case has been assigned chairs the conference. The complainant and the respondent are both expected to be present in order that there can be a detailed discussion of the complaint.

The purpose of this meeting is,

1. to determine the positions of the complainant and the respondent with respect to the complaint; and
2. to obtain evidence from both parties about the facts that gave rise to the complaint.

(b) Extended Investigation

Complaints that cannot be resolved in the Fact Finding Conference often require further investigation.

In carrying out the investigation, the Human Rights Officer may:

1. enter business premises—request the production of documents; and
2. speak to witnesses who may have information relevant to the complaint (when questioning witnesses, the Officer may exclude any person who may be adverse in interest to the complainant, but not the witness' lawyer or chosen representative).

(c) Formal Conciliation

Following the extended investigation, the investigating officer will meet with the parties, review the investigation findings and endeavour to conciliate the complaint. In most instances a settlement can be arrived at that is satisfactory to the complainant, the respondent and the Commission.

Where a resolution is achieved, the case is forwarded to the Commissioners for their approval. Officers of the Commission are not empowered under the Code to accept a settlement without the approval of the publicly-appointed Commissioners.

(d) The Ontario Human Rights Commission

The Ontario Human Rights Commissioners, as distinct from the officers and staff of the Commission, are members of the public who are appointed by the Lieutenant Governor in Council to administer the Code.

For this reason, and in order to ensure that in each instance the public interest has been served, cases that are settled or otherwise resolved are approved by the Commission before they are closed.

Similarly, any case that cannot be settled must be referred to the Commissioners for their decision whether or not to request that the Minister of Labour appoint a Board of Inquiry.

These cases are considered at regularly scheduled meetings of the Commission, and any decision made by the Commission is based primarily upon a summary of the information collected by the investigating officer. This summary is made available to the parties, and an opportunity is provided to make written submissions before the case appears on the Commission agenda.

If the Commission decides not to request the appointment of a Board of Inquiry or not to deal further with the complaint, the Chairman of the Commission will inform the parties in writing of the reasons for the decision. The parties will also be advised of the procedure set out in the Code for the reconsideration of this decision.

(e) Reconsideration

An application for reconsideration may be made by the complainant within 15 days of the date the Commission decision is mailed, and must include a statement of the facts upon which the application is based. Under certain circumstances, the Commission will consider a late application provided that there are good reasons for the delay.

The respondent will be notified that the complainant has made a request for reconsideration and will also be provided with an opportunity to reply. The Commissioners will then make a final decision on the disposition of the case.

The decision of the Commission upon reconsideration is communicated to the complainant and respondent in writing by the Chairman of the Commission.

(f) Board of Inquiry

A Board of Inquiry is an independent adjudicative body that is appointed by the Minister of Labour at the request of the Commission.

The Board will hold a hearing to determine whether or not a right under the Code has been infringed. The Board's decision will be based on the evidence and the law.

If the Board finds that there has been no infringement of the Code, the case is dismissed.

If the Board finds that the Code has been infringed, the Board may issue an order providing compensation for any losses suffered by the complainant and providing a remedy for any discriminatory practices that gave rise to the complaint. Additionally, where the Board finds that the infringement has been wilfully or recklessly engaged in, the Board may award general damages up to $10,000 for mental anguish.

The decision of the Board must be made within 30 days of the conclusion of the hearing.

Any decision or order of the Board may be appealed to the Divisional Court of the Supreme Court of Ontario.

PART I

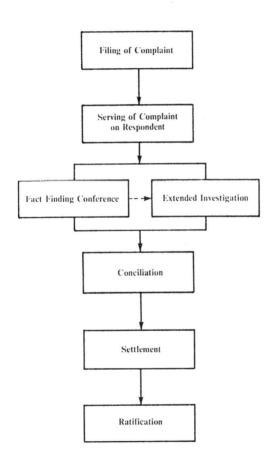

PART 2

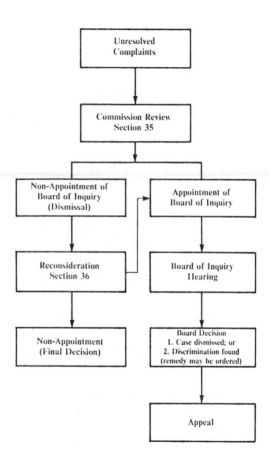

25

Conclusion

The private security industry is one of Canada's major growth industries and as such is in a constant state of flux and modernization. Because crime is increasing daily, private security must and does fill the void created by the heavier burden continually placed on the public police. This contribution is not meant to replace the public police, but rather enhances their role, allowing them to devote more of their valuable time to the general public.

We have attempted to promote loss control with the emphasis on *prevention* rather than *reaction*. Losses, such as theft, fire and, most importantly, injury to employees and the general public can greatly reduce the potential of any given industry. An effectively functioning private security force can help greatly in eliminating these potential losses.

Through the use of modern training techniques and modern technology, losses can be severely curtailed, if not eliminated.

Advances in technology will no doubt continue to be vast and in the future will greatly change the role of the private security officer. However, the personal approach can never be removed from the private security field. Al-

though modern machinery has greatly changed our lifes-
tyles, both at home and the worksite, the personal element
must still be present.

This is especially true in the private security field. All
the modern technology available can never replace the well
trained private security officer.

Index

Abuses. *See* **Purchasing**
Access
    Control, 172, 182
    Hotel, 195
    Property, 92
Accounting
    accounts payable, 61
    auditors, 2
    controller, 59
    invoice, 62
    packing slip, 62
    tenders, 5
Affidavit
    Private investigator/
      security guard, 19, 25
Agency
    detective, 15
Alarms. *See* **Responses**
    survey, *see* **Security**
    systems, *see* **Burglar** *and*
      Fire
Alcohol, 255
Application
    Private investigator/
      security guard
        Manitoba, 16–19
        Ontario, 20–25

Arrest
    authority, 77–79
    occupier, 94
    powers, 80–81
    procedure, 81–84
    recording, 82
    shoplifting, 192
Assault, 2
Attorney General, 79
Audit
    internal, 59
    trail, 60
Auditors, 2
Bags. *See* **Shopping**
Barbiturates. *See* **Drugs**
Base Radio. *See* **Radios**
Birth Certificate, 15
Bomb
    recipient, 229
    threat, 226
Broadcaster, 156
Budget
    authority, 60
    duration, 36
    expenses, 37
    financial standing, 38
Building Security. *See* **Security**

Burglar
   alarms, 167, 104
   resistant, *see* **Safes**
   system, 156
By-Law Enforcement, 1
Cannabis. *See* **Drugs**
Carbon Dioxide, 206
Card. *See* **Entry**
Casualty, 216, 225
Central Registry, 178
Central Returning Area, 188
Charter of Rights, 81, 87
Citizenship
   documentation, 15
Classification
   casualties, 225
   complaints, 141
   confidential, 177
   documents, 98, 177, 182
   procedure, 143
   restricted, 177
   requirements, 287–291
   routine, 143
   secret, 133, 177
   types, 145, 178
   unclassified, 177
Cleared
   by charge, 145
   otherwise, 145
Closed Circuit Television, 170
Cocaine. *See* **Drugs**
Codeine. *See* **Drugs**
Codes
   Phonetic Alphabet, 159
   10-Code signals, 157
Collective Agreement, 85
Colour
   marking signs, 95
   marking systems, 94
Communications, 162, 215, 236

Consulting, 8
Controlled Drugs. *See* **Drugs**
Contract. *See* **Security**
Corporate. *See* **Security**
Courier Services, 2
Credit Cards, 198
Crimestoppers, 4
Criminal. *See also* **Arrest**
   act, 79
   activity, 92
   Code of Canada, 75
   detention, 79
   dual procedure, 79
   enforcement, 75
   indictable offences, 75
   offences, 75
   pertaining to Canada, 76–78
   prosecution, 89
   provincial statute, 76
   summary conviction, 75
Criminology, 30
Criticality, 97
   See also **Probability**
Cylinders, 174
Dead Spots. *See* **Shoplifting**
Detective. *See* **Agency**
Detention. *See* **Criminal**
Detex. *See* **Patrols**
   clock, 151
Diary Date, 143, 145, 179
Dignitary, 201
Disaster
   factors, 216, 224
Discharge, 88
Discrimination
   by association, 324
   constructive, 324
   direct, 259
   exception, 262, 319
   indirect, 324

Documents. *See* **Classification**

Drugs
    abuse, chronology of, 259
    barbiturates, 268
    cannabis, 272
    cocaine, 270
    codeine, 267
    controlled, 263
    diethlyamide (LSD), 270
    Food and Drugs Act, 76, 264
    hashish, 273
    librium, 266
    lysergic acid, 270
    meperidine, 268
    morphine, 266
    Narcotic Control Act, 76, 261
    phencyclidine (PCP), 271
    schedules, 263, 266
    solvents, 257
    tranquilizers, 269
    valium, 266

Dual Procedures. *See* **Criminal**

Duties
    Division of, 63

Emergency
    plans, survey, 123

Emergency Measures Organization, 228

Employee
    entrance, 196
    relations, 85, 133
    safety, 120
    termination of, 89

Enforcement. *See* **Criminal**

Entry
    card, 172
    digital, 172
    prohibited, restricted, *see* **Colour**

Equipment
    fire, 124, 126, 211
    safety, 124, 125
    transport, 164

Evacuation. *See* **Plan**

Evidence
    preservation of, 83

Excise, 1

Expenses, 37

Explanatory Report. *See* **Reports**

Extinguishers
    fire, 208, 211

Fencing, 164

File Numbers. *See* **Reports**

Financial. *See* **Budget**

Fingerprints, 15

Fire
    alarms, 104
    classification, 207
    control, 2, 167
    elements, 206
    equipment, 125, 211
    manuals, 212
    marshall, 205
    prevention, 5, 118
    protection survey, 118
    routes, 125, 127
    sprinkler system, 211

First Aid, 125

Fixed Surveillance. *See* **Surveillance**

Flux
    state of, 34

Food and Drugs Act. *See* **Drugs**

Foot Patrol. *See* **Patrol**

Force
    excessive use of, 81

Gambling, 195, 199, 200

Guard Services, 2
Hand Signals. *See* Signals
Hardware. *See* Security
Hashish. *See* Drugs
Heat, 206
Highway Traffic Act, 76
Holiday, 45
Hotel
    housekeeping, 195, 211
    receiving, 195
    registration, 196
Human Rights
    accommodation, 325
    areas of discrimination, 323
    commission, 321, 328
    complaint, process for filing,
      327
    grounds, 323
    harassment, 325
      responsibility to prevent, 326
Identification Card, 12
Immigration, 1
Implied Invitation, 195
Index Cards, 143
Indictable. *See* Criminal
Infrared Lighting. *See* Lighting
In-House. *See* Security
Inkeepers Act of Ontario, 199
Insurance, 5
Internal Accountability. *See*
  Audit
Introduction, 130
Investigation. *See also*
  Application
    internal, 137
    interviews, 138
    priorities, 138
    procedures, 138
    senior personnel, 141
Investigator. *See also* Application
    private, 12

Invoice. *See* Accounting
Jurisdiction
    occupier, 79, 94
    provincial, 15
Justice System, 4
Keys. *See* Locking Devices
Kleptomaniac, 185
Labour, 85, 205
Law and Security Courses, 30
Librium. *See* Drugs
Licence. *See* Application
Licensing. *See* Security
Lieutenant Governor of
  Canada, 321
Lighting, 105, 124, 171
Liquor Control Act, 76
Locking Devices
    blank keys, 174
    control of, 175
    master, 176
    survey, 113
Locksmithing, 174
Loss Prevention, 3, 55
Lysergic Acid Diethlyamide
  (LSD). *See* Drugs
Manpower
    deployment of, 41
Material Receiving. *See* Report
Meperidine. *See* Drugs
Mobile. *See* Surveillance
Morphine. *See* Drugs
Narcotic Control Act. *See* Drugs
Neighbourhood Watch, 4
Observation. *See also*
  Surveillance
    categories, 145
Occupiers' Liability Act of
  Ontario, 91
Old-Boy System, 29
Operation Identification, 4
Overt. *See* Surveillance

Oxygen, 206
Packing Slip. *See* **Accounting**
Park Warden, 1
Patrols
    detex, 151, 153
    foot, 149
    observation, 152
    random, 150
    services, 1
    types, 149
    vehicle, 150
Pay Standards, 4
Pedlars, 76
Personal Search. *See* **Search**
Petty Trespass Act, 76
Phencyclidine (PCP). *See*
  Drugs
Phonetic Alphabet, 159
P.I.N./U.N., 289
Plan
    evacuation, 203, 215
Police
    auxiliary, 2
    public, 2
    railway, 76
Premises, 91
Preserving Evidence. *See*
  Evidence
Prevention, 4, 8, 40, 205
Preventive Role, 4
Private Detective. *See* **Agency**
**Private Security Guards Act of
  Ontario,** 12
Probability, 97
    See also **Criticality**
Probationary Licence, 16
Proceedings
    internal, 88
Prosecution. *See* **Criminal**
Prostitution, 195,, 199
Protected Property, 93

Provincial Statutes. *See* **Criminal**
Public. *See* **Security**
Purchasing
    abuses, 63
    agent, 61
    department, 60, 139
    order numbers, 61
    process, 45
    requisition, 60
Radios, 156
Railway. *See* **Police** *and*
  Security
Random Patrol. *See* **Patrols**
Reaction, 9, 205
Reactive Role, 4
Receiving. *See* **Hotel** *and*
  Security
Registry, 141
Release. *See* **Discharge**
Reports
    appendix, 134
    contents, 129
    explanatory, 130
    file numbers, 131, 143, 145
    master, 134
    material receiving, 62
    surveillance, 242
Responses
    alarm, 1
Restricted. *See* **Classification**
  and **Security**
Rights
    conferred by law, 93
    Human Rights Code, 321
Risk, 92
Roof Lighting, 164
Routes. *See* **Fire**
Safes, 102, 168
Safety, 123
Schedules G, H, F. *See* **Drugs**
Search, 81, 87

Secret. *See* **Classification**
Security
    analysis, 32
    budget, 36
    clearance, 179
    consulting, 2
    contract, 3, 5, 6, 8, 11, 15, 38
      89, 196
    corporate, 2
    defined, 1
    force, 6
    government building, 4
    guard, 12, 55, 57
    hardware, 161
    in-house, 2, 15, 89, 196
    licensing, 11
    manager, 29, 34
    private, 1
    public, 1, 4
    railway, 2
    standards, 11
    store, 2
    system, 97
Seizure
    stolen property, 82, 87
Shifts
    distribution, 55
    part time, 42
    projection, 41
    rotation, 42
    switching, 41
Shoplifting, 185, 191
Shopping
    bags, 189
Shredding Machines, 183
Signals, 235
Solvents. *See* **Drugs**
Sprinkler System. *See* **Fire**
Stand-By, 156

Summary Conviction. *See*
  Criminal
Surveillance
    check list, 243
    control vehicle, 240
    covert, 233
    fixed, 233, 244
    mobile, 106
    overt, 233
    parallel, 239
    patterns, 239
    reports, 242, 246
    teams, 235
    vehicles, 237
Tenants, 91
Tenders. *See* **Accounting**
Theft, 4,
    control, 114
    hotel, 195
    mobile objects, 81
Tool, Torch Resistant. *See*
  Safes
Training, 3
Tranquillizers. *See* **Drugs**
Transport. *See also* **Equipment**
    dangerous goods, defined, 278
Trespassers, 77, 92
Trespass to Property Act, 93
Trespass Notice, 200
Triage, 220
Unclassified. *See* **Classification**
Underwriters Insurance, 205
Underwriters Laboratories of
  Canada, 168
Unidentified Female (U.F.), 242
Unidentified Male (U.M.), 242
Unfounded, 145
Union, 85
U.N./P.I.N., 289